Cyber Sovereignty

Cyber Sovereignty

THE FUTURE OF GOVERNANCE IN CYBERSPACE

Lucie Kadlecová

STANFORD UNIVERSITY PRESS
Stanford, California

Stanford University Press
Stanford, California

Printed and bound by CPI Group (UK) Ltd, Croydon, CR0 4YY

Library of Congress Cataloging-in-Publication Data

Names: Kadlecová, Lucie, author.
Title: Cyber sovereignty : the future of governance in cyberspace / Lucie Kadlecová.
Description: Stanford, California : Stanford University Press, 2024. | Includes bibliographical references and index.
Identifiers: LCCN 2023040291 (print) | LCCN 2023040292 (ebook) | ISBN 9781503638549 (cloth) | ISBN 9781503639386 (ebook)
Subjects: LCSH: Sovereignty—Case studies. | Cyberspace—Government policy—Case studies. | Internet—Government policy—Case studies.
Classification: LCC JC327 .K335 2024 (print) | LCC JC327 (ebook) | DDC 384.3—dc23/eng/20231221
LC record available at https://lccn.loc.gov/2023040291
LC ebook record available at https://lccn.loc.gov/2023040292

Cover design: Matt Avery, Monograph
Cover images: iStock
Typeset by Newgen in Adobe Jenson Pro 10.75/15

Contents

# *Acknowledgments*

I worked on the overall idea of this book for several years, and I was fortunate to be able to discuss it with outstanding scholars who helped me advance my arguments. These brief acknowledgments do little justice to their contributions.

First and foremost, I give my deepest thanks to Tomáš Weiss, my mentor, who patiently helped me all the way from formulating and developing the initial arguments up to polishing the final manuscript. I would not have finished my research or published this book without his encouragement and advice.

I conducted this project while working at the Institute of International Studies in the Faculty of Social Sciences at Charles University. I received funding from the Charles University Research Center program, grant UNCE/HUM/028 (Peace Research Center Prague). I am grateful to the faculty for providing me with the most flexible, friendly, and stimulating working environment I could wish for. Further thanks are due to Michal Smetana and participants of research seminars at the Institute of International Studies and the Peace Research Center Prague for providing valuable comments on the later versions of the manuscript. The initial research was undertaken with support from the Grant Agency of Charles University under grant no. 288217.

I am very grateful to Nazli Choucri, my host and advisor during my visiting scholarship at the Massachusetts Institute of Technology, who helped me immensely to deepen and sharpen my research on state sovereignty in cyberspace. The MIT Political Science Department was the most inspiring institution I could have wished to conduct my research at. I also thank the MIT Sloan School of Management, especially Stuart Madnick and his working group, and Harvard's Belfer Center for Science and International Affairs, especially Michael Sulmeyer. They, and their colleagues at their respective institutions, offered their insight into the conduct of multidisciplinary research, which helped me develop my ideas and arguments. None of this would have been possible without the generous funding and support of the Czech Fulbright Commission, for which I am deeply thankful.

I thank Vicki Nash of the Oxford Internet Institute at the University of Oxford and participants of the OII Summer Program for challenging an earlier version of my research project and helping me sharpen it.

Parts of this manuscript went through several iterations and have benefited from the generous comments of many scholars, often at international conferences, and I have no doubt failed to recognize all specific individuals. I thank them as well.

The following people were kind enough to comment on drafts of the manuscript or advised me on the research or publication process: Pierre Allan, Helena Farrand Carrapiço, John Cawley, Keir Giles, Berta Jarošová, Kateřina Králová, Michal Raška, and three anonymous reviewers from Stanford University Press.

I am most appreciative of the understanding, patience, and flexibility that I received from my employers from the public and private sectors whom I had the pleasure of working for while attending to my academic career. They all allowed me to conduct my research and develop my academic path while juggling my professional one. Any opinions, findings, and conclusions in this book are purely mine and do not necessarily reflect the views of any of my current or former employers.

I also thank Daniel LoPreto at Stanford University Press for his support and for steering the manuscript through the phases of the review process, always with great patience and helpfulness. Working with him and his colleagues at SUP was a pleasure.

Finally, a very special thank you goes to my mom, my dad, and my family, who always supported and stood by me, and without whom I would not have gotten this far. Thank you.

Cyber Sovereignty

Introduction

Governments of the Industrial World, you weary giants of flesh and steel, I come from Cyberspace, the new home of Mind. On behalf of the future, I ask you of the past to leave us alone. You are not welcome among us. You have no sovereignty where we gather.[1]

These are the opening lines of "A Declaration of the Independence of Cyberspace," a manifesto formulated at the 1996 World Economic Forum in Davos, Switzerland, by John Perry Barlow, a poet, political activist, cyberlibertarian, and founding member of the Electronic Frontier Foundation, an institution defending online civil liberties. Back then, cyberspace was at its onset, and a group of the first cyberspace theorists believed that cyberspace should be free from state interference and thus also immune from state sovereignty. Barlow was the loudest proponent of this paradigm, which claimed that a new community with its own norms and internal regulations was being constructed in cyberspace and that governments' presence was neither necessary nor welcome. Despite these hopes and wishes, it soon became clear that states would not follow Barlow's demands and would try to impose their sovereignty on cyberspace.

State sovereignty is a fundamental concept of the modern international order whose origins can be found in the Peace of Westphalia of 1648. It is not a specific style of governance or type of constitution. State sovereignty is rather a legal and political groundwork on which different styles of governance can be executed and different types of state constitution can be built. It is a remarkably long-lasting and ever-changing concept that has continually evolved and transformed with time to accommodate particular historical periods. Despite all these transformations, state sovereignty has always preserved its fundamental idea. It is the supreme authority exercised within a distinct territorial jurisdiction that is free from foreign interference but asserts its place in the international system. Sovereignty is the ultimate precondition of modern law and politics.

Sovereignty has faced serious challenges and undergone occasional existential crises. The most recent challenge for states and their sovereignty materialized in the form of cyberspace, whose wild and fast spread worldwide was, at one point, predicted to erode the concept. Cyberspace is complex, requiring more than a simple description of hardware and software. I interpret it through four distinct layers that, together, create the cyber domain. These are its physical infrastructure, its code, its regulations, and the data and information it contains.[2] The main concern has been the supposedly borderless nature of the cyber domain, where data can be exchanged from one corner of the planet to another in the blink of an eye, diminishing the relevance of physical territory.

Governments became conscious of the capacity of cyberspace in its early stages, as indicated by their actual practice, and wanted to extend their sovereign position into it. Increasingly, states seek greater sovereignty over the cyber domain, previously seemingly ungoverned. In the broader context of cyberspace as a domain, this behavior appears logical. The concept of state sovereignty in cyberspace is crucial to any debate about regulation of the domain. Achieving a cyber order broadly accepted by the international community requires, first, a consensus on basic regulations. These basic regulations, then, are inherently based on the application of state sovereignty in this new domain. If states cannot apply and rely on their sovereignty in the cyber domain, they will not accept even the weakest attempt to establish order in cyberspace. Hedley Bull's *The Anarchical Society* proclaims that states try to preserve the international order because it is in their own interest.[3] From this logic, international order in cyberspace cannot exist without a solid basis of sovereignty, hence states' activity in this regard.

The puzzling situation this creates is the subject of this book. I argue that we find ourselves in an exploratory phase; governments try new options for extending their sovereignty into cyberspace. States globally stretch their muscles and probe the limits to their sovereignty in the cyber domain. Nevertheless, a state is still a territorial entity, and imposing sovereignty in a seemingly nonterritorial man-made cyber domain is very different from imposing it in the physical domains of sea, land, air, and space in which sovereignty was previously developed. I examine how our understanding of state sovereignty has been transformed by state practice under the pressure of new cyber challenges. This is a crucial question because the debate on sovereignty in cyberspace is being framed at the moment, and its outcome will offer a framework for addressing further cyber-related topics.

I aim to answer three related questions. The principal question asks *How does state practice of sovereignty in cyberspace change the traditional understanding of the concept?* Two working questions delve into sovereignty in cyberspace and feed into the answer to the principal question. The first working question asks *What kinds of tools do states employ to exercise their sovereignty in cyberspace?* The second working question asks *In what way is the exercise of authority and control by states in cyberspace different from traditional domains?*

I argue that the unique environment of cyberspace requires states that desire to retain their sovereignty therein to adjust their behavior to fit the characteristics of the cyber domain. State sovereignty exists in cyberspace, and states are not willing to cede it to other cyber actors. However, because cyberspace does not have the same characteristics as the traditional domains of air, sea, land, and space, states need to adapt their practice of sovereignty in cyberspace accordingly. Consequently, state behavior influences our approach toward the concept of sovereignty, which must be more adaptive and accept a modification of its classical understanding. Distribution of authority and control in cyberspace likely differs substantially from noncyber environments, and the tools used by states to enforce sovereignty in cyberspace are more miscellaneous, closely interconnecting modern technologies and legal frameworks. Ultimately, I argue that sovereignty as applied to cyberspace is the latest stage of its evolution, and so sovereignty once again transforms itself to keep up with the latest developments in modern politics and law: cyber governance.

Although state sovereignty in cyberspace has been studied before my examination, I show in chapter 1 that the research has focused solely on narrow and specific segments of the issue so far, such as territoriality or framing the concept within one particular state activity. It has not taken the crucial further step of exploring in depth and in a more complex manner how the cyber domain transforms our understanding of state sovereignty with respect to democratic rule. This book addresses this gap and moves the debate forward by exploring how democracies in the transatlantic area enforce their sovereignty in cyberspace.

To do this, I use Stephen Krasner's typology of sovereignty, which constitutes the most suitable theoretical framework for this book. The typology is simultaneously complex, covering the whole range of states' activities, and flexible enough that it can also be applicable in different conditions and environments. According to Krasner, states exercise sovereignty in four ways: Westphalian sovereignty, international legal sovereignty, domestic sovereignty, and interdependence sovereignty. Westphalian sovereignty centers on the exclusion of external actors from authority structures, and international legal sovereignty deals with a state's behavior as a juridical equal in international law and relations. Domestic sovereignty focuses on the organization of political authority and the ability to exercise effective control, and interdependence sovereignty concerns the regulation of transborder movement.[4] Embedded in these four sovereignty types are a fundamental distinction between authority and control. Authority Krasner defines as a mutually acknowledged right for actors to become involved in specific activities, and control as attainable through the simple use of brute force without a need for mutually recognized authority.[5] I do not always neatly apply all the aspects of the typology as originally defined, because the nature of cyberspace simply does not allow it (for example, it is impossible to use brute force in relation to control), but I am positive that it is the most suitable analytic foundation, which will become self-evident during the course of the book.

I transfer Krasner's typology of sovereignty into the cyber domain and match each sovereignty type with a case study. To do so, I first identify four long-term trends in states' approaches to cyberspace: efforts to preserve the confidentiality, integrity, and accessibility of governmental data in the digital era; international negotiations on norms of behavior in cyberspace; the push toward state control of the internet; and protection of national infrastructure. With minor exceptions, almost every state worldwide with at least a minimal interest in cyberspace has faced all four topics and come to a decision about how to approach them. Using purposive sampling, I then identify the most suitable case study per sovereignty type, those whom I perceive to be democratic pioneers in the transatlantic region that stretch the limits of state sovereignty in cyberspace the most. To operationalize the cases, authority and control are the variables. Authority in cyberspace is assessed through respective state legislation, and control is measured through the cyber capabilities that are necessary for the state's exercise of the respective type of sovereignty.

I limit the territorial definition to democracies, because they are guided by the general will of the people and do not tend toward extreme solutions. I also narrow it to the transatlantic region, because those states have similar perceptions of cyberspace matters. I intentionally avoid the study of authoritarian regimes for two reasons: first, previous research on state sovereignty has already substantially explored the approach of authoritarian governments to state sovereignty in cyberspace; second, the source of legitimacy of authoritarian regimes is not the will of the people to whom they would be answerable. Their source of sovereignty is different, and hence their sovereignty limits can be set differently too. Ultimately, these different limits could distort the results of this book.

Westphalian sovereignty is represented in chapter 3 by Estonia and its decision to build a network of data embassies. These are data centers under the full control of the Estonian government but located outside Estonian territory. The data embassies can serve as backup providers in times of emergency in Estonia, thereby ensuring the digital continuity of Estonian e-government. This progressive and innovative idea clearly secures the exclusion of external actors from the authority structures of a state within its territory as defined by Westphalian sovereignty. The subsequent adoption of the same far-reaching practice by other states and institutions confirms Estonia's leadership in this sovereignty type.

The engagement of the Dutch leadership in international negotiations in chapter 4 on responsible state behavior in cyberspace embodies the most advanced case of international legal sovereignty. The Netherlands has been a keen and progressive proponent of establishing international forums for discussion about norms in cyberspace while also playing an active role in already-established negotiations. This leadership resides in the Netherlands' efforts to include in these negotiations the broadest range of stakeholders possible while working on both bottom-up and top-down approaches. Their proactive steps and eagerness have paid off in a recognition by other stakeholders of their initiatives, including significant successes in clarifying norms of responsible state behavior in cyberspace.

Turkey and its approach to internet restrictions in chapter 5 represents the most advanced case of domestic sovereignty. I intentionally limit this case to the time frame of 2007 to 2016 because that is when Turkey could still be considered a democratic or partially democratic state. In 2007, the first internet governance law in Turkey created its main legal framework. Since then, the law has gradually evolved into a tool of the state that facilitates its reaction to political events unfavorable to governmental policy, culminating in the military coup of 2016. Because this is when Turkey began transforming into a semiauthoritarian regime both inside and outside cyberspace, I believe it is a good example of the delicate moment when the extension of sovereignty by a government violates democratic values and so serves as a warning for other democracies.

Finally, the United States' approach in chapter 6 toward the Chinese telecommunications company Huawei Technologies and its attempts to enter the US market is the most advanced case of interdependence sovereignty. Governments globally have discussed the threats and risks from Chinese information technology (IT) companies to their critical infrastructures for several years. The United States, however, has most strongly advocated excluding Chinese companies from their markets because investigations indicate the companies might pose a significant threat to US national security. The US leadership went one step further when it launched a global campaign to persuade US allies to adopt the same approach.

In chapter 7, I draw conclusions on the theoretical implications of state sovereignty's application to cyberspace. The distribution of authority and control in cyberspace compared with noncyber domains is diametrically different. In fact, the very nature of cyberspace requires that the distribution be much more nuanced, such that one variable might be needed to exercise a particular type of sovereignty but does not play the decisive role. This contrasts with Krasner's view of authority and control being either present or absent in the exercise of a sovereignty type. Authority and control are also closely linked to the methods and tools that states employ to exercise their sovereignty in cyberspace. I come to the conclusion that governments must carefully balance legal frameworks and cyber capabilities, because sole reliance on one is not sufficient. Depending on the type of state sovereignty that states want to enforce, they need to work with domestic legislation or international law and international relations on both multilateral and bilateral levels. Interestingly, the word "innovation" is often associated purely with technologies in cyberspace. I show, however, that that is a mistake, because cyberspace requires us to innovate and think outside the box with respect to authority and law too. In terms of cyber capabilities and capacities, I conclude that the technical tools used by governments are more miscellaneous than the legal ones. Technology constantly evolves and so must governments and their willingness to use them. Governments can no longer rely on only their own cyber capabilities but must create strong, reliable, and safe partnerships with the private sector and other stakeholders. Nonstate actors are often owners of cyber capabilities that states must have to exercise a particular type of sovereignty.

This ultimately leads me to the answer of how the state practice of sovereignty in cyberspace changes the traditional understanding of the concept. I see two major changes compared with noncyber domains. First, authority and control are much more interconnected and strongly interdependent, and they often influence each other in cyberspace. This is why governments, when considering a particular type of sovereignty in cyberspace, must employ a more comprehensive approach to cover both of these factors and their potential interactions and dependencies. Second, governments and the cyber community need to be more open-minded, flexible, and creative in their thinking about sovereignty in cyberspace than in their thinking about other traditional tangible domains. Cyberspace is a man-made domain that is far from static, which is most visible in terms of cyber capabilities. Similarly, governments must use lateral and out-of-the-box thinking in relation to legal frameworks and negotiation platforms. If states wish to retain their sovereignty in cyberspace, they must keep up with the rapid pace of development and react swiftly with the tools at hand.

In addition to the theoretical implications of my research, I also discuss practice-oriented conclusions. These brief findings and observations might have particular relevance for decision-makers and policy-oriented practitioners in general. I lay out several findings for each of the case studies in the conclusion, and I mention just few here.

Estonia is a showcase country, having built up and continuing to develop its novel e-government under the watchful observation of the international community. Its government is open and transparent about most of its efforts, including the feasibility analysis of the solutions for how to secure its digital continuity. This transparency is a valuable resource for other countries trying to achieve the same goal, but even more importantly, it greatly enhances the Estonian reputation globally and raises its profile and credibility in the eyes of the cyber community.

The example of the Netherlands teaches us that the territorial size and population of a country do not really matter in cyberspace. What is far more important is for a nation to have a good strategy and the dedication to achieve its goal. The Dutch have aptly demonstrated this with their approach to norms building and shaping. They are aware that, for a norm to be successfully accepted by the international community, it is crucial to bring to the negotiation table states and nonstate actors from the broadest spectrum of interests and opinions. Consequently, to keep them interested in the negotiation process, it is a smart strategy to start with less controversial, more basic topics to reach a consensus that serves as a foundation to build on.

The Turkish case shows the perils of a state-centric approach to regulation of the internet. Compared with a multistakeholder approach, a state-centric one is based on a hierarchical system of mutually interconnected entities that is ultimately controlled by the government. That can lead to the dangerous situation of the government misusing its powers and hiding its misuse behind national security concerns or some other similar justification. Thus, the multistakeholder approach is, in my opinion, a safer option because it incorporates checks and balances of power.

The most crucial observation of the United States' case is the importance of cooperation between a government and the private sector. The time when governments were fully able to sustain and secure their infrastructures using solely domestic sources is long gone, and so they need to create a supply chain of trustworthy and reliable international partners. At the same time, however, it is necessary to sufficiently diversify providers and not to rely on just one supplier or one other country. That can create the dangerous situation where the potential interruption of production can have far-reaching implications, as happened in the early 2020s with the supply of semiconductors.

States desire to retain their sovereignty in cyberspace and are willing to adjust their behavior accordingly to fit the particular nature of the domain. This book explores the most advanced cases of states exploring and stretching their sovereignty's boundaries in cyberspace while holding on to their democratic values (with one precautionary exception). After all, we are still in the exploratory stage, where states are testing new methods and tools, establishing important precedents for the future. I analyze this behavior to offer a new understanding of the concept of state sovereignty in cyberspace. Ultimately, state sovereignty is one of the foundational building blocks of the modern international order, and thus it is important to fully explore and comprehend how it functions when it is exercised in the new domain of cyberspace.

ONE
The Transformation of State Sovereignty over Time

The nature of state sovereignty has been debated among political theorists, international lawyers, and social scientists for centuries. The understanding and interpretation of it has constantly changed, depending on contemporary political developments and the international environment. Flexibility in the use of the term has allowed it to find utility across different ideologies, political systems, and styles of governance. State sovereignty featured in the work of Jean Bodin and Thomas Hobbes in the era of absolutism, in John Locke's and Jean-Jacques Rousseau's philosophy emphasizing the will of the people and democratic rule, and in the modern globalist interpretation of the appropriate world order.[1] The concept of state sovereignty has traditionally been based on two rules: the sovereign must exercise supreme authority over its territory and population, and it cannot allow other states to apply their rules within its borders.[2] Those rules underline both the domestic and the international character of state sovereignty, and they highlight state sovereignty's two fundamental elements: territory and population. From the Peace of Westphalia, traditionally identified as the origin of state sovereignty, to the moment when globalization stepped in, sovereignty has always involved authority being exercised over a certain territory and population, no matter the political system.

In this chapter, I make a brief tour of the key moments of state sovereignty's transformation through its early roots up to the modern time of globalization and the era of cyberspace. This might benefit readers not strongly familiar with the historical evolution of sovereignty as a concept and its significance for international relations and international law in the modern world order. I also briefly touch on the latest major crisis of sovereignty, that caused by the arrival of globalization, and the first studies of sovereignty applied in cyberspace.

The Evolution of State Sovereignty

Early Roots

State sovereignty is a historic innovation that marked a transition from medieval times to the modern era. No states in antiquity or the Middle Ages, such as the Roman Empire and medieval Latin Christendom, knew the notion of state sovereignty; they were governed by principles differing according to their ruling systems and surrounding political conditions. State sovereignty is a postmedieval idea. Under its banner, European political and religious authorities sought to escape papal and imperial subjugation and to establish their independence from those powers and also from each other.

The power politics of the Middle Ages displayed a diverse, disjointed, almost chaotic structure of mutually interdependent layers of authority. Although there was royal authority, personified by kings and queens, there were also layers of political and theological power above and below that significantly restrained royal authority. The Roman Catholic Church and the pope at its head were political-theological authorities that ruled above the kings and queens of the Middle Ages. Below the king, or even rising to the same level at times, were spiritual and secular authorities who wielded significant religious and political influence, such as archbishops and cardinals. Despite their role as administrative servants to the king, they were also loyal to the pope, who had bestowed on them their religious offices. The political order of the Middle Ages in Europe was a truly cosmopolitan world rather than the collection of independent territorial jurisdictions that is typical of the later system of sovereign states. The overlapping regulations and laws of the various authorities inevitably set the stage for repeated struggles for supremacy and independence.[3]

The Peace of Westphalia

Growing tensions over power and authority in the late medieval period escalated into the Thirty Years' War, which raged in central Europe between 1618 and 1648. Besides the struggle of the European states for political power, the main reason for one of the longest and most disruptive armed conflicts in European history was enmity between those countries influenced by the Reformation of the sixteenth century (represented by Calvinism and Lutheranism) and those that remained loyal to the Roman Catholic Church. The Protestants' main goal was to gain absolute authority, independent of both the Holy Roman emperor and the pope in Rome, as well as from one another. Those countries sought recognition of the right of all states to full independence, which subsequently evolved into what is now known as sovereignty.[4]

The objective of ending the political and religious subjugation of the European political elites of Latin Christendom to papal and imperial authorities, who had exercised power over most of Europe, was finally accomplished with the Peace of Westphalia in 1648. The Peace of Westphalia is traditionally considered the origin of the concept of state sovereignty. Sovereigns agreed on, among others, two crucial principles that were meant to shape the political future of Europe and potentially that of territories beyond European shores. First was the principle of religious tolerance, which espoused equality between Catholic and Protestant sovereigns and their states and provided certain guarantees to religious minorities. More importantly, no authority could contest how religious affairs were settled within another ruler's territory. The principle of religious equality set an influential precedent, which has since been followed by powerful historic documents such as the preamble of the United Nations Charter. Second, the Peace of Westphalia articulated several rules for peaceful settlement of future disputes among sovereigns. This step is generally considered to be one of the most important taken in the direction of modern international law and the contemporary system of international relations.[5]

The Peace of Westphalia should be understood as a symbol of a key political transformation in Europe, which freed European sovereigns from a transnational, overarching politico-theological system and established the modern secular community of sovereign states. It marked the end of the medieval world order, characterized by the idea of a Christian commonwealth governed by popes and emperors, and the beginning of a new era in which sovereign states were free from any external authority and coexisted in equality with one another.[6] Since then, state sovereignty has provided, first European and later world, leaders with a powerful concept that has been adapted to various political systems in various epochs.

The Divine Right of Kings

By the end of the eighteenth century, state sovereignty had become a well-established concept, respected across the whole of Europe in both international and domestic politics. Sovereign states and their rulers recognized one another and their right to nonintervention in their domestic affairs. Legal norms, which were slowly developing into what is today called international law, did not rule sovereign states from above but were rather a mutually agreed arrangement among sovereign states. In any era, sovereigns need legality and legitimacy for their governments to be stable and long lasting. The exercise of sovereign power alone would not suffice. Thus, given that persistent powerful religious ideas were widespread across the continent, most European sovereigns embraced a new doctrine of the divine right of kings. They believed that kings did not need a papal blessing to exercise their office, because their monarchic rule was inherently lawful and legitimate in the eyes of God. In other words, rulers were sovereigns because God made them so. They were his servants, anointed to execute his plan for humankind. This new interpretation weakened the pope's influence, because he was no longer needed to confirm and bless the godly rule of sovereigns over their patch of the Earth.[7]

The earliest political thinkers who most powerfully influenced the form and transformation of state sovereignty had already started to formulate their ideas and interpretations of this concept in the pre-Westphalian age. One of the first such thinkers who elaborated the divine right of kings and influenced it the most was Jean Bodin. This French lawyer and humanist philosopher of the sixteenth century lived at a time of religious upheaval, which escalated into the civil war in France between Catholics and Huguenots. Bodin's work focused on offering a solution to that bloody conflict and building a strong base of power for the French king to stabilize the nation and restore order and security. Bodin's thesis was that the end of the war and the restoration of peace could be achieved through religious tolerance and, more importantly, by submission to the absolute and indivisible power of a strong, sovereign king to govern the state. He considered the king to be accountable only to God and his sovereignty to be unlimited and perpetual. Bodin's analysis and interpretation of sovereignty is most famously detailed in his *Six Books of the Commonwealth*.[8]

Dynastic Sovereignty

The divine right of kings was not a universal doctrine respected in the whole of Europe. It had power only in European states where the majority of society unconditionally believed in God-granted powers. Some European societies—namely, the English, French, and Dutch—started to regard religion as a matter of private conscience rather than state authority at the turn of the eighteenth century, and the doctrine of the divine right of kings rapidly eroded and lost its political efficacy. By that time, however, a number of royal dynasties, such as the Habsburgs and Romanovs, had established strong claims to their thrones. They exercised supreme authority justified in itself, without reliance on God's will, enforcing a new concept of dynastic sovereignty that lasted until World War I. Through this dynastic sovereignty, state sovereignty became a purely secular form of authority, and it has remained so into modern times.[9]

It was in this environment that Thomas Hobbes, an English philosopher and Bodin's intellectual successor, formulated his ideas about the absolute yet resolutely secular power of a ruler. Hobbes's work and ideas on the state and society, like Bodin's, was influenced by the political upheaval of his time: the English civil war in the 1640s. Hobbes's main concern was how to secure social and political order, so that people could live together peacefully without fear of armed conflict. He argued that the people must rise above the state of nature, which he deemed to be insecure, chaotic, and violent, much like the civil war in England. Hobbes offered an alternative path: all individuals should agree to submit to the state in a social contract and swear allegiance to a (preferably absolutist) sovereign. Hobbes called the result of this universal surrender to state power the "Leviathan." The people would retain only the right to self-defense in the face of an immediate threat to their lives, in a state where no distinction would be made between the state and society because they would be united as one. He argued that chaos can be avoided only when the sovereign is omnipotent and has strong centralized power; the people must obey the absolute sovereign. They are justified in rebelling against him only if he is unable to secure the peace, which is the main reason for his existence. In that case, the social contract is invalidated.[10]

Imperial Sovereignty

With the territorial expansion of European states overseas and the arrival of colonialism, international relations among states soon reached a new level of development with the evolution of a new form of sovereignty. This was imperial sovereignty, sometimes also labeled territorial sovereignty. Imperial sovereignty became the most powerful conception of sovereignty in the nineteenth century because of its strong emphasis on territory as the fundamental basis for the existence of a state. Robert Jackson defines imperial sovereignty as "an assertion of superiority by a foreign power and a rejection of an independent right to rule of an indigenous government or people, thereby imposing a dependent status on the territory and its population."[11] Europeans claimed that non-Europeans lacked legal claim to state sovereignty because of their lesser civilizations as perceived by the Europeans, thereby justifying Europeans' imperialist behavior and claim to the right to rule over indigenous people. Colonialism peaked in the second half of the nineteenth century under the influence of European, and later also US, assumptions of racial superiority. At that time, it was proclaimed that the privileges and obligations of state sovereignty could be bestowed solely on those of the white race, who could bear the heavy burden of creating a racially exclusive sovereignty.[12] The global spread of colonialism and European (and later Western) imperialism entailed not just the subjugation of indigenous people. It also slowly transformed sovereignty itself into a globally accepted doctrine that was soon turned against the colonialists themselves in colonies' fight for independence.

In the meantime, the European continent itself was undergoing yet another revolution in the conception of state sovereignty. The technological progress of the nineteenth century had two features that shaped sovereignty for the future. First, industrialization facilitated and deepened national administrations, giving central governments more power and forcing the integration of economic, political, and social spheres within state borders. Second, modern nationalism, unleashed and empowered by the French Revolution, highlighted the importance of society and the people and provided a unifying essential ideology for future types of political entities.

Popular Sovereignty

The French Revolution and the slow, gradual decline of the legal rights and legitimacy of dynasties and kings, whose claims of authority were no longer taken for granted, required new grounds for the sovereign authority of the secular governments of the new era. The people, with growing power and privileges derived from the French Revolution and industrialization, became the basis for state sovereignty. "Popular sovereignty" is the trust and political will of the people of an independent state that confers authority on the ruling government.[13] The notion of popular sovereignty was powerful, and it soon dominated the political discourse of the newly independent British colonies, which pioneered the hegemony of the political will of the people. The Declaration of Independence of 1776 proclaimed that "whenever any form of government becomes destructive of these ends, it is the right of the people to alter or to abolish it, and to institute new government."[14] The rise of popular sovereignty marked yet another transformation of state sovereignty, this time identifying its source of authority in the people.

Recognizing the slowly growing power of the people, and reacting to Hobbes's influential idea of the Leviathan, John Locke, another English philosopher and political theorist of the seventeenth century, published *Two Treatises of Government*, which offered a different opinion about the relationship between the people and the sovereign. Locke agreed that, in the beginning, all people were in a state of nature, without government, in which everyone had certain natural rights. The state of nature was unstable, however, and all individuals were under constant threat of harm. The people realized that if they yielded some of their rights to a central authority, the state would become more stable and secure to live in. In exchange for those rights, the government would become the protector of people's property and guardian of individuals' physical security and the system's stability. This relationship between the individual and the government formed a social contract. Locke, however, argued that the sovereign could not claim absolute power over the people, because in establishing the government, the people yielded only some of their original, natural rights, not all. Therefore, sovereigns must not only be responsive to the needs and the voice of their people but also leave enough space for the exercise of certain individual liberties and rights. Those rights would be most useful if the government misused its authority or failed to safeguard the interests of its people. In that case, citizens are entitled to revolt against the sovereign and ultimately replace him. Thus, Locke was an advocate of limited government that exists to preserve and protect individual rights, deriving its legitimacy as a sovereign from the consent of the citizens. Locke rejected Hobbes's view of state sovereignty as an absolute coercive power.[15]

The debate about state sovereignty that followed, and the growing importance of "the people" in the eighteenth century, was influenced and shaped by the Enlightenment movement. That movement was mainly represented in the works of Jean-Jacques Rousseau and Immanuel Kant. Rousseau, like Hobbes, asserted that all individuals had agreed to subordinate themselves to the sovereign under a contract and that sovereign power is indivisible and limitless. Unlike Hobbes, he argued that government is simply a commission, which he believed should be formed in accord with the general will of the people, in their common interest, and should be honored by the people in absolute terms. The exercise of sovereignty was, then, nothing but the execution of the general will of the people. This helped Rousseau minimize the difference between the state and its citizens, between the political apparatus and society, and between power and authority. Sovereignty based on the general will of the people expected that all individuals would recognize it and put aside their own self-interest. In exchange, each citizen would have a chance to become a member of the political community, along with the rest of the nation, and so wield a share of state sovereignty. The people would do what is best for the nation, not just for themselves, their family, or the closest community. Ultimately, this meant that Rousseau entrusted sovereign authority entirely into the hands of the political community.[16] The general will of the people quickly became one of the most well-known themes in political science, as well as a powerful tool of political regimes.

Another prominent sovereignty theorist of the Enlightenment, the Prussian philosopher Immanuel Kant, was also interested in the relationship between the people and the government. Kant held that the optimal form of governance is a republic. In a republic, the people elect their representatives, and the representatives formulate and agree on laws on behalf of the voters and in the voters' best interest. Kant then projected this relationship between individuals living together with an equal degree of freedom inside their national borders into international relations. He argued that this is the only way to achieve world peace and that states must be understood as individuals, whose rights to self-determination must be respected by others. No state should meddle in the affairs or the government of another sovereign state. In the sense that citizens are organized into just societies, so states ought to create a global federation of equal sovereign members. Only such a setting can guarantee a state of perpetual peace. In the meantime, wars are an inevitable evil resulting from imbalances in international relations. Although wars are destructive and undesirable, they can also have a positive result if they establish new and potentially more balanced relationships that can ultimately bring the international system to its most desirable goal: world peace.[17] Kant offered not only his views on the proper domestic relation between society and government but also a fascinating cosmopolitan theory that has provided much food for thought for theorists of international relations, especially in the light of events of the twentieth century.

Parliamentary Sovereignty

Although popular sovereignty means that the people are the source of sovereignty, it would be technically impossible for the people themselves en masse to govern the state directly. For the sake of order, the people cannot act purely on their own. Their voice needs to be heard and recognized—for instance, through the creation of democratic constitutions—but it must also be organized by an agent for it to rule efficiently. Hence, an entity that is given sovereign authority and power by the people is needed. This idea gave birth to several forms for the exercise of state sovereignty, the most prominent in the twentieth and twenty-first centuries being parliamentary sovereignty.

Parliamentary sovereignty organizes politicians into parties, to which they are answerable. These parties lead discussions in parliament according to agreed parliamentary rules, a traditional one being decision-making by a majority vote. The members of parliament are elected to voice the will of the people and to represent them. This relationship is most effective when the entire adult population is enfranchised without reference to gender or social class. Parliamentary representatives legitimately represent the people only if they are elected by them in fair elections, in which case a parliament can truly express the collective will of the people and claim that its exercise of sovereignty is based on a foundation of popular sovereignty.[18]

Max Weber's work on the theory of the modern state helps reconcile the evolution of sovereignty over the past four hundred years with the events of the twentieth and twenty-first centuries. Although this German sociologist is not a thinker on sovereignty or a political theorist per se, he offers a new perspective on states and state sovereignty. According to his popular definition, the state is "a human community that (successfully) claims the monopoly of the legitimate use of physical force within a given territory."[19] The Weberian definition of a modern state highlights two crucial issues.

In his definition of the modern state, Weber adheres to the two traditional elements of state sovereignty: the people and the territory. His reference to the "human community" implies that it has a certain degree of organization and institutionalization. In his famous essay "Politics as a Vocation," he says, "The state is a relation of men dominating men," in which "the dominated must obey the authority claimed by the powers that be."[20] The territorial element in his definition refers to limiting the exercise of authority and force to the territory within the state's borders. Authority and the use of force cannot legitimately be extended beyond the state's territorial boundaries, except when exercised in self-defense. The second important issue according to Weber is the state's monopoly on the legitimate use of physical force. The modern state has the absolute ability to marshal, institutionalize, and control the exercise of coercive force. This monopoly over the use of legitimate physical force is the hallmark of the sovereignty entrusted to the hands of public authorities and is best based on a codified legal order. In short, the state is the only rightful source of violence.[21]

Global Spread of the Concept

The concept of state sovereignty evolved into the modern era as movements for colonial independence peaked and the colonial empires rapidly dissolved after World War II. State sovereignty became the highly prized goal of non-European territories under the rule of the United Kingdom, the Netherlands, France, Spain, and other Western colonial powers. The domestic elites of the colonies realized that only by achieving their own state sovereignty could they be accepted as equal to their former colonial masters. The first colonies to reach this goal were in South and North America, in the eighteenth and nineteenth centuries. The real peak of the decolonization effort came in the aftermath of World War II, when dozens of new sovereign states were established in Africa, Asia, the Middle East, and the Caribbean. Ultimately, the fight against the old imperialism and the subsequent disbanding of empires multiplied the number of sovereign states and strengthened the position of the international system of sovereign states as it is known today. The revolution of state sovereignty brought about by decolonization was finally complete when the European states recognized that state sovereignty was a fundamental right of other peoples around the globe. The concept of state sovereignty then reached its maximum extent, being recognized all over the globe.

De Jure versus De Facto Sovereignty

With the global spread of state sovereignty, international lawyers started to distinguish between de jure and de facto sovereignty, depending on the domestic and international state of affairs in concrete cases. "De jure sovereignty" refers to the formally recognized legal right to exercise control over a territory. "De facto sovereignty" concerns the ability to practice control; in other words, it means sovereignty that exists in practice, regardless of legal recognition.

Although most states are both de jure and de facto, meaning their sovereignty exists in practice and in law, some common, special, and anomalous variations of de jure and de facto sovereignty have been observed over the last century or so. Some states are recognized as de jure, the legitimate governments of a territory that they possess no actual control over; the governments-in-exile of several states during World War II (including Czechoslovakia, Poland, the Netherlands, and Belgium) are examples from recent history. These governments maintained strong diplomatic ties with the Allies despite their territories being occupied by Axis forces. De facto states have control over their territory but have no or only partial legal recognition from the international community. These states are de jure according to their domestic laws and to the governments that officially recognize them. For example, Somaliland is "one of the most stable de facto states in the world" today and has been waiting for international recognition since 1991.[22] The world of geopolitics has also spawned several extreme examples of states with ambiguously de jure and de facto sovereignty, the case of Taiwan being one of the most glaring. Taiwan is known as a legal sovereign state, the Republic of China, enjoying recognition and formal diplomacy as a de facto state with paradiplomatic ties. This status quo of ambiguously being a de facto independent state that lacks de jure statehood is mostly accepted because it leaves the legal status of Taiwan open, thereby allowing a flexible interpretation that is politically acceptable.[23] All in all, our understanding of state sovereignty clearly continues to evolve in the modern era as it has throughout history.

A Living Concept

In less than four hundred years, sovereignty as a concept has grown from its earliest roots in the Peace of Westphalia to the global system of sovereign states we know today. Even if the core idea has remained unchanged, the shape of the concept has continuously morphed to accommodate the needs and demands of political organizations and regimes, providing kings and governments with legitimate authority to rule. It has developed from the sovereignty recognized by the Peace of Westphalia through the divine right of kings to dynastic and imperial sovereignty, and into popular sovereignty. This list of types of sovereignty is not exhaustive, nor does it pretend to be. Moreover, the names of types of sovereignty can differ from author to author. The taxonomy used by Robert Jackson[24] is different from, for instance, the "absolutist, constitutional, national, democratic and welfare state" typology of sovereignty employed by Edgar Grande and Louis W. Pauly.[25] Although the names of types of sovereignty may differ, the main message and ideological core are always the same, or at least very similar.

The work and ideas of thinkers about state sovereignty such as Bodin, Hobbes, Kant, and Weber, from the sixteenth century up to modern times, show a transformation of the philosophical debate that has mirrored contemporaneous political and social developments. Bodin and Hobbes, two of the first and most influential such thinkers, conceived state sovereignty in terms of an absolutist state that would impose order on Europe after the traumatic ending of the medieval world and the Christian commonwealth ruled by popes and Holy Roman emperors. Later, Locke, Rousseau, and Kant offered more democratic interpretations of state sovereignty under the rising influence of the popular masses who gained respect owing to the French Revolution and industrialization. Finally, work by Weber suggested that the concept of state sovereignty still had a role to play at the turn of the twentieth century.

The historical trajectory of the literature of sovereignty demonstrates that philosophers were more concerned with the source of sovereignty than how it was exercised. The perceived source of authority for sovereignty has changed over time. Before the Peace of Westphalia, Europe was governed by the cosmopolitan political-theological authority of the pope as head of medieval Latin Christendom. The Peace of Westphalia and the new order created immediately afterward freed monarchs from the need to seek a papal blessing in order to exercise their royal office. Kings were lawful, legitimate rulers by the will of God, the direct source of their sovereign authority. This arrangement remained unchanged until the French Revolution and industrialization, which shifted the source of authority from God to the people and gave rise to the concept of popular sovereignty. Although the will of the people as the source of sovereign authority was at first limited to certain groups of people on the basis of gender and social class, that limitation soon began to vanish. "The people" in the end included the entire adult population as we consider it today.

The changes in the source of sovereign authority are linked with another important observation. Although the territory and the people, the two elements of state sovereignty, were always recognized from the beginning, the balance between them changed. At first, the emphasis was put on territory and external respect for sovereignty. As the people started to play a more important role as the source of authority, the balance changed in their favor, and the state's internal respect for their rights and sovereignty gained more importance. State sovereignty is a living concept that has survived throughout history up to modern times. It continues to provoke long-lasting debate over its proper form, its implementation, and occasionally, even its very existence.

The Modern Debate on State Sovereignty

The way the sovereignty debate developed in the latter decades of the twentieth century offered new empirical and theoretical challenges to established concepts. The most notable of these is the slowly blurring distinction between the internal and external aspects of sovereignty resulting from globalization. The debate has evolved into a controversy about whether state sovereignty is an outmoded concept or still has validity in the modern globalized world. In one camp are those arguing that state sovereignty is a failed concept in the modern era. In the other are those who defend state sovereignty as still functional and much needed by nation-states.

The Camp of State Sovereignty's Skeptics

The first camp, those skeptical about state sovereignty, points to global phenomena such as international trade, electronic telecommunications, multinational corporations, supranational organizations, and transcontinental passenger transport and shipping, which together create a truly cosmopolitan society and a global marketplace. They argue that this new society and marketplace bypass, and in some instances replace, the sovereign state and the old world order. Consequently, states cannot effectively police their territorial borders as they once did, and so borders lose their significance. In short, the camp of the skeptics argues that modern times are forcing a transformation of the system of sovereign states into something different, even if they are unsure about the form the postsovereignty world order will look.

The traditional proponents of the thesis that sovereignty is eroding through globalization, which was very powerful in the 1990s, are Joseph A. Camilleri with Jim Falk, Susan Strange, and Richard Rosecrance, among others.[26] According to Camilleri and Falk, "Not all is well with the theory of sovereignty, neither as a description of how the world is, how it is evolving, or how it might be shaped. . . . Not only is the world being progressively integrated but, perhaps paradoxically, it is also experiencing a process of progressive decentralization of authority and fragmentation of society."[27] They perceive an urgent need to rethink the concept of sovereignty.

Strange talks about the declining authority of states, which has been accompanied by the transfer of their authority to other actors. She asserts that the power of most governments weakened during the 1980s and 1990s, along with their political authority over the societies they control within their national borders. The authority they have lost has not disappeared altogether and sparked chaos, but it has been transferred to nonstate actors that have increased their influence on society. She adds that "the impersonal forces of world markets . . . are now more powerful than the states to whom ultimate political authority over society and economy is supposed to belong. Where states were once the masters of markets, now it is the markets which, on many crucial issues, are the masters over the governments of states."[28] Strange blames the loss of sovereignty on the rapid technological evolution of recent decades, which she sees as the primary reason for the change in the balance of power between the state and the markets. In the last century, there have been more radical technological changes than ever before in the history of humankind, which she says have slowly caused the state to lose its main reason for existence: the capacity to protect its people from harm.[29]

Rosecrance also bases his argument on the growing power of the market. The main argument of his book *The Rise of the Virtual State: Wealth and Power in the Coming Century* is that states do not need territory to exist because the factors of capital, information, and labor exceed the outdated factor of land in importance. Moreover, states should concentrate their efforts on the most beneficial factors for production, which are a well-trained labor force and high-quality services and products. Hence, states' attention diverts from the material factors that were dominant in the past to the products of the mind, which are preferred today.[30] Rosecrance also introduces a new phenomenon, which he calls the "virtual state"—that is, a state that has downsized its domestic, territorially based production capacity and lodged it abroad, specializing instead in production of intangible goods (for example, finance, marketing, product design, and high-level technical and research services). This results in the emancipation of the virtual state from the land, negating the need to acquire new territories, focusing instead on entering the world market with products of the mind. By moving its production capacity abroad, the virtual state makes its security dependent on keeping trade routes open and the inflow of products manufactured abroad uninterrupted.[31]

Rosecrance's identification of virtual states bridges the differences between critics and defenders of state sovereignty in the modern era. He claims that sovereignty has failed but at the same time offers a new type of state.

The Camp of State Sovereignty's Defenders

The second camp claims state sovereignty is not a failed concept at all and offers perspectives on the apparent weaknesses of modern state sovereignty with respect to its key elements of territoriality and authority. The first grounds for defense of the continued viability of state sovereignty are offered by those who argue that the concept is still valid because it is ever changing. They usually base their arguments on historical evidence. Most typical of them is Robert Jackson, who argues that state sovereignty continually evolves, taking on new forms over time to fit the demands of successive ruling political regimes. He illustrates his argument by exploring the concept of sovereignty in a long list of historical periods, and he shows that, although the character of sovereignty has evolved, it has not fundamentally changed, and its core remains the same.[32]

Similarly, Daniel Philpott argues that the system of sovereign states has been shaped by revolution, two in particular: the transformation of Europe from the medieval system to the modern international order, which was embodied in the Peace of Westphalia of 1648, and the fight for colonial independence and the fall of the colonial empires, which disseminated the sovereign state system across the globe. Philpott claims that revolutions in sovereignty are always preceded by ideological revolutions in political authority and law. For example, the Protestant Reformation of the sixteenth and seventeenth centuries saw a century of turmoil that escalated into the Thirty Years' War and ended with the Peace of Westphalia. Likewise, nationalism and the fight for racial equality in the twentieth century began in protest movements in the colonies and continued with wars for independence that expanded the system of state sovereignty around the globe.[33]

Philpott further names several major constitutional revolutions. Besides the Peace of Westphalia and colonial independence, he lists the 1878 Treaty of Berlin, which redrew the map of the Balkans; the Treaty of Versailles and other post–World War I treaties; the creation of the European Coal and Steel Community in 1950 and the integration of Europe it commenced; and the post–Cold War internationally sanctioned interventions in the internal affairs of states by the United Nations and other international organizations.[34] Philpott, like Jackson, tracks and describes the development of state sovereignty throughout history; unlike Jackson, he focuses on historical breakpoints, or in his words, revolutions.

Edgar Grande and Louis W. Pauly are two strong proponents of sovereignty who also recognize its continuous evolution. They agree that we are eyewitnesses to a comprehensive yet partly contradictory transmutation of authority that is changing the elementary principles, institutions, and structures of modern policy making. They contend, however, that this does not necessarily mean that states are an antiquated institution. On the contrary, according to Grande and Pauly, "in most parts of the world, states seem to be more important than ever for the production of public goods such as security and welfare. Where states have failed, it seems quite clear that it is certain specific structures of the state that have failed, rather than the idea of the state itself."[35]

Perhaps even more important for my discussion is their argument regarding the transformation of state authority. They assert that the hierarchy of contemporary political control is no longer clear-cut, yet it is not chaotic either. Grande and Pauly outline a coherent but highly complicated system of numerous overlapping hierarchies that make up global political authority. They call this "complex sovereignty."[36] This kind of sovereignty results from a redistribution of responsibility for the production of goods between the private and public sectors. It creates new avenues for cooperation between them, such as public-private partnerships. Furthermore, Grande and Pauly describe new, multilevel systems of governance: transnational policy networks and international regimes governed by new arrangements and rules.

They stress that the new governance formats are not a substitute for the modern nation-state, nor will they likely be in the future. States continue to play an indispensable role in and remain a functional element of the global system, but they are not the only powers dictating the rules of the world order anymore. In other words, "state sovereignty is not obsolete; it is, however, being reconstituted."[37]

As a follow-up to the work of Grande and Pauly, Rodney Bruce Hall and Thomas J. Biersteker offer a detailed look at the contemporary forms of authority. Their initial assumption is that "at the beginning of the twenty-first century there are so many examples of sites or locations of authority that are neither states, state-based, nor state-created. The state is no longer the sole, or in some instances even the principal, source of authority, in either the domestic arena or in the international system."[38] They point out the rising importance of private authority alongside public authority and organize their book *The Emergence of Private Authority in Global Governance* around three varieties of private authority: moral authority, market authority, and illicit authority, the latter of which is exercised, for example, by organized crime groups. Hall and Biersteker conclude their analysis of private authority by pointing out the growing importance of private actors, not only in international trade but also increasingly in other crucial spheres of political and social life, such as social welfare and national security.[39]

This brings us to the last, but probably the most robust issue in the modern-day debate about sovereignty: the influence of globalization. Jean L. Cohen defends sovereignty in her book *Globalization and Sovereignty: Rethinking Legality, Legitimacy and Constitutionalism*, arguing that although globalization has brought about a number of momentous shifts in world power, we live in a cosmopolitan world where sovereign states continue to play an important role. We must not abandon the traditional concept of sovereignty to conceptualize the changes that accompany the establishment of a new globalist regime. Cohen further asserts that we are witnessing the emergence of a new sovereignty, which redefines the legal prerogatives of sovereign states. She immediately adds, however, that states remain the key players that produce international legal norms for themselves.[40]

Jackson also disagrees with the contention that globalization has crippled sovereignty. In his defense of sovereignty, he recounts its historical development and asserts that, rather than sovereignty losing its importance, "it is more reasonable to suppose and expect that the sovereign states system will adapt to globalization just as it adapted to previous transformations of science, technology, economy, and society."[41] Globalization is not unprecedented. Some elements of today's global civil society have existed for a long time: world trade and traffic routes, religious missionary work, criminal activities, and piracy, to name just a few. Such historical activities are not the same as the contemporary aspects of globalization that result from high technology facilitating a tightly integrated global economy. Jackson notes that, nevertheless, this does not change the historical fact that people and their goods have traveled and moved across the globe for centuries.[42]

Finally, another critic of the thesis that globalization has seriously eroded state sovereignty is John Agnew, who explains his argument in *Globalization and Sovereignty*. He disputes the idea that global networks that know no borders are replacing the previous, territorialized world. Agnew says that state sovereignty is not, and never has been, clearly contained within state territory, as is generally believed. Agnew develops an innovative mode of thinking about the geography of sovereignty. He says that states have never possessed a total economic, regulatory, or political monopoly over their territories because challenges to the territorialism of sovereignty have always existed, such as dual citizenship, flows of refugees and migrants across borders, denationalized currencies, and supranational organizations.[43] Agnew formulates an idea on spatiality that is important for this book: "Alternative spatialities (modes of geographical organization) of political and economic activities, particularly hierarchical networks (as in the world-city network) or reticular networks (as with the Internet), can challenge or supplement the use of territoriality."[44]

The Performance of Sovereignty

The sovereignty debate today focuses on the fundamental question of whether the sovereign states system is sustainable in the modern era. The question is existential: is state sovereignty a totally failed concept, or does it still have meaning in the modern, globalized world? Those who say it has failed believe we are witnessing the formation of a new type of society and marketplace that bypasses or even replaces the sovereign states system. This camp, which was most popular in the 1990s, concludes that the old world order has been transformed into something new and different and that state sovereignty is no longer an effective concept.

Defenders of the viability of state sovereignty argue that it is still relevant and much needed. Some focus on the transformation of sovereignty, either from a long-term historical perspective or the perspective of just the past century. Others are well aware of the current weakness of the two key elements of sovereignty (authority over persons and territory) and offer new perspectives that reinterpret those weak spots in the light of the most recent changes in the international world order, including globalization. Finally, a group of scholars criticizes the thesis that globalization is eroding sovereignty and assert that, although sovereign states may no longer play the principal role in international relations, they are still very important to the functioning of the world system.

The modern debate over sovereignty has also undergone a significant shift in content compared with the previous debate. Historically, thinkers mainly focused on the source of sovereignty and how sovereignty has been transformed. They tracked the evolution of the source of sovereignty from the pope's blessing in the Middle Ages to God's direct grant of absolute power to the monarch, to a natural, secular source in "the people." The modern debate, in contrast, is not much interested in the source of sovereignty anymore. It assumes the people to be the source by default. Modern-day thinkers focus on the performance of sovereignty itself rather than its source. Their concern is the current situation, when the state, as sole executor of sovereignty, is being endangered and weakened by political, economic, and sociological developments. According to those who believe state sovereignty is eroding, sovereignty is no longer the monopoly of the state but is shared with other actors such as international organizations and the private sector. Nonetheless, even they still have to admit that the state remains the main actor, even if it must adapt to the new globalized world.

This analysis of the debate about state sovereignty confirms a pattern, pointed out in works of Jackson, Philpott, and Grande and Pauly: the continual change and development in state sovereignty. State sovereignty is a living concept that was first recognized in 1648 and has continued to develop into modern times. Although it has experienced numerous transformations, it survives in the twenty-first century. The majority of scholars agree that it still has a role to play, even in the now-globalized world. In the following section, I show that the concept of state sovereignty does not lose importance, even when it encounters the seemingly borderless cyberspace.

State Sovereignty in Cyberspace

Cyberspace is a constructed domain that, in contrast to the four domains of land, sea, air, and outer space, is not an element of nature. Therefore, the construction, regulation, and potentially the destruction of cyberspace is in the hands of humankind. Although cyberspace is a modern construct, numerous definitions reflect the specific understanding of a particular actor. Yet definitions of a more complex character emerge from time to time too, accepting that cyberspace features two main elements: hardware and software. One of them is a definition by Ronald Deibert, Rafal Rohozinski, and Masashi Crete-Nishihata that acknowledges the interconnection between the informational and physical characters of cyberspace by breaking it into four constitutive elements. First is the physical infrastructure, which consists of hardware such as cables and routers. Second is the code level, which includes software operating communications traffic. Third is the regulatory level, which is understood as the norms, laws, and principles governing the domain. Fourth is the sphere of ideas, which is reified, for example, as videos or pictures and is present above all three previous layers.[45] This definition stresses the complexity of cyberspace, which encompasses both physical and informational elements. Furthermore, this complicated nature of cyberspace is even more important when studying the broad spectrum of states' activities in the domain.

States' activities in cyberspace are the basis of the two main streams of debate on state sovereignty in the cyber domain. As soon as cyberspace and the internet spread worldwide and became a new international-relations arena, a question arose as to whether state sovereignty applies to the seemingly borderless cyber environment. This was a crucial question given that state sovereignty is traditionally a cornerstone of both international relations and international law that would potentially govern states' behavior in cyberspace. Not long after, the first stream of debate on territoriality and borders emerged, asking whether territoriality plays a role in cyberspace and, if it does, whether it is possible and feasible to build borders in this environment. The growing activity of states in cyberspace prepared the ground for the second debate dealing with state sovereignty in cyberspace. Initially, the second stream of debate focused on the official proclamation that the concept actually applies to cyberspace. Later, it discussed the rules of state sovereignty applicable in the cyber sphere. Thus, the debate is both broadening and deepening in scope, and given the growing spectrum of state activities in cyberspace, it can be expected to further develop.

The Debate on Territoriality in Cyberspace

International relations experts, who shape the discussion on territoriality in cyberspace the most, explore the territorial aspect of state sovereignty, cyberspace, and borders. Geoffrey L. Herrera discusses in "Cyberspace and Sovereignty: Thoughts on Physical Space and Digital Space" the relation between cyberspace and politics and analyzes the national security threats derived from it. He rightly argues that information and communications technology (ICT) and globalization are interdependent and that business and information flows being bolstered by globalization is a crucial factor shaping the intersection between the technologies and international security. Modern threats to national security are often facilitated by this synergistic relationship, and thus a state's vitality and survival depend on its control of information flows.[46] According to Herrera, the cyber domain has been sculpted by geopolitics, and the internet's characteristic features of anonymity and ubiquity exist because of politics. Consequently, technologies reshaped in the future could potentially rebuild cyberspace into a more territorial domain.[47] The internet is traditionally characterized as a network of networks, in which private and public sector networks connect to national network backbones. These backbones join worldwide via international gateways. The internet is a "socio-technical system" that reflects its "state-centric origins," and it is highly unlikely that its structure will be reshaped or unmade in the future.[48] Thus, it is not difficult for governments to control and even censor the information flows into and out of their territory, particularly if the state is the owner of the internet backbone. Herrera makes an important observation: we need to abandon the modern binary debate of whether the sovereign state is or is not relevant anymore and instead study the current transformation of sovereignty and territoriality.[49]

Forrest Hare follows Herrera by asking whether borders, as an element of sovereignty, can be pertinent to addressing issues of cybersecurity. He argues that borders are indeed a relevant construct because they help people make informed national policy decisions and deal with cybersecurity topics.[50] Hare predicts that the more cyber threats become securitized, the more states will feel pressured to play an active role. For example, the United States might try to regain the control it had over the internet during the initial phase of its development. Rather than merely a symbolic proclamation to "regain control," such an attempt could take the concrete form of technological control points at the border crossings between fiber-optic lines and undersea cables or of labeling inward and outward internet traffic to identify its country of origin and destination.[51] Hare further asserts the importance of a state's borders in a domain dependent on the state's ability to exercise its sovereignty within them. If states remain the main target of security threats, and the sole legitimate source of response to threats, states' borders will preserve their relevance as well. Hare concludes, "Borders can be equally important in cyberspace because borders define boundaries of sovereignty regardless the domain and the ability to locate them physically. Even though borders have become less significant for all legal commerce, they have become even more significant for policing action against transnational threats."[52]

Chris Demchak and Peter Dombrowski follow up on this line of argumentation in introducing their "cybered Westphalian age."[53] Demchak and Dombrowski contend that, although states have not recognized it publicly, regulation in cyberspace has already begun creating the basis for national virtual borders. Not only cyber superpowers such as China and the United States but also other states want to know and control what is happening inside their borders, giving birth to the "emerging cybered territorial sovereignty."[54] According to Demchak and Dombrowski, the Stuxnet worm[55] marks the emergence of a new Westphalian system of virtual borders in cyberspace that is characterized by building national cyber commands as an integral component of cybered governments. Uncovering the Stuxnet worm was a watershed moment in conflict in cyberspace, and states must now delineate safe and secure territory to guarantee the economic well-being and safety of their citizens. States attempt to achieve control by building both technological and organizational capacities and capabilities. In the end, these efforts will escalate into the formation of national borders in cyberspace. Demchak and Dombrowski argue that "states are learning that everything about today's grid can be technologically regulated," and thus "a cybered national border is technologically possible, psychologically comfortable, and systematically and politically manageable."[56]

Demchak and Dombrowski's later work "Cyber Westphalia: Asserting State Prerogatives in Cyberspace" brings far more theory of state sovereignty into cyberspace when they ask, "To what extent are states recreating in cyberspace the older Westphalian process of delineating borders and reaffirming state sovereignty?"[57] Traditionally, a Westphalian sovereign state has been characterized by its territory, control over it, autonomy from other states, and mutual recognition by other states. Demchak and Dombrowski use these four attributes to assess developments in the new interstate system. According to them, this new system of the digital information age most likely will not possess the same characteristic features as the old, nondigital period: "If, as we expect, current states develop for cyberspace the necessary authorities, domestic institutions, and international regimes for exercise [of] political sovereignty, 'territoriality,' and non-intervention/mutual recognition, then the existing Westphalian system will have to adapt."[58] Demchak and Dombrowski admit that it would be beneficial to study more deeply how states are dealing with their sovereignty in cyberspace under the Westphalian model, yet they leave it for future research; besides that, they argue that the current situation indicates the transformation to a cyber Westphalian structure is underway.[59]

Herrera, Hare, and Demchak and Dombrowski are thus representatives of the first stage of the debate on sovereignty in cyberspace, the question of the applicability of borders, a crucial element of state sovereignty, in cyberspace. They all agree that cyberspace is not immune to state efforts to establish borders in cyberspace for very practical reasons. The discussion on borders in cyberspace marks the beginning of the sovereignty debate. The second part of the debate asks whether and, more importantly, how state sovereignty is applied to cyberspace—that is, from the points of view of international legal norms and international relations.

The Debate on the Rules of Sovereignty in Cyberspace

Benedikt Pirker studies the application of sovereignty in cyberspace, focusing on the diverse legal issues stemming from the violation of territorial sovereignty.[60] He asserts that states have the exclusive right to exercise their powers on their territory and therefore any cyber infrastructure within the state's borders is protected under the state's territorial sovereignty and subject to its territorial jurisdiction. He lists several examples of a territorial sovereignty violation, such as the use of cyberspace for political influence by one state against another, cyber espionage, cyber sabotage, and cybercrime.[61] But, Pirker suggests, the exact content of certain rules of international law remains to be shaped by future state practice.

Wolff Heintschel von Heinegg goes one step further, expressing a preference for the application of customary international law in cyberspace, including the principle of territorial sovereignty. He appreciates that the voices calling for development of completely new international legal norms for cyberspace, because of its unique and distinct character, have not been heard and notes that states seem to prefer the application of customary international law in cyberspace instead.[62] Heintschel von Heinegg shows that the principle of territorial sovereignty (the claiming of a state's exclusive authority over a territory) indeed applies to cyberspace. He then immediately adds that it is uncertain whether the principles and rules of customary international law, including territorial sovereignty, can be applied to cyberspace unconditionally in their traditional understanding and interpretation. Thus, it is important that states reach agreement on not only the general application of these rules to the cyber sphere but also a joint interpretation reflecting the extraordinary character of emerging technologies.[63] Therefore, according to Heintschel von Heinegg, the rules and principles of customary international law apply to cyberspace, but because of the necessary modifications to their interpretation to reflect the unique cyber environment, it will take time to clarify certain aspects of this application of customary international law.

To enhance and support the state practice of international law in cyberspace, the international community launched two initiatives that developed important insights about the applicability of state sovereignty in cyberspace. The first initiative was by the United Nations Group of Governmental Experts (UN GGE) on Developments in the Field of Information and Telecommunications in the Context of International Security.[64] The UN GGE's membership was drawn from the United Nations. This is both an advantage and a disadvantage. The membership is diverse, but the diversity makes reaching a consensus hard or can even result in a stalemate. The UN GGE also discussed state sovereignty during its meetings, and in its 2013 report concluded that "State sovereignty and international norms and principles that flow from sovereignty apply to State conduct of ICT-related activities, and to their jurisdiction over ICT infrastructure within their territory."[65] Its 2015 report reiterated the statement and added that "in their use of ICTs, States must observe, among other principles of international law, State sovereignty, sovereign equality, the settlement of disputes by peaceful means and non-intervention in the internal affairs of other States."[66] The last UN GGE report, published in 2021, also mentioned sovereignty several times but did not present a major breakthrough either.[67] Although the UN GGE had the difficult task of reaching a consensus on the governing principles of cyberspace, its outcomes were of a general character and lacked concrete details.

Another initiative of the international community in this regard seems to be more successful and substantial. The project began in 2009 with the support of the Cooperative Cyber Defense Center of Excellence of NATO (North Atlantic Treaty Organization), based in Tallinn, Estonia. It brought together a group of distinguished international legal scholars and practitioners to examine extant legal norms and suggest how they can be applied to cyberspace. The result was *Tallinn Manual on the International Law Applicable to Cyber Warfare*. Although the *Tallinn Manual*'s content is nonbinding for states, it offers them a useful framework on which to base their behavior in the cyber domain and, later, for creating customary international law or crafting international agreements.

The *Tallinn Manual* project has had three iterations so far; two published in 2013 and 2017, respectively, and the third's publication projected to be 2025. The first manual, *Tallinn Manual 1.0*, was written by group of twenty experts mainly from the transatlantic area and addressed international law applicable in cyber warfare.[68] The second, *Tallinn Manual 2.0 on the International Law*

Applicable to Cyber Operations, covers international law applicable to cyber operations, updates the 2013 manual, and extends the scope to include international legal norms applicable to more common cyber incidents that states face daily and are below the threshold of the use of force. *Tallinn Manual 2.0* involved nineteen experts from all around the world, representing a much greater diversity of nationalities than the first edition. Given that each member of the expert group had veto powers over the black-letter rules, the broader number of nationalities lent the manual higher credibility. Furthermore, fifty states reviewed chapter drafts to provide feedback during its writing.[69]

Tallinn Manual 2.0 elaborates rules on state sovereignty in more depth than its predecessor. The first and only rule on sovereignty in *Tallinn Manual 1.0* merely stated that "a State may exercise control over cyber infrastructure and activities within its sovereign territory,"[70] whereas *Tallinn Manual 2.0* lists five related rules on different aspects of state sovereignty. The first rule states that "the principle of State sovereignty applies in cyberspace."[71] The commentary to the first rule then discusses the territorial aspect of sovereignty.[72] The second and third rules and commentaries discuss the interrelated internal and external elements of state sovereignty. The fourth rule proclaims that one state must not violate the sovereignty of another state by any cyber means. The extensive commentary to this rule mentions the idea of Estonian digital embassies and says that interference with critical governmental data backed up in digital embassies in other states "in a way that affects the performance by Estonia of its inherently governmental functions would . . . amount to a violation of this rule."[73] The final sovereignty rule of *Tallinn Manual 2.0* discusses sovereign immunity and inviolability.[74] Hence, *Tallinn Manual 2.0* clearly proclaims that state sovereignty does exist in cyberspace and develops the elements, issues, and possible sovereignty violations in rules and commentaries, reflecting prior debate.

The comprehensive content of *Tallinn Manual 2.0* has served as a starting point for scholars and state representatives to develop the discussion on how state sovereignty applies to cyberspace from the international legal perspective, which is continuously unfolding. The debate has grown robust, sometimes controversial, in the late 2010s and early 2020s. It is not my goal to capture all the subtle nuances of it here, but two points of the debate have future impact. First, academic debate, building on previous efforts, centers on the application of state sovereignty in cyberspace. It discusses the implications, rights, and obligations tied to sovereignty in cyberspace in times of war, but also below the threshold of the use of force.[75] Scholars have also explored the physical dimension of sovereignty in cyberspace by focusing on physical infrastructure, linking state sovereignty in cyberspace with a state's territorial sovereignty.[76]

Second, a growing number of states around the globe are publishing their stands on the application of law in cyberspace, including state sovereignty in the domain. Authoritarian states like Russia and China have been clear in their positions on state sovereignty in cyberspace for some time, be it through official or unofficial channels.[77] Other states around the world, including democracies, are also publicly putting forward their positions. The majority of negotiations over the rules of international law applicable in cyberspace have taken place throughout the 2010s and early 2020s as multilateral negotiations within the UN (most notably by the Group of Governmental Experts on Developments in the Field of Information and Telecommunications in the Context of International Security and its later incarnation, Advancing Responsible State Behavior in Cyberspace in the Context of International Security, as well as the Open-Ended Working Group on Developments in the Field of Information and Telecommunications in the Context of International Security[78]). After initial success, these initiatives have not since pushed the frontiers of the field forward in a substantial way. This situation has encouraged states to unilaterally publish their views on the application of international law in cyberspace (also in relation to sovereignty).[79] The United States and the United Kingdom were the first to publish their views. France, Estonia, and the Netherlands followed in 2019 with written positions or public speeches delivered by leading governmental officials; others are now joining in. Thanks to these events, we can, for example, observe the debate unfolding over whether state sovereignty in cyberspace operates as a rule of international law (and when breached, gives rise to state responsibility) or as just a principle of international law (and thus may guide state interactions).[80] Proponents of it being a rule of international law include the Netherlands and Estonia, and it being a principle is supported by the United Kingdom.[81] These debates are key for the nascent order of international law in cyberspace, and so states need to take a clear stance to help clarify the application of international law, including in terms of state sovereignty in the domain.[82] The discussions also include certain aspects from the perspective of international relations, which I elaborate later.

From the point of view of international relations, Patrick W. Franzese asserts that recognizing state sovereignty in cyberspace provides the necessary basis from which the international community can address the new challenges arising from the cyber environment.[83] Franzese lists four reasons why cyberspace is not resistant to state sovereignty. First, an absolutely key and inseparable element of cyberspace is its physical infrastructure, which is located in the territory of a state and thus logically falls under the authority of that state. Second, the financial market and its movements in cyberspace needs rules and laws that would govern these transactions. Without state sovereignty in cyberspace, any business relationships in cyberspace would face uncertainties and the peril of substantial financial loses. Third, the content of cyberspace has its significance outside cyberspace, and states to which data are sent, received, and stored express interest in exercising control over it. Fourth, it is not unusual for states nowadays to operate their critical infrastructure via cyberspace. It is thus in their best interest to assert and strengthen their role in cyberspace because national security is at stake.[84] Franzese contends, "Because sovereignty in cyberspace will be an extension of territorial sovereignty," it is crucial to also study sovereignty's historical developments within the domains of sea, air, and space, which might suggest how state sovereignty in cyberspace will unfold in the future.[85]

Andrew Liaropoulos also opposes a borderless cyberspace immune to sovereignty and international regulations. Cyber infrastructure is physically located on states' territories and is thus not immune from sovereignty. Liaropoulos argues that cyberspace is a simple reflection of the modern international system and as such is deeply affected by its rules.[86] Cyberspace is partially defined by its physical structures in state sovereign territories. This characteristic of cyberspace is then reflected in states' behavior; they have continuously exercised their jurisdiction over cyber events on their territory and have exercised control over cyber infrastructure in their territory, which they protect from transborder attack by other states or nonstate actors. Liaropoulos therefore concludes that, despite the nonterritorial nature of cyberspace, state behavior proves that the cyber sphere is not immune from state sovereignty or regulations. On the contrary, the increasing trend in the regulation of cyberspace suggests that a new international cyber order is gradually coming to be.[87]

Liaropoulos briefly discusses a few of the challenges in the cyber environment facing the four types of sovereignty developed by Stephen Krasner: Westphalian, domestic, interdependence, and international legal sovereignty.[88] Unlike international legal sovereignty, which is the least challenged type according to Liaropoulos, Westphalian sovereignty is under constant pressure by activities in cyberspace. This is caused mainly by external cyber attacks against the information infrastructure of states, which constitutes a violation of Westphalian sovereignty. Similar examples are the challenges to interdependence sovereignty caused by the unrestricted flow of data and information in cyberspace. It is highly difficult for states to control or even monitor information such as terrorist propaganda online. Finally, domestic sovereignty is also challenged in cyberspace, for example, by states that try to control their citizens' access to online information, justifying such control as defense of domestic order and national security. Liaropoulos concludes that, although state sovereignty can be exercised in cyberspace, states have not yet established an effective system of authority and control.[89]

Ben Buchanan also outlines how sovereignty in cyberspace works and employs Krasner's four types of state sovereignty. Buchanan looks into how state sovereignty is exercised as implementation of cryptographic systems increases. For example, where domestic sovereignty is concerned, a government might mandate that cryptographic systems produced on its territory must include a so-called back door, or golden key. Such systems with back doors provide users with cryptographic protection but allow the state to access messages produced within its borders and so retain its domestic powers.[90] Likewise, states can decide to exercise their interdependence sovereignty in relation to cryptography. Any state has information flowing across its borders in cyberspace, and states have two options to manage that flow. States can either monitor the traffic and exercise surveillance to ensure their national security or block certain information from crossing their borders because they deem it illegal or subversive.[91] Similarly, because of the ease with which computer code and data can cross borders, the principle of noninterference in other states' domestic affairs embedded in Westphalian sovereignty is also challenged.[92] Yet Buchanan admits that the cryptography debate does not substantially affect international legal sovereignty, the fourth type of sovereignty.[93]

David Betz and Tim Stevens also employ Krasner's typology and dedicated a whole chapter to it in *Cyberspace and the State: Toward a Strategy for Cyber-power*.[94] Like Buchanan, Betz and Stevens admit that international legal sovereignty has not been substantially affected by cyberspace compared with the other three types of state sovereignty.[95] They give some examples of how cyberspace influences these sovereignty types. The best illustration of the interaction between cyberspace and Westphalian sovereignty is computer network operations targeting assets located in another state, a clear breach of sovereignty. A massive cyber campaign against Estonia in 2007, cyber attacks against Georgia during the Russian-Georgian war in 2008, and the Stuxnet worm discovered in Iran in 2010 were violations of Westphalian sovereignty. Betz and Stevens also contemplate these breaches of Westphalian sovereignty increasing globally and possibly becoming the new status quo.[96] Regarding interdependence sovereignty, Betz and Stevens point to states' efforts to restore it. They give the example of terrorists sending undesirable content and ideas flowing over borders to introduce terrorist ideology to citizens and potentially radicalize them. States can order web companies to filter harmful political material on their behalf, but that can lead to highly regulated online environments like China's Golden Shield Project, also called the Great Firewall of China.[97] According to Betz and Stevens, the clearest examples of states' exercise of domestic sovereignty in cyberspace are governments' efforts to control and regulate citizens' access to information online within its territory. This is especially true for content deemed unfavorable, possibly threatening internal order or national authority and interests.[98] Betz and Stevens, along with the other authors discussed in this section, thus confirm the urgent need for states to exercise their sovereignty in cyberspace.

Sovereignty of Authoritarian Regimes in Cyberspace

The study of authoritarian regimes and their approach to state sovereignty in cyberspace is a specific stream of academic inquiry. Owing to growing cyber capabilities and influence of certain authoritarian regimes (such as China, Russia, and Iran) in cyberspace, experts have paid more attention to how these countries exercise their sovereignty in cyberspace than to democracies so far. Authoritarian states, China being their visionary and leader, prefer a state-centered approach to sovereignty in which the government holds ultimate authority in the cyber domain. By growing their regulatory and technological capabilities, they seek to fully control transborder and domestic data flows and online content, and some aim to seal themselves off from the global internet and establish their own national online spaces. Russia and China have been the most researched states seeking this expansive and aggressive redefinition of cyberspace.[99]

Lacking a Comprehensive Picture

State sovereignty in cyberspace is becoming an established topic among the international community. At first the debate was rooted in the discussion on borders in cyberspace. Then the community agreed that state sovereignty in cyberspace is still a legitimate topic, definitely not a needless one. Later, it moved to debate about exercise of sovereignty. I observe two points of view here. One is that of international lawyers, debating norms of behavior that might become international customary law. Second is that of experts on international relations contemplating states' behavior in cyberspace. But a deeper unified and comprehensive picture eludes us still. Authors either discuss the topic on a very theoretical level or limit themselves to examples of states' practices when sovereignty is exercised, challenged, or eroded. They all fail to explore in depth and in a more complex manner *how* cyberspace changes the understanding of state sovereignty and its applicability in this unique environment. I aim in this book to explore the complexities of how democratic states enforce their sovereignty in cyberspace.

Krasner's Typology of Sovereignty

The typology of state sovereignty developed by Stephen Krasner is comprehensive, covering the whole spectrum of activities of states, but it is also flexible enough to apply to cyberspace. That is why I believe it constitutes the most suitable theoretical framework for this book. Krasner's typology having been previously used by Liaropoulos, Buchanan, and Betz and Stevens adds weight to my assumption that it is the most suitable typology of state sovereignty for transposition into cyberspace.

Krasner is an opponent of the thesis that state sovereignty is a dead concept. He argues that no matter how strong or weak the state is, sovereignty remains attractive and desired. Even if it guarantees only recognition by the international community, this recognition provides a status to individual leaders and access to international organizations.[100] State sovereignty has always been challenged and "those who proclaim the death of sovereignty misread history. The nation-state has a keen instinct for survival and has so far adapted to new challenges—even the challenge of globalization."[101] Krasner admits that the revolutionary technological innovations of the past two centuries have boosted the global flow of goods, people, ideas, and money but contends that states today are much better prepared to face the challenges that have concurrently arisen. To give a practical example, the influence of modern media on political authority cannot be fairly compared with the massive turmoil in the aftermath of the introduction of the printing press in the fifteenth century.[102] Thus, state sovereignty remains a desired concept, and states quickly adapt to new challenges to preserve it.

With this crucial prerequisite in mind, we now more fully consider the idea in Krasner's book *Sovereignty: Organized Hypocrisy* that states exercise sovereignty in four ways:

1. Westphalian sovereignty: "Political organization based on the exclusion of external actors from authority structures within a given territory"
2. International legal sovereignty: "The practices associated with mutual recognition, usually between territorial entities that have formal juridical independence"
3. Domestic sovereignty: "The formal organization of political authority within the state and the ability of public authorities to exercise effective control within the borders of their own policy"
4. Interdependence sovereignty: "The ability of public authorities to regulate the flow of information, ideas, goods, people, pollutants, or capital across the borders of their state"[103]

Krasner defines Westphalian sovereignty as an "institutional arrangement for organizing political life that is based on two principles: territoriality and the exclusion of external actors from domestic authority structures. . . . Westphalian sovereignty is violated when external actors influence or determine domestic authority structures."[104] The fundamental criterion of Westphalian sovereignty is that states rule over a specific territory and local authorities are the exclusive arbitrators of legitimate conduct within its borders. The structures of these domestic authorities can be infringed, and thus Westphalian sovereignty can be compromised either coercively or voluntarily through intervention or invitation, respectively. The former has received much more political and academic notice; this is unsurprising given that the rule of nonintervention is considered by many to be the crucial element of sovereign statehood.[105] Krasner argues, however, that despite voluntary invitation of an external actor by domestic authorities causing the same erosion of Westphalian sovereignty as intervention by coercion or imposition, invitation has received much less attention in the literature. This is probably because Westphalian and international legal sovereignties are often confounded when it comes to the voluntary infringement of the domestic autonomous polity. According to Krasner, free choices do not violate international legal sovereignty, as they do Westphalian sovereignty. An invitation does infringe Westphalian sovereignty when the domestic authority structures become subjected to external compulsions.[106]

Under the umbrella of international legal sovereignty, states are preoccupied with securing the status of a political entity within the international system. They deal with issues such as their recognition by other states, acceptance as a juridical equal, membership in international organizations, facilitation of treaty making, and provision of defense against legal actions initiated in other states. International legal sovereignty is most often employed in the realm of international law, but it has been used by international relations researchers in a broader sense too.[107] Thanks to this kind of sovereignty, states can secure resources to uphold their security, economy, and ideational interests. It promotes the role of representatives from internationally recognized states to sit as equals at the negotiation table in international organizations, as well as be equal in the eyes of other states.[108] International recognition is typically granted to entities that possess both formal juridical independence and a territory. Occasionally, other criteria have been employed, and a specific government was recognized rather than a state. In such cases, the recognition is a political act that may undermine or enhance the specific governmental establishment.[109] All in all, international legal sovereignty is a precious concept that offers numerous benefits while not imposing high costs. Thus, state entities, including those lacking juridical autonomy or even territory, have universally desired international recognition by other states in order to secure their material and normative resources. Throughout history, the majority of states have achieved international recognition, but not all have enjoyed Westphalian sovereignty.

"The intellectual history of the term sovereignty is most closely associated with domestic sovereignty," Krasner notes.[110] Domestic sovereignty deals with how public authority is organized in a state and how it is effectively practiced. No matter if the polity is democratic or authoritarian, parliamentary or presidential, or republican or monarchical, the effectiveness of political authorities may vary substantially. "They might, or might not, be able to maintain order, collect taxes, regulate pornography, repress drug use, prevent abortion, minimize corruption, or control crime."[111] Furthermore, the authority's organization within a state and the level of its effectiveness is not in any way dependent on Westphalian or international legal sovereignty. A state with ineffective domestic control can still be regarded as a juridical equal by other states and can successfully continue to exclude any external actors from its domestic matters.[112] The strength of domestic sovereignty is thus entirely determined by the organizational capability and effectiveness of its authority.

Interdependence sovereignty, the fourth type of Krasner's sovereignty typology, deals with the state's ability to regulate transborder movements. For this, Krasner argues against the discourse that "the inability to regulate the flow of goods, persons, pollutants, diseases, and ideas across territorial boundaries has been described as a loss of sovereignty" and that globalization is eroding state sovereignty.[113] He reminds us that the increased transborder movements have not prevented states from pursuing their national policy agendas or undermined state control. On the contrary, modern states have become acclimatized to handling global flows, which started long ago. In some areas, the impact of these global flows was much higher in the nineteenth century than they are now, two hundred years later. State control has been tested by transborder movements, but these issues are not substantially more challenging than they were in the past.[114] Interdependence sovereignty thus remains a relevant concept for many states today.

When introducing the types of sovereignty, Krasner addresses the relations and balances among them. Some actions of states in favor of one type of state sovereignty can undermine another type and vice versa. An excellent example of this is membership in the European Union. When a state enters the European structures, it exercises and strengthens its international legal sovereignty but, by doing so, enters into an agreement that recognizes external authority structures, undermining the state's Westphalian sovereignty.[115] Therefore, states can exercise the four kinds of sovereignty on different scales of advancement, based on their national interests, preferences, and conditions.

As I previously outlined, the four meanings of sovereignty have embedded in them an elemental distinction between authority and control. Krasner defines authority as a mutually acknowledged right for actors to get involved in specific activities. Authority is crucial, because if it is effectively enforced, force does not need to be used. Control, in contrast, is attainable through brute force, without the need for mutually recognized authority. In certain instances, authority and control are reciprocally interlinked; effective control can create new structures of authority over time, and weakening of control can potentially also cause weakening of authority.[116] Distinction between authority and control is therefore important.

Krasner further argues that the distribution of authority and control among the four different types of state sovereignty varies depending on a state's behavior within the framework of the respective type. Thus, Westphalian and international legal sovereignties are based on authority but not control. They pivot on whether the state possesses the right to exclude external actors from its affairs and whether other states recognize the authority of the state to participate in international negotiations and agreements. Interdependence sovereignty exclusively involves control and not authority. It is based on the ability of a state to control flows across its borders. Domestic sovereignty is the only type concerned with both authority and control. Domestic sovereignty depends on the recognized authority structures within the state and on their effective level of control.[117] This binary distinction that was developed for the noncyber domains can be translated into the following table 1.1. An X in a column represents the dependence of the respective kind of sovereignty on authority, control, or both.

TABLE 1.1 Binary distribution of authority and control based on typology by Stephen Krasner.

Sovereignty type	Authority (and legitimacy)	Control
Westphalian	X	
International legal	X	
Domestic	X	X
Interdependence		X

Source: The author, based on Krasner (1999, pp. 4, 10).

This distribution of authority and control together with the four types of sovereignty introduced by Stephen Krasner constitute the main framework of this book. Krasner's *Sovereignty: Organized Hypocrisy,* in addition to explicating his typology, expands on his thoughts about state sovereignty in modern times and explains the subtitle "Organized Hypocrisy."

In contrast to my identification of the state as the key actor, Krasner understands the rulers (the policy makers) to be the ontological givens and starting points for his work. He argues that it is a ruler, not a state or international system, that makes decisions about policies and institutions. Krasner assumes that the rulers desire to stay in power, and to achieve that end, they aim to secure the prosperity, security, and interests and values of their people. The methods rulers use to achieve these goals differ from one state to another; for example, some rulers rely on the military, some endorse exclusionary nationalism, and others rely heavily on financial support coming from external actors.[118]

Krasner continues by focusing exclusively on the study of Westphalian and international legal sovereignty, which constitute the empirical core of his book. He claims that the principles of these two sovereignty types have always been violated. "Neither Westphalian nor international legal sovereignty have ever been a stable equilibrium from which rulers had no incentives to deviate. Rather, Westphalian and international legal sovereignty are best understood as examples of organized hypocrisy. At times rulers adhere to conventional norms or rules because it provides them with resources and support (both material and ideational). At other times, rulers have violated the norms, and for the same reason."[119]

Alternative norms have been invoked by rulers to justify breaches of Westphalian principles. Among Krasner's examples are "the illegitimacy of revolutionary regimes (the Holy Alliance), the provision of national security (the Platt amendment imposed on Cuba by the United States), problems of drug running (the 1989 U.S. invasion of Panama), or the protection of the Soviet commonwealth (the Brezhnev doctrine)."[120] Because the goal of rulers is to stay in office, in instances such as these, they may rhetorically call for Westphalian principles, although in actuality they are supporting contradictory norms or taking decisions that weaken their autonomy or the autonomy of other polities at the same time.[121]

Another example of organized hypocrisy is international legal sovereignty, although its hypocrisy is less pronounced. Usually, recognition is granted to territorial entities with juridical independence. In certain specific cases, however, rulers have decided to follow a different strategy. These alternative paths have been less disputatious than some breaches of Westphalian sovereignty because they have been based on a voluntary agreement rather than coercion or imposition.[122]

To sum up Krasner's typology, the concept of sovereignty has been applied in four different ways. These four distinct sovereignty practices are based on two elements, which are authority and control. The weakening or absence of one type of sovereignty does not necessarily mean an erosion or violation of others, although the sovereignty types can be empirically interlinked. Thus, a state can be officially recognized by other states, but the state's authority structures might be subordinated to external control and authority. Similarly, a state can remain autonomous despite having lost control of movement across its borders. In practice, states might prioritize a particular kind of sovereignty on the basis of their national preferences and the interests of their domestic constituents. All in all, Krasner's typology offers a flexible and suitable framework that embraces the whole spectrum of a state's activities in different conditions and environments. This is why I apply the four sovereignty types together with authority and control as my main framework, although because the subject is complex and novel, it is not possible to rigorously follow their definitions all the time, as becomes clear in chapter 2.

TWO

The Transposition of State Sovereignty into Cyberspace

Understanding and interpretation of state sovereignty, a living concept that has existed for centuries, have continually evolved to accommodate contemporary political developments and reflect the international ambience. The flexibility of state sovereignty has allowed it to be employed across different political systems, ideologies, and styles of governance. The first research and literature on state sovereignty in cyberspace has further established that the cyber domain, the latest challenge to state sovereignty's existence, is no exception to the rule and that states do indeed desire to project their sovereignty also in this seemingly borderless virtual environment. Yet the existing literature, despite tackling the issue in depth, usually covers only a subsection of the subject, such as territoriality. I offer here a deeper, unified view on state sovereignty in cyberspace.

A Novel Approach to the Study of State Sovereignty in Cyberspace

My point of departure is the assumption that states that want to retain their sovereignty in cyberspace must adjust their behavior to fit the unique environment of the cyber domain; this has an impact on the understanding of state sovereignty itself. State sovereignty does exist in cyberspace, and states are not willing to give up their sovereignty entirely to other cyber actors. States try to protect their interests despite the unpredictable character of the cyber domain. Nevertheless, because the nature of cyberspace is different from the other domains (air, sea, space, and land) to which the concept of sovereignty traditionally applies, states must adapt their sovereignty practice in cyberspace accordingly. If governments desire to retain their sovereignty in cyberspace, they must take a more creative and flexible approach. This particular state behavior must be projected with a more adaptive approach toward the concept of sovereignty, one that accepts certain modifications of the classical understanding of sovereignty. As the exploration in chapter 1 of the historical debate on the transformation of state sovereignty illustrates, the concept develops according to the practices of states. It is hence necessary to closely examine those practices in order to understand the concept of sovereignty, especially including its application in cyberspace. The four case studies of state practice in cyberspace of democratic nations in the transatlantic region in the following chapters show how their actions have influenced the traditional understanding of state sovereignty.

States started to implement their authority and control over cyberspace from the moment it became clear that it is an important environment for the development of national and international affairs. As discussed in chapter 1, state sovereignty being applicable to cyberspace is acknowledged by experts, academics, and politicians worldwide. No research, however, has yet investigated how democratic states exercise their sovereignty and, more importantly, what impact this state practice has on our traditional perception of the concept of state sovereignty. To address this lack, this book poses the principal question *How does state practice of sovereignty in cyberspace change the traditional understanding of the concept?*

Cyberspace is a relatively new domain, and so states are still exploring their powers, testing new limits in the cyber environment. States introduced in the case studies are democratic pioneers of different methods for applying state sovereignty in cyberspace. I study these states' behavior to offer an answer to the working question *What kinds of tools do states employ to exercise their sovereignty in cyberspace?*

State sovereignty developed outside cyberspace, in the traditional, tangible physical domains of land, sea, and air. Because the characteristics of these natural domains are diametrically different from those of man-made cyberspace, we can expect that the methods by which state sovereignty is exercised in the cyber domain differ too. These methods can be defined through practice of two elements: authority and control. Therefore, I also offer an answer to the second working question *In what way is the exercise of authority and control by states in cyberspace different from the traditional domains?*

The Four Types of Sovereignty and Cyberspace

To assess a state's approach toward sovereignty in cyberspace, I use Stephen Krasner's four types of state sovereignty as the analytic foundation. I chose Krasner's conception of sovereignty because it offers the most suitable theoretical framework for my research thanks to its comprehensiveness, flexibility, and applicability in different environments and conditions, including cyberspace. Krasner's types of sovereignty comprehensively cover the whole spectrum of a state's behavior in terms of its sovereignty. At the same time, the definitions of sovereignty are sufficiently flexible to apply in the cyber domain, despite having been developed in noncyber domains. The case studies and variables do not always exactly match all relevant aspects of Krasner's original definitions, given the novel nature of cyberspace, and required me to use Krasner's typology in a more flexible manner. For example, Krasner's definition of control is based on the use of brute force; that is impossible in cyberspace, and so when I transpose the variable into cyberspace I substitute and assess it through the cyber capabilities and capacities that are necessary for a state to exercise a particular type of sovereignty.

I apply Krasner's typology in cyberspace so that each type of state sovereignty is matched with one of the four case studies. They were selected from a pool of demonstrative examples of the actions of democratic regimes in the transatlantic area and its close neighborhood that have occurred mainly during the 2010s. I chose this geopolitical arena because states there similarly perceive cyberspace matters; they are all members of NATO and other international organizations and maintain close bilateral dialogues with each other.

I limit the territorial definition to democracies because the general will of the people guides governance in those regimes and steers them away from extreme solutions. The case studies have extended state sovereignty into cyberspace the furthest and thus represent the current outer limits under democratic, nonauthoritarian rule. Including nondemocratic regimes such as China or Russia would twist the results in an unrepresentative way. Authoritarian regimes are not necessarily elected in free and democratic polls, and their legitimacy does not come from the will of the people. Their source of sovereignty is different. Contrary to democracies, they do not need to be answerable to their people. Therefore, authoritarian governments can set sovereignty limits that are more intrusive than democracies'.

Having a time frame of recent years encompasses the most relevant information and provides enough empirical material. Furthermore, the internet and cyberspace change rapidly, and thus it makes sense to focus on more recent developments. This territorial and time framework guarantees that the four types of sovereignty have the same points of departure to provide the most objective results. Despite the case studies having this similar understanding of cyber matters at about the same time, I do not aim to compare the four types of sovereignty.

To find cases most representative of the four types of sovereignty, I identified four long-term trends of state behavior that particularly relate to key attributes of the sovereignty types: (1) determined efforts to preserve the confidentiality, integrity, and accessibility of governmental data in the digital era (exclusion of external actors from authority structures in Westphalian sovereignty); (2) international negotiations on norms of behavior in cyberspace (state activities as a juridical equal in international relations and international law in international legal sovereignty); (3) a push toward state control of the internet (a state's organization of political authority and its ability to exercise effective control in domestic sovereignty); and (4) protectionism of national infrastructure through the supply chain (the ability to regulate transborder movement in interdependence sovereignty). Almost every state worldwide with at least a minimal interest in cyberspace has experienced all four trends and has had to consider a response, some responding conservatively, others in a more forward-looking manner.

I then applied a purposive sampling method, which relies on the researcher's best judgment to select cases that provide the most suitable data to realize study objectives. This method is most appropriate when the research needs information-rich case studies or needs to make the most of limited resources, as in cybersecurity. My efforts resulted in the following: The Estonian data embassy project is a pioneer in state efforts to preserve the confidentiality, integrity, and accessibility of governmental data online, or Westphalian sovereignty. The Dutch leadership in international cyber negotiations is the best illustration of negotiations on norms of behavior in cyberspace, or international legal sovereignty. The Turkish government's actions in domestic online affairs best show the extent a state can go in pushing toward state control of the internet, or domestic sovereignty. The US approach toward Huawei Technologies is the most advanced case of protectionism of national infrastructure through the supply chain, or interdependence sovereignty.

Estonia is one of the most digitally connected states in the world with all its governmental data stored in the cloud, and thus it is highly important for Tallinn to protect its digital continuity and cross-border services for its e-residents in case of emergency. "Data embassies" are the most progressive part of the Estonian plan because they would serve as back-up providers under the full control of the Estonian government despite being outside Estonian territory.[1] It works to ensure that, in case of emergency or danger, the country runs its services from abroad, a need brought to the fore by the aggressive behavior of Russia, the eastern neighbor of Estonia, since the invasion of Crimea in 2014. Estonia's decision to move governmental data to the cloud and secure it in data embassies is a clear attempt to exclude external actors from authority structures within its territory, as embodied by Westphalian sovereignty.

The Netherlands demonstrated progressive leadership in establishing international forums for discussion about norms in cyberspace. A good example of this is The Hague Process, used in drafting *Tallinn Manual 2.0 on the International Law Applicable to Cyber Operations*. When drafting the manual, The Hague Process was a series of meetings of fifty states from around the globe whose representatives convened in The Hague to review and comment on draft chapters. Another excellent example is the 4th Global Conference on Cyberspace hosted in The Hague in 2015, where the Global

Forum on Cyber Expertise was launched. The Dutch are also the initiators and the supporters of the Global Commission on the Stability of Cyberspace, launched at the Munich Security Conference in February 2017. These and other Dutch activities show that the Netherlands plays a leading role in the development of international legal sovereignty in cyberspace by creating platforms for negotiations that facilitate state engagement in norms building in cyberspace.

While some states such as Iran and China are notorious for their harsh internet restrictions, more and more democratically elected governments have been using domestic sovereignty to influence free speech rights on the internet. Turkey is a leader in applying domestic sovereignty to cyberspace in this sense. As early as 2007, the law Regulation of Publications on the Internet and Combating Crimes Committed by Means of Such Publication was enacted.[2] Law No. 5651 was passed to protect families and minors from harmful and illegal online content, and it created the legal framework for internet governance in Turkey. After passage of the law, the official political discourse of the Turkish government shifted, and amendments to the internet law in 2014 made it a tool of the state for reacting to political events unfavorable to governmental policy, including filtering and blocking of popular social platforms and communication apps.[3] Turkey is keen to take advantage of its domestic sovereignty in cyberspace and does not hesitate to justify doing so through the domestic legal framework, although its restrictive actions are not always directly supported by court decisions, sometimes being based solely on administrative orders of the authorized governmental body.

The expansion of Chinese IT companies into global markets has caused heated discussions around the world. The Chinese products are sold cheaply, and have immense potential in competitive foreign markets, but suspicions exist that the companies' commodities are a vehicle for Chinese government espionage and may endanger the national security of the states they are sold in. The US stance on attempts by the Chinese telecommunications company Huawei to enter the US market is the most radical approach toward this potential threat and illustrates interdependence sovereignty. After a yearlong investigation, the Permanent Select Committee on Intelligence of the US Congress concluded in its report,

"The United States should view with suspicion the continued penetration of the U.S. telecommunications market by Chinese telecommunications companies. . . . U.S. government systems, particularly sensitive systems, should not include Huawei or ZTE [another top Chinese telecommunications equipment manufacturer] equipment, including component parts."[4] A similar recommendation was addressed to governmental contractors and the private sector. Although Huawei has been trying to allay US concerns ever since, the apparently invincible governmental protectionism clearly displays the ability of US authorities to oversee transborder movement as embraced in interdependence sovereignty.

These four case studies illustrate how democracies of the transatlantic area have tested the boundaries of state sovereignty in cyberspace in the 2010s and early 2020s, be it through leadership, innovation, or political attitude. What they have in common are the unprecedented steps they have taken in exercising sovereignty in cyberspace. Estonia was the first state to implement data embassies, which other states are slowly adopting (e.g., Monaco). The Netherlands took leadership on negotiating responsible state behavior in cyberspace, and many other states have followed. Turkey had an originally democratically elected government that used its domestic sovereignty to influence rights around free speech. From 2007 to 2016, Turkey went from being a democracy to being a semidemocratic regime, both inside and outside cyberspace. It is an ideal example of the delicate moment when the extension of sovereignty by a government violates democratic values, which is a typical behavior of hybrid regimes. Finally, the distinctiveness of the US case lies in two points. First, the United States was the first government to openly proclaim that Chinese companies (and Huawei in particular) could be a threat to its national security and to broadly implement measures to expel said companies from its critical infrastructure. Second, the United States went a step further with its global campaign to persuade its allies to follow the same approach. These four cases, one per sovereignty type, represent unprecedented state behavior in cyberspace and show us how states approach their sovereignty in this new domain, how they attempt to stretch and explore its limits, and what tools and methods they employ to do so.

I apply to the four case studies the variables of authority and control as originally described by Krasner. I apply them in a more relaxed manner, however, because the nature of cyberspace makes it impossible to employ them neatly and rigidly in their original definition. Krasner defines authority as the mutually recognized right of a state to engage in specific kinds of activities.[5] I measure authority in cyberspace through legislation—domestic laws or international legal actions, depending on the character of the studied type. For domestic legislation, I investigate whether preexisting domestic legislation specifically addressing the issue in question has been used. If it has, I examine in more detail the conditions and frequency of where the law is employed. I also assess the importance of the legal framework on the basis of its reach and the issuing authority within the government. Finally, I appraise the necessity of the invocation of the legal framework by the state for the fulfillment of its objectives. For international legal sovereignty, negotiations on establishing international law are the focus. I study, for example, international legal agreements and negotiating platforms created to discuss and help establish the norms of international law applicable in cyberspace. The fundamental point of interest here is the role of the state in the negotiations and the importance of the respective platforms in the global picture.

Krasner defines control as the use of brute force with no mutual recognition of authority at all in general terms.[6] Given that brute force does not exist in cyberspace, I measure it by proxy: the cyber capabilities and capacities necessary for a state to exercise a particular type of sovereignty. First, I assess which cyber capabilities have a role in the respective sovereignty type and whether they have been employed. If they have, I investigate the conditions under which they were employed and whether they were decisive in the result. Determining cyber capabilities and capacities can be difficult because states often do not want to reveal the true cyber potential at their disposal, to preserve their strategic advantage. To avoid or at least minimize this limitation, I chose transparent and open examples for the case studies.

Table 2.1 summarizes the operationalization of authority and control for the case studies. For details, see the case study chapters.

TABLE 2.1. Measuring authority and control in cyberspace

	Westphalian Sovereignty and Estonia
Authority	Legal framework securing Estonian jurisdiction over its governmental data hosted abroad: the bilateral Agreement between the Republic of Estonia and the Grand Duchy of Luxembourg on the Hosting of Data and Information Systems
Control	Infrastructure necessary for secure operation of a data embassy: X-Road data-exchange layer, KSI blockchain technology, and the highest standard of data centers
	International Legal Sovereignty and the Netherlands
Authority	The government's initiatives and activities during international negotiations on cyberspace-related issues, such as the 2015 Global Conference on Cyberspace, the Global Forum on Cyber Expertise, the Global Commission on the Stability of Cyberspace, and The Hague Process
Control	Infrastructure that makes the state the digital gateway to Europe, which motivates the Dutch government to actively engage in international negotiations on cyber norms
	Domestic Sovereignty and Turkey
Authority	Legislative framework for internet restrictions on Turkey's territory: Law No. 5651, Regulation of Publications on the Internet and Combating Crimes Committed by Means of Such Publication
Control	Exercise of internet restrictions by public authorities, in particular the Information and Communications Technologies Authority and the Presidency of Telecommunication and Communication, and their partners
	Interdependence Sovereignty and the United States
Authority	The government's administrative and legislative actions preventing Huawei Technologies from entering the US market, and the US outreach campaign abroad in this regard
Control	The government's strong interest in and approach to building critical infrastructure, particularly telecommunications infrastructure and the 5G technology standard, to retain US tech superiority

Source: The author, inspired by the typology of state sovereignty by Stephen Krasner.

The book uses qualitative research methods, which are explanatory in nature. Each case study concerns a unique situation in which a state stretches the limits of the respective state sovereignty type to its extreme in practice. I aim not to compare the four case studies but rather to generalize and draw theoretical propositions. I employ multiple sources of evidence, analyzing all sources together and basing the outcomes of the case studies on the confluence of collected information from sources. This data triangulation ensures that the findings are as accurate and convincing as possible.

Occasionally, sources were difficult to acquire or access. For instance, some had a limited lifetime, which is common for the ever-changing content of the internet, as was the case for some of the sources published online by the Turkish government. This was mitigated by using nongovernmental sources like Engelliweb, an anonymous interactive online database, and the WayBack Machine, a digital archive of the World Wide Web. Some primary sources were in languages other than English and had no official translation available—for example, Turkish Law No. 5651. In these cases, I compared multiple unofficial translations to verify the quality of the sources.

THREE

Estonia and Westphalian Sovereignty

Stephen Krasner defines Westphalian sovereignty as an "institutional arrangement for organizing political life that is based on two principles: territoriality and the exclusion of external actors from domestic authority structure."[1] The government of the Republic of Estonia projects these principles into cyberspace and sets new limits on Westphalian sovereignty in the cyber environment via its data embassies. But first, the Estonian government needed to move the life of its population to the cyber domain, transforming itself from a poor and digitally underdeveloped state to a digital society and the paperless state of today. The digitalization of Estonian society and people's lives from the physical to the cyber environment culminated in progressive projects such as online voting, e-ID, and e-residency. These individual projects were shaped by the Estonian approach to cybersecurity and its information and communications technology (ICT) principles. Moving Estonian society into cyberspace led to the need to also secure Estonian Westphalian sovereignty in this domain. The initial question was how to preserve data in a digital form and secure it against an external element that could interfere with the Estonian government's authority. Estonian experts explored several options, discussed later, and determined that data embassies provide the best guarantee of excluding external elements' intrusion while also offering a possible solution to the question of territoriality in cyberspace. The concept of data embassies is an innovation in diplomatic relations and international law; the embassies securely host sensitive and confidential data in a friendly country and have guarantees of immunity because the data centers are considered the sovereign territory of the state that owns the data.[2]

This chapter describes the journey Estonia has taken since the 1990s to move the life of its people from the physical to the digital world, as well as the first realization of the risks accompanying this decision. It then moves to the initial lines of thought and ambitions of the Estonian government and the debate about the feasibility of the data embassy initiative as a possible solution to these risks. I apply and examine the two variables of authority and control when discussing the data embassies' implementation. I examine authority through the study of the legal framework, which is indispensable for the smooth running of data embassies' services, and consider both domestic and international legal arrangements. International legal arrangements establish Estonian jurisdiction over its data hosted outside its territory, and are thus the core of the analysis of the variable of authority. More specifically, it is the role played by the bilateral Agreement between the Republic of Estonia and the Grand Duchy of Luxembourg on the Hosting of Data and Information Systems. Control, the other variable, is embedded in the state's cyber capabilities and capacities. Estonia's X-Road infrastructure and KSI blockchain technology—both detailed later—and its use of the highest standard for data centers are key for securing the data's confidentiality, integrity, and accessibility, and I thus consider them in the analysis of the variable of control. I then assess which of the two variables is more dominant or whether they carry the same weight.

Estonia in Cyberspace

Estonia has advanced immensely in the past few decades, from being an integral yet poor part of the former Union of Soviet Socialist Republics to becoming a European or perhaps even world leader in implementing modern technologies. In 1991, when this tiny country in the Baltics regained its independence after the collapse of the USSR, Estonia struggled with a flatlining economy and decrepit infrastructure, the legacy of the former regime. The Estonian government succeeded in turning problems such as the absence of a land registry or less than half of Estonian households having telephones to its advantage. It started from scratch, deciding to develop an ambitious digital infrastructure that would become the center point of the country's economic and social transition. For example, when Finland offered Tallinn its archaic 1970s analogue telephone exchange for free because Helsinki was upgrading to a digital phone connection, Estonia declined and built its own digital infrastructure.[3] These kinds of decisions of the 1990s, when the government sought out technologically driven innovation, very much helped counteract the post-Soviet economic and political crises in the country.

The government knew it was also necessary to educate the nation in understanding of the digital solutions and prepare it for future technological innovations. Thus, a special program was launched in 1996 to provide all schools with computers, connect them to the internet, and train teachers to teach coding. By the end of the decade, computer infrastructures had been supported by large investments, and all classrooms in Estonia could access the internet. In addition, public libraries received more support and soon became internet hubs, bringing online governmental services to the population.[4] The next step was taken in 2000, when Estonia became the first country in the world to declare access to the internet as a basic human right, and internet connections spread to the most rural regions of the country. Soon, free Wi-Fi followed as a common standard.[5] This progress set a solid basis for the Estonian population to understand the benefits of digitalization, and it supported the government's steps in this direction, foreshadowing the expansion of Estonian society's life from the physical domain to the cyber one.

In 2000, the Estonian government passed a law giving digital signatures equal importance to handwritten signatures, the first step to becoming a paperless state. Since the law's passage, no physically signed hard copies of official documents are required for day-to-day tasks such as filing taxes, obtaining a medical prescription, or having a bank account. Voting online in elections, which Estonia allowed in 2005 as the first country in the world to do so, was only another phase in it becoming a completely paperless state.[6]

The introduction of digital signatures into the Estonian administration inevitably led to establishing a digital identity for all Estonian nationals, the peak of moving the life of the Estonian population to cyberspace. This happened with the introduction of e-ID in 2002. At birth, every Estonian is given a unique digital identifier, an eleven-digit number, that can be used in the majority of everyday aspects of that person's existence. The e-ID is a tool for citizens to access all governmental e-services, business transactions, and banking services. For example, it can be used as a national health insurance card or a travel document within EU borders or for internet voting and digital signatures, submitting tax forms, or checking medical records. According to Estonian government statistics, there were 1,333,624 active ID cards as of the beginning of November 2019, which processed 37,748,670 transactions in October 2019.[7] In other words, approximately 98 percent of Estonians have an ID card, and 67 percent use it regularly.[8] These numbers illustrate that the e-ID has become an integral part of the everyday life of the vast majority of Estonians. E-ID and e-governmental infrastructure constitute the chief components of the consolidation of e-Estonia, a common trademark for the Estonian government's technological ecosystem, along with e-residency, which extends beyond Estonian borders.

With 1.3 million citizens, Estonia is a relatively small market, and to boost its economic growth the country needs more market participants. It is not easy for such a small country in northern Europe to attract masses of highly skilled immigrants, and thus the government came up with another first: virtual residency for non-Estonians. In some respects, e-residency resembles Estonian e-IDs. The holders of e-residency also receive an ID card, which comes with the same microchips as those in Estonian e-IDs. The cards of e-residents allow them to sign digital documents, including those that are legally binding; encrypt sensitive documents; establish a company in Estonia and manage it from abroad; or access local online banking. All this is possible without the need of the physical presence of the card holder on Estonian territory. However, in contrast to Estonian e-ID, e-residency does not grant any citizens' rights such as Estonian citizenship, voting rights, public pensions, or tax residency, and it does not guarantee its holders access to the EU. Nor can it be used as a travel document.[9] Still, Estonian e-residency, the first digital residency of its kind in the world, offers non-Estonians opportunities, such as registering companies in Estonia and thus accessing the attractive EU common market for only several dozen euros paid as an administrative fee. The e-residency is a demo version of the Estonian population's life in cyberspace offered to non-Estonians, significantly contributing to the ultimate Estonian goal of building a paperless state. The first e-residency card was issued in December 2014, and the government hopes to reach ten million e-residents by 2025, boosting the number of market participants in Estonia almost tenfold.[10]

Over time, Estonian digital leadership has helped define several ICT principles specific to Estonia and its approach to shaping systems and processes related to Estonian society's life in cyberspace. One principle is the single digital identity, in which a unique identifier assigned to a citizen at birth links to a secure digital identity. Another principle stresses that citizens control their data and know how it is being accessed and used. A principle is dedicated to information systems of the government being centrally catalogued and registered. Another principle says that government should request information from a citizen only once, and that governmental agencies should be ready to share information among themselves when needed. This principle is facilitated by the X-Road, which is the only channel for data exchange among information systems. X-Roads are a special layer for information systems for secure data exchange and are discussed in more detail later. Finally, a principle states that the government must ensure that any ICT system that is about to reach the end of its lifetime should be phased out as early as possible.[11] These principles underlie Estonia's digitalization and e-government, and they shape its future direction. Although a main purpose of these principles is enhancement of security, spreading digitalization inevitably creates serious vulnerabilities in digital dependency and unprecedented sensitivity to system interruption.

The Estonian government was reminded about its growing digital dependency and vulnerability in 2007 during an unprecedented massive cyber campaign against its infrastructure, which was perhaps somewhat hyperbolically called "Web War One" by *Wired*.[12] This cyber attack was a major crisis that greatly contributed to the shaping of digital Estonia as we know it today. The truth is that it was indeed the first cyber attack that targeted a whole country. The 2007 cyber campaign portended how vulnerable to intrusion by external actors Estonian Westphalian sovereignty in cyberspace could become when the expansion of its society's life into the cyber domain is complete.

The triggering moment of the attack seemed harmless at first. In April 2007, the Tallinn municipality decided to move a memorial statue of a Soviet soldier of World War II from the city center to a nearby military cemetery. The bronze statue, unveiled in 1947 by Soviet authorities, was originally called *Monument to the Liberators of Tallinn*, and to the Russian-speaking minority of Estonia (almost 25 percent of the population today[13]) it is a symbol of the Soviet victory over the Nazi regime, even today. Ethnic Estonians, however, never thought of the Soviet army as a liberator but rather as an occupier that denied them their freedom for half a century, and the bronze soldier was a reminder of this painful part of Estonian modern history. Thus, the decision to move this iconic statue from the center of Tallinn to the outskirts of the city aroused unexpected outrage among the Russian-speaking population, and two nights of street riots and looting resulted. Besides hundreds of people being detained, dozens being injured, and one person killed during the riots, the events had unexpected repercussions in cyberspace.

While people were taking to the streets, Estonia was hit by a massive cyber campaign that lasted several weeks. The cyber attacks took different forms. The most serious ones were distributed denial of service attacks targeting online banking services, websites of governmental bodies, and media outlets, which were repeatedly overwhelmed by one of the biggest-ever overloads of internet traffic. Other attacks consisted of enormous waves of spam sent by botnets, defacement of prominent internet websites, and spamming of comments sections of news portals. An Estonian cyber expert said of the events, "We are back to the stone age, telling the world what is going on with phone and fax."[14] Although no clear evidence attributes the cyber attack to the Kremlin, the attacks were initiated from Russian IP (internet protocol) addresses and online directions to join the attacks were published in the Russian language. Appeals by the Estonian authorities to Russia for assistance in stopping the attacks were left unanswered. The serious consequences for Estonian society and the government included governmental employees unable to communicate with each other via email, outages of cash machines and online banking, and media unable to reach their audience.[15]

These cyber attacks against the Estonian infrastructure are the strongest and most far reaching so far. Although the attacks took place in 2007, when Estonia's digital society and technologically advanced government was not as refined as it is today, when practically every governmental service is paperless, it still caused considerable damage. The cyber attacks of 2007 highlighted that the great advantages of cost-effectiveness and convenience brought by a paperless state are also a dangerous drawback in the long term: growing dependency on information systems and the data stored on them increases vulnerability to interruption of online services. This was the first serious endangerment by an external actor's intrusion to Estonian cyber Westphalian sovereignty. Consequently, the Estonian government has been seeking to minimize the risk of the unavailability of crucial online services, an indivisible component of today's Estonian digital society.

Debate on the Feasibility of the Data Embassy Initiative

All vital governmental databases such as the land, population, and business registries are currently available exclusively in digital form in Estonia and have evidentiary value only in electronic form, and the government has been preoccupied for several years by how to safeguard all its essential services and data to resist an external actor in a cyber or military attack. Its aim is to ensure digital continuity, or "the capacity of a state to maintain its services and digital data relevant for the functioning of the state, regardless of any adverse changes or interruptions. It includes processes that enable stability, ensure recovery and help restore governmental services rapidly in the event of a crisis or natural disaster, so that those services can continue to be available and operate without being compromised."[16] The government formulated several possible responses to this dilemma, and a long discussion on their feasibility ensued, illustrating how progressive and unprecedented these ideas themselves were.

The feasibility discussion matured in 2015 and 2016 when the Estonian Ministry of Economic Affairs and Communication, responsible for the task, teamed up with Microsoft to explore three of the most discussed solutions to digital continuity. Although some aspects of the solutions proved unfeasible, the resulting discussion is a unique opportunity, thanks to the Estonian government's transparency and openness, to observe how states reflect on their sovereignty in cyberspace, their ambitions, and their direction of thinking and compare it with what the reality is.[17]

The discussion led to the Data Embassy Initiative, whose central point was that data backups are not enough for Estonia. Online services need to be continuously available and operational, even if a crisis develops on Estonian territory. Thus, the Estonian Data Embassy Initiative "consists of additional security measures that would allow Estonia to ensure continuity in government and operations, including: digital and data continuity (backup); data integrity (non-repudiation); and core governmental services in the event of a physical or cyber emergency."[18] This quote captures the fundamental criterion of Westphalian sovereignty; a state rules over a specific territory, and local authorities are the exclusive arbitrators of legitimate conduct within the borders.

The three solutions to digital continuity explored in the Data Embassy Initiative are a government-operated cloud, virtual data embassy, and physical data embassy. A government-operated cloud would maintain data backups and live online services within the physical borders of Estonia. The government planned to add additional data centers and e-governmental services backups.[19] Estonia has a long history of cloud computing; it made use of cloud services by large international companies as early as 2009.[20] During the Data Embassy Initiative discussion, Taavi Kotka, the chief information officer of the Estonian government, and Innar Liiv from Tallinn University of Technology identified five reasons for building an Estonian government cloud, and some apply to virtual and physical data embassies too. The first reason is the fragmentation of governance ICT services. The IT architecture of the Estonian government is distributed, managed separately by diverse institutions. These information systems are often in facilities constructed by the agencies themselves and do not meet modern standards for security, cost efficiency, and energy requirements. Thus, according to Kotka and Liiv, the government needed to build data centers that would comply with the necessary service standards required to build a governmental data cloud. The second reason is protection of so-called digital monuments. These are public websites, such as those of the Ministry of Defense and president of Estonia, with symbolic status. Estonia has already experienced cyber attacks targeted at these websites. Each successful attack, such as defacement that changes the visual appearance of the website, seriously damages Estonia's reputation in the eyes of its public as well as Estonian allies. A cyber attack against a digital monument is like a conventional attack against a physical monument with national symbolism. The third reason is digital continuity, addressed in the preceding. The fourth reason for building a strong governmental cloud solution is to ensure trustworthy and high-quality cross-border services. This was particularly valid when Estonia introduced the idea of e-residency for nonresidents of the country in the spirit of building a state without borders. E-residents must be sure that their money, stocks, and property are safe from being lost owing to a security breach in the land registry or commercial registry. The fifth reason is the flexibility and cost effectiveness of a governmental cloud, which are particularly important characteristics for local municipalities.[21]

A governmental cloud solution indeed would contribute to the exclusion of external actors and factors from the domestic authority structures of Estonia, thus strengthening digital continuity in terms of Westphalian sovereignty. But it has the disadvantage of a heavy dependency on the Estonian territory in which it is located. The Government Cloud Policy of Estonia admits that developing capabilities outside Estonian territory, in addition to the government cloud, is necessary to secure data continuity and services functionality. This was supposed to be achieved through establishing physical data embassies in allied foreign states and virtual data embassies in the public cloud.[22]

Virtual data embassies would hold backups of nonsensitive data in the public cloud of private companies. These embassies would strengthen the digital continuity in several ways, indisputably increasing the resilience of the nation against common cyber campaigns and providing a greater guarantee of availability because their capacity surpasses that of many organizations. Another asset is their location outside Estonian territory and within the globally managed cloud environment. On one hand, turning again to Westphalian sovereignty, the virtual data embassies would help exclude external elements from Estonian domestic authority structures and significantly contribute to solving the dilemma of territorial dependency. On the other hand, the ownership of the public cloud by private companies leads to concerns about data integrity, personal data protection, and privacy because the Estonian government might not be the exclusive arbitrator of legitimate manipulation of the data.[23] Thus, only nonsensitive data could be stored in virtual data embassies, leaving the digital continuity problem not entirely solved.

The virtual data embassy initiative would involve giving privileges similar to governmental privileges to data centers owned by private sector companies. This is not currently done, and it is hard to imagine that it would be in the foreseeable future.[24] Siim Sikkut, the ICT policy adviser to the Estonian government, said, "The cloud technology provides a good opportunity, but the state also wants to maintain the full control and jurisdiction of their data and systems. For this reason the private cloud services are not exactly suitable for us."[25] Still, the government uses the public cloud in certain circumstances, and it is incorporated in the security standard. The governmental cloud is technically ready, and transfer into the cloud is underway. Some agencies have already moved there.[26] Nevertheless, it is a limited solution that remains dependent on the security of the physical borders of Estonia.

The physical data embassies of the Data Embassy Initiative make Estonia the pioneer of Westphalian sovereignty in cyberspace and are why they constitute the core of this chapter. In the following discussion "data embassies" refers to physical data embassies, not virtual data embassies. Data embassies were conceived as a server resource entirely under the control of the Estonian government but situated outside its borders. It was designed not only as a backup of governmental registers but also as an active copy that could operate services in real time and be updated accordingly, even if data centers within Estonian borders are not under the control of Estonian government anymore.[27]

The idea of data embassies was presented for the first time in a document, Digital Agenda 2020 for Estonia, published by the Ministry of Economic Affairs and Communications in 2014. The document presents an additional strategy to the Cybersecurity Strategy for 2014–2017: to facilitate "the use of ICT and the development of smart solutions in Estonia in general. The ultimate goal is to increase the economic competitiveness, the well-being of people and the efficiency of public administration."[28] Digital Agenda 2020 defines several priority projects for the coming years, data embassies being listed alongside e-residency. The document also promises that "the interoperability solutions of the common service space will be further developed to make sure they are up-to-date with technological development and function both nationally and cross-border in a secure manner."[29] This task and others would be fulfilled by "creating conditions for the secure digital storage of critical applications and registries abroad (for example in 'digital embassies') to ensure the continuity of the state information system."[30] Data embassies are data centers located in countries friendly to Estonia that would store the data of key governmental information systems and house critical service applications.

In the initial phase of the project, the government explored two approaches to data embassies. The first considered having Estonian embassies host registry backups, such as the population registry or the land registry. The advantage of this option was the existing diplomatic status of the embassies, which would extend the jurisdiction of Estonia to the respective online services. This would offer the e-governmental services protection such as immunity, which is granted to the embassy itself and the residence of the ambassador, for example.[31] There were also substantial drawbacks, however, that the government needed to consider. The data embassies and their infrastructure require technical support, especially in a crisis, but existing embassies did not have sufficient technical competence in this regard. Furthermore, the telecommunications services provided to the embassies are not under their control. Kotka and Liiv give an example of an attack whose perpetrator takes control of a telecommunications operator that then disables an embassy's internet connection. That would substantially impair the functioning of data embassies. Relying solely on data embassies at Estonian embassies abroad is therefore not an ideal solution.[32]

The second option considered using governmental cloud solutions constructed and owned by allied states. A bilateral agreement to procure an already established cloud computing solution in specialized data centers could be signed between Estonia and one of its closest allied countries.[33] Such a data embassy would have Estonian jurisdiction, applicable within an agreed-on perimeter, and it would possess privileges similar to a traditional physical embassy's. Another advantage would be the fulfillment of the specific requirements for service quality assurance and professional staff, who would be trained in handling not only the day-to-day services but also emergencies that could jeopardize service availability.[34] In the end, the government appraised the latter option of dedicated data centers as more likely to succeed.

In terms of Westphalian sovereignty, the data embassy project assists in organizing the political life of Estonia while addressing both Westphalian principles. When the intended network of data embassies is constructed, they will exclude external actors and factors from Estonian domestic authority structures because of the backups and ability of the data embassies to run governmental services. At the same time, they will contribute to solving the problem of dependency on territory and the need to protect it. The data embassies do remain dependent on a government-protected territory to a certain degree, because the data is stored in data centers in allied countries; however, the territorial dependency is diversified because if Estonian territory is endangered by a threat such as a conventional attack, governmental services will remain up and running through data embassies located abroad. Hence, the data embassy project helps anchor Westphalian sovereignty in cyberspace.

The Implementation of Data Embassies: The Legal Framework

On June 20, 2017, the prime ministers of Estonia and Luxembourg, Jüri Ratas and Xavier Bettel, respectively, signed the Agreement between the Republic of Estonia and the Grand Duchy of Luxembourg on the Hosting of Data and Information Systems in Luxembourg. The bilateral agreement deals with the storage of Estonian critical and confidential data and related systems in Luxembourg's government-owned high-security data center.[35] This unprecedented agreement sets the stage for establishment of the world's first data embassy, serving not only as a backup of Estonian data critical for the running of the state outside its physical territory but also for the operation of services. In March 2018, Riigikogu, the parliament of Estonia, ratified the agreement.[36]

The implementation of data embassies rests on two pillars, which constitute the two variables here: legislation as the variable of authority and modern technology as the variable of control. The Estonian government had to address both during implementation. Initially, it was thought that they would need many adjustments in both the legal and the technological domains. It soon became clear, however, that a previously established legal framework and technology innovations adopted in reaction to the previous Estonian efforts to become a digital world leader were sufficient, and thus the implementation would be easier than originally calculated.

With respect to the legal pillar, the Estonian government initially thought that the peculiar and unprecedented character of data embassies would mean that Estonia's Emergency Act, which addresses crisis management, might not sufficiently cover data embassies and a special act would be needed. Such a digital continuity act would cover "the *de jure* 'complete preservation and persistence' of Estonia" if an unstable international security situation occurred.[37] It would, for example, specify the circumstances under which critical services must be operational from outside Estonian borders within twenty-four hours in the event of a serious security threat to the Estonian state. A digital continuity act could define procedures for a secondary site becoming a primary one and when the services could be returned to Estonian physical territory.[38] In the end, the government concluded that there was no need for any adjustment or amendment to Estonian domestic law or for a digital continuity act, because existing legislation such as the Emergency Act applies to data embassies.[39]

A different approach, however, had to be adopted in terms of public international law. The international document governing most diplomatic relations between states is the Vienna Convention on Diplomatic Relations.[40] The UN adopted the convention in April 1961, and it entered into force three years later. It is one of the cornerstones of the modern framework of international relations, defining the prerogatives granted to diplomatic missions abroad and creating the legal basis for diplomatic immunity. The closely related Vienna Convention on Consular Relations defines standards of behavior for states in international relations.[41] The UN adopted this second convention in April 1963, and it entered into force in March 1967. It sets the framework for consular relations, including immunity, although the protection defined by it is more limited compared with the diplomatic premises defined in the first convention.[42] Thus, the diplomatic relations convention was the document considered most often when discussing the possible international legal status of the Estonian data embassy.

A data embassy cannot be considered a diplomatic mission, possessing the same immunity and privileges as a traditional physical embassy; according to the Vienna Convention on Diplomatic Relations, an embassy can be used for diplomatic functions. The data embassy's purpose exceeds the primary purposes of diplomatic missions.[43] The concept is so innovative, it would be too difficult to create an embassy in a data center, as well as being impractical and less flexible.[44] The Estonian and Luxembourgian governments therefore had to find a new solution. The sensitivity of the data embassy's substance necessitated a solution that would grant it very similar protection, in the spirit of the diplomatic relations convention. "Under the Vienna Convention [on Diplomatic Relations], embassies, ambassadors, and the diplomatic pouches they carry are given special protections. For a data embassy to be meaningful, that same protection needs to be applied—effectively creating a corner of Estonian sovereign territory in cyberspace, via a data centre in Luxembourg."[45] Ian Walden, a professor of information and communications law at Queen Mary University of London, explains that although the diplomatic relations convention was formulated almost sixty years ago, it could support the data embassies and the idea of housing data remotely but securely. But he cautions that "the point with the Vienna Convention [on Diplomatic Relations] is there are a set of rules, but their enforceability is somewhat doubtful."[46] Enforceability largely depends on the state hosting the data and its interpretation of the respective laws drafted for the physical world, not the digital age. To avoid these potential risks, Estonia has conditioned the creation of a data embassy outside of its physical border by signing a bilateral agreement. Such an agreement would define the rights and responsibilities of sending and receiving states, which are crucial for the protection of the integrity of Estonian critical and sensitive data and information systems abroad.[47] And so the Agreement between the Republic of Estonia and the Grand Duchy of Luxembourg on the Hosting of Data and Information Systems came into existence, the first agreement of its kind worldwide.

Its preamble states the agreement "is in the spirit of the Vienna Convention on Diplomatic Relations" and adds that "the Vienna Convention on

Diplomatic Relations is not sufficient to set a legal framework for the hosting of data and information systems."[48] The agreement is heavily inspired by many elements articulated in the diplomatic relations convention, but because that convention does not contain provisions on data hosting, the agreement deviates from common practice regarding a traditional physical embassy in several crucial ways. Furthermore, certain privileges of the diplomatic relations convention are in the agreement but not in full, as if it were an embassy.[49]

For example, this is clearly visible in the definition of the premises in question and their privileges. The main issue here was to make it evident that, although the data embassy's premises enjoy prerogatives similar to those of traditional embassies, it is not an embassy per se or a diplomatic mission.[50] Article 1(i) of the Vienna Convention on Diplomatic Relations notes that the premises "are the buildings or parts of buildings and the land ancillary thereto, irrespective of ownership, used for the purposes of the mission including the residence of the head of the mission."[51] The related Article 1(b) of the agreement between Estonia and Luxembourg states, "The premises shall mean a dedicated data centre space provided by the Grand Duchy of Luxembourg and meant for the purpose of hosting Estonian data and information systems and equipment," and the agreement's Article 1(a) further specifies that "the data centre shall mean a facility used to host the data and information systems, the equipment and licences and associated components, such as telecommunications and storage systems."[52] Thus, the bilateral agreement clearly expresses that the premises in question are not the traditional embassies in the sense of the diplomatic relations convention but are data centers.

Still, some crucial elements of the bilateral agreement strongly resemble the diplomatic relations convention and reflect the raison d'être and importance of the data embassies; for instance, the inviolability and immunity of premises. Article 22(1) of the diplomatic relations convention provides that "the premises of the mission shall be inviolable. The agents of the receiving State may not enter them, except with the consent of the head of the mission,"[53] and Article 22(3) further specifies that "the premises of the mission, their furnishing and other property thereon and the means of transport of the mission shall be immune from search, requisition, attachment or execution."[54] The archives and documents of the mission enjoy inviolability according to the diplomatic relations convention too.[55] The bilateral agreement similarly articulates inviolability of data embassies' premises. Article 3(1) states, "The premises shall be inviolable and thus exempt from search, requisition, attachment or execution."[56] The same is true for the archives of the premises.[57] Furthermore, any official or public authority's representative of Luxembourg who wishes to enter the premises must first seek the approval of the authorized representative of Estonia, although prior approval can be assumed in emergencies such as fires.[58]

Certain articles in the bilateral agreement cover elements not addressed in the diplomatic relations convention at all or that are substantially different from paragraphs of the diplomatic relations convention on the same topics. One such example is the immunity for licenses. Article 5 of the bilateral agreement provides that "the equipment and licenses required to operate the data centre and put in place on the premises by the Republic of Estonia shall be regarded as assets of the Republic of Estonia and shall enjoy immunity from every form of legal process."[59] The diplomatic relations convention has no mention of licenses or their inviolability. Bartołomiej Sierzputowski also points to the beginning and end of the inviolability of a data center's premises, which differs significantly from the diplomatic relations convention. According to Sierzputowski, "It might be thought that, based on analogies with the [Vienna Convention on Diplomatic Relations] and [Vienna Convention on Consular Relations], [premises inviolability] would be from when they are ready to be occupied and used for their designated functions."[60] Article 10(4) of the bilateral agreement, however, adjusts the established practice for data centers: "The inviolability of those premises ends with the termination of the agreement. However, the Estonian archives, equipment and the licences remain inviolable—until they are handed over to an Estonian legal representative."[61] These two examples reflect the bilateral agreement having been created to cover problems and realities that were unknown in the 1960s when the diplomatic relations convention was formulated.

Data centers, in sum, do not possess the status of a diplomatic mission, despite their label of data embassies. In fact, "data embassy" is not found in the bilateral agreement between Estonia and Luxembourg or in any other official document. This caused some confusion at the beginning of negotiations on the bilateral agreement and had to be clarified straightaway, especially in relation to the diplomatic relations convention.[62] "Data embassy" is more of a marketing label, catchy and easy for people to understand and explain.[63]

Despite that, the bilateral agreement between Estonia and Luxembourg sculpts the status of data embassy premises in the spirit of the Vienna Convention on Diplomatic Relations, "with almost all of the agreement being analogous to it."[64] Most importantly, the bilateral agreement establishes that the data stored in Luxembourg is under Estonian jurisdiction.[65]

The Implementation of Data Embassies: Cyber Capabilities

The other pillar on which the concept of the data embassy is built, which also constitutes the control variable, is cyber capabilities. Given the innovative nature of data embassies, Estonia needs a technical infrastructure and implementation that ensures data synchronization between two sites while securing data integrity and preventing data loss.[66] Estonia is a leader in modern technologies in general, but one deserves special mention here: X-Road, a data-exchange layer that is the true backbone of e-Estonia.[67] Other technical infrastructure pertains to security measures and standards. The data embassy is protected against cyber attacks and crisis situations with KSI blockchain technology, and the data centers require the highest level of security certification. All three of these cyber capabilities are indispensable for building a reliable and secure data embassy and are discussed in the following paragraphs.

The main purpose of the X-Road infrastructure, launched at the end of 2001, is interoperability between various organizations and their information systems, an essential feature for a functioning and developed e-government. Estonia does not use a single, central database to offer its citizens governmental services. Quite the opposite; data are stored in different databases managed by the respective departments and agencies, such as the population registry or the land registry. If one governmental institution needs information possessed by another governmental institution, the former does not need to request it from the citizen again. Estonian law mandates that data retrieved from one institution must be securely transferred to another via the X-Road data-exchange layer.[68] For example, drivers do not need to carry a hard copy of their driver's license with them. A police officer can request the information about the license from the database of the Estonian Road Administration via X-Road using only the driver's ID card.[69] Thus, the X-Road infrastructure allows a new generation of e-service information systems of the public and private sectors to interconnect and work in harmony, collecting specific data from a citizen only once.

X-Road has developed into a powerful tool. To ensure safe transfer of data and protection of confidentiality and integrity, all outgoing data is digitally signed and encrypted, and all incoming data is authenticated and logged. X-Road can transfer large data sets, send a message to several information systems, and search for data across multiple information systems. It is also possible to join two X-Road ecosystems in a federation, or a "one to one relationship between two ecosystems. Members of the federated ecosystems can publish and consume services with each other as if they were members of the same ecosystem. Federation enables easy and secure cross-border data exchange between these ecosystems."[70] A federation of X-Road environments was created between Estonia and Finland in February 2018.

The power of X-Road technology is apparent from statistics provided by the Estonian government. As of May 1, 2022, the X-Road has listed as indirect users of its services 688 institutions and enterprises, 164 public sector institutions, and approximately 52,000 organizations. Around 3,155 different services can be used via the X-Road ecosystem.[71] Furthermore, "3% of requests on [the X-Road] are submitted by citizen[s]. Assuming that every request saves 15 minutes—those requests have saved 2,391 working years during [the] previous calendar year."[72] Hence, the X-Road ecosystem is a crucial part of the functioning of the Estonian e-governmental system and ensures data availability, integrity, and confidentiality, the three core tenants of information security. Without the X-Road infrastructure, Estonia probably could not have developed into one of the most digitalized countries in the world.

KSI blockchain technology is another cyber capability without which Estonian digital society would not be as secure and reliable as it is today.[73] KSI blockchain technology protects the data embassy against cyber attacks and any cyber crisis. The development of a scalable blockchain technology in

Estonia started in 2008 in the aftermath of the 2007 cyber attacks related to relocating an unknown soldier's statue. At that time, the keyless signature infrastructure (KSI) method, developed by the Estonian company Guardtime, was chosen as an appropriate blockchain infrastructure. In 2012, Estonia became the first country in the world to deploy blockchain technology in production systems, with the succession registry, the record of wills, of the Ministry of Justice.[74] Since then, KSI blockchain technology has spread across Estonian state agencies and their registries.

KSI blockchain technology secures the integrity of data stored in governmental repositories and protects the networks and data against compromise while ensuring data privacy. The strength of the blockchain technology stems from the impossibility of changing data on the blockchain. Thus, "with KSI blockchain deployed in Estonian governmental networks, history cannot be rewritten by anybody and the authenticity of the electronic data can be mathematically proven. It means that nobody—neither hackers, nor system administrators, nor even government itself—can manipulate the data and get away with it."[75] This allows absolute trust in governmental data in any situation. This trust is important given that blockchain technology backs state registries such as the property registry, the business registry, the digital court system, and the state gazette of laws and regulations. Access to the blockchain network for state institutions is guaranteed via X-Road infrastructure by the Estonian Information Systems Authority, the internal service provider for the Estonian government.[76]

The final cyber capability indispensable for the secure and reliable functioning of data embassies is the required level of standards for data centers. The US-based company Uptime Institute has developed a globally recognized standard for the design, construction, and operation of data centers. The Tier Standard is a "standard for data center reliability and overall performance. It allows for various levels of performance to be chosen based on the intended applications and business parameters associated with those applications."[77] The Tier Standard has four levels, Tier IV being the most advanced and most appropriate for data stored and processed at data embassies. Estonia itself does not possess a Tier IV data center on its territory, but Luxembourg owns a data center with Tier IV certification. Having a high-security data center was a chief benefit of placing the data embassy in Luxembourg, in addition to its flexible, forward-looking, and open approach to technology innovation.[78] The data center standard joins the X-Road and KSI blockchain technology as one of three cyber capabilities indispensable for securing confidentiality, integrity, and availability of data for Estonian data embassies.

Currently, Estonia operates one data embassy, in Luxembourg. The embassy's funding and the lease with Luxembourg expires after five years, the time period for testing the overall vision of storing and operating governmental data in data centers owned by friendly countries to secure digital continuity. If the concept is proved, Estonia will develop a decentralized system of at least three data embassies in other allied states. If one of them is hit by a cyber attack such as a distributed denial of service, the other two could replace it, because they would store the same data and would work as an active system.[79]

A complete picture of the data embassy concept must include the Luxembourgian point of view and its motivation to host the initiative. After all, Estonia needed a similarly innovative and like-minded counterpart to realize this unprecedented project. The grand duchy was a fine candidate for that for several reasons. Luxembourg, in the center of western Europe, has excellent connectivity due to its telecom network being hyperconnected to primary internet access centers in other countries. Furthermore, it has a well-developed infrastructure of data centers with the Tier IV standard as mentioned earlier. On top of that, the Luxembourgian long-term digital initiative aims to position the country as a leader in the ICT field. Therefore, when the grand duchy noticed the increasing demand among its allies to store data outside their own territory, the Luxembourgian government decided to step forward as a trustworthy international partner for such negotiations. An agreement with Estonia on data embassies, however, must not limit or influence the state sovereignty of Luxembourg itself. The bilateral treaty, which covered the requested immunities and was in line with the constitutions, satisfactorily addressed this important point. In the end, the implementation of the Estonian data embassy was perceived as a success and attracted a wave of attention not only in the grand duchy but also abroad; the Luxembourgian government had its embassies abroad introduce this attractive project to others.[80]

The idea appealed to not only other states but also international organizations, setting an important precedent. Luxembourg is a progressive state with a reputation for reliability and an agile business-oriented government that realizes that data storage has a promising future. Not surprisingly, Luxembourg has become the seat for the second data embassy in the world.[81] On March 5, 2018, Luxembourg and the European Patent Organization signed the Complementary Agreement concerning the inviolability of the archives of the European Patent Organization.[82] The agreement, which entered into force July 25, 2018, establishes that the patent organization's digital archives together with correspondence, manuscripts, films, recordings, photographs, and accompanying materials are to be hosted by Luxembourg in government-owned data centers. The agreement stresses the inviolability of the archives and employs the model of the Estonian data embassy.[83] On the government-to-government level, Luxembourg and Monaco formed a partnership on digital innovation in December 2018 for saving Monaco's sensitive data in a data center in Luxembourg with guarantees of immunity in line with the Estonian data embassy model. Luxembourg and Monaco signed a bilateral treaty July 15, 2021, for a data embassy of Monaco in Luxembourg.[84]

Conclusion

To apply Westphalian sovereignty and its two principles, territoriality and the exclusion of external actors in domestic affairs, in cyberspace, a state first needs to expand the life of its society into the cyber realm. Estonia achieved this during its transformation from a poorly developed country right after the dissolution of the USSR to the paperless state of today. The government's efforts in this direction culminated with the declaration of access to the internet being a basic human right, the guarantee of digital signatures having equal importance to handwritten signatures, the introduction of online voting, and ultimately the launch of e-ID for native Estonians and e-residency for non-Estonians. The expansion of society to the cyber environment has, however, also created serious risks that have the potential to undermine the state's Westphalian sovereignty in cyberspace. Estonia experienced this threat to its government's functions for several weeks in 2007 during a severe cyber attack. This experience and the realization of the risks of running the government's services in cyberspace forced Estonia to find a solution to securing its digital continuity and strengthening its Westphalian sovereignty in cyberspace.

A lengthy debate ensued on what solutions would protect governmental data, securing their confidentiality, integrity, and accessibility, and how to ensure governmental services could stay up and running even during a major cyber or conventional attack. The Data Embassy Initiative introduced three elements to the feasibility debate. A government-operated cloud was an idea for how to maintain data backups and live online services at data centers within the physical borders of Estonia. Although the governmental cloud solution has the indisputable advantage of excluding external factors from the domestic authority structures of Estonia, it has a large drawback in terms of Westphalian sovereignty; this solution is heavily dependent on Estonian territory and hence cannot ensure digital continuity during, for example, a conventional attack across Estonian physical borders. A solution to this could be the second element of the Data Embassy Initiative; virtual data embassies. Virtual data embassies could serve as a backup of nonsensitive data in the public cloud of private companies. Although this solution based on commercial cloud computing would help solve the territorial dependency, there is a chance that the government might not be the exclusive arbitrator of manipulation of the data. Sensitive data therefore could not be stored in virtual data embassies, thereby not ensuring digital continuity, which is based on the processing of different kinds of data, including the most sensitive. Therefore, although cloud technology is to a certain degree employed by the Estonian government today, the governmental cloud and virtual data embassies as described under the Data Embassy Initiative appear to be currently unfeasible and too ambitious, while not providing the required level of security for governmental data in terms of Westphalian sovereignty in cyberspace.

The third element of the Data Embassy Initiative has more promise. Although the "physical" data embassy is more of a PR term and in reality is like a regular data center, its value is embedded in the uniqueness of the concept. The data embassies are designed as data centers under the control of Estonia's government but located outside Estonian borders in an allied country. The data embassy would not only back up essential governmental databases and registers but also be an active copy that could operate services in real time in times of crisis when data centers on Estonian territory are not under

Estonian control. Thus, the data embassy project satisfactorily addresses both Westphalian principles. It secures the maximum possible exclusion of external actors from Estonian domestic authority structures while diversifying the territorial dependency by extending the storage of governmental data to safe data centers beyond Estonian borders. Ultimately, the data embassy project helps establish and enforce Westphalian sovereignty in cyberspace.

Two crucial building blocks of the data embassy constitute the variables of this book: the legal framework as the authority variable and cyber capabilities as the control variable. I considered both the domestic and the international legal frameworks and found that the international framework was more crucial. International public law ensures Estonian jurisdiction over its data hosted outside its territory and ensures data embassy immunity. The bilateral agreement between Estonia and Luxembourg builds on and expands the Vienna Convention on Diplomatic Relations, and it represents the authority variable of this chapter. Cyber capabilities ensure the inviolability of data as part of e-government and data embassies. The X-Road infrastructure, KSI blockchain, and Tier IV standard for data centers are indispensable for the safe functioning of data embassies. These cyber capabilities represent the control variable of this chapter. For smooth and safe functioning of data embassies, both legislative framework and cyber capabilities are vital. Authority and control are equally important for Estonia to enforce its Westphalian sovereignty in cyberspace.

FOUR

The Netherlands and International Legal Sovereignty

Stephen Krasner defines the classical understanding of international legal sovereignty as "the practices associated with mutual recognition, usually between territorial entities that have formal juridical independence," although history has shown that juridical independence and territory are not indispensable prerequisites.[1] Various activities can come under the definition, the most crucial one being the state's recognition by other states, followed by the state's acceptance as a juridical equal, a membership in international organizations and platforms, facilitation of treaty making, and providing defense against legal actions initiated in other states. Thus, international legal sovereignty, stretching into both international law and international relations, is a powerful tool for strengthening a state's security, economy, and interests.[2]

States' mutual recognition of each other's existence outside cyberspace is not challenged in cyberspace. The international legal sovereignty of a state usually expands from the physical world into the cyber domain. Hence, a state enters the cyber arena as a recognized actor by others, and its government solely decides how to build and strengthen the already-established international legal sovereignty. International legal sovereignty cannot be taken from a government in cyberspace unless it ceases to exist outside this domain.

Generally, a state has two options for how to approach its international legal sovereignty in cyberspace. First, it can be disinterested in participating in international developments regarding cyberspace, such as negotiations on creating cyber norms in international organizations or treaty making on the topic; consequently, its international legal sovereignty in cyberspace exists, but it is not boosted in any way by the government's activities. Alternatively, the government realizes the leverage cyberspace has on its security, economy, and ideological interests and decides to fortify its international legal sovereignty. To do so, the state must be accepted as a juridical equal by the others in cyber discussions, seek membership in international organizations interested in cyber developments, and take part in international negotiations on, for example, treaties related to cyber issues. If the state wants to boost its international legal sovereignty in cyberspace to the maximum, it needs to take the lead itself and attempt to influence global developments in international relations and law in cyberspace through initiatives, reaching out not only to its closest allies but also the broadest range of stakeholders possible. A state that successfully engages in international negotiations on cyber issues with as many stakeholders as possible heightens its recognition in the cyber community and maximizes its international legal sovereignty in cyberspace.

In the case of international legal sovereignty in cyberspace, identifying the cyber capabilities that represent this book's variable of control is not straightforward, given that this sovereignty type centers on the state's legal actions. Thus, I take the variable of control to be the cyber capabilities the state has at its disposal to establish itself as an important actor in international cyber negotiations. I then assess the variable of authority through the various activities around cyber issues of a state in the international community, such as setting new platforms for negotiation and formulating new agenda topics. In this regard, the Netherlands, with its cyber initiatives in the second half of the 2010s and in the early 2020s, is the leader of the transatlantic area and its neighborhood.

I start by focusing on the Netherlands' role as the "digital gateway to Europe."[3] The Netherlands hosts digital infrastructure crucial not only for its own benefit but for the whole of Europe and beyond. The "digital gateway" consists of infrastructure such as internet exchange points and a dense network of data centers. Although this infrastructure is not necessarily owned by the government, it is a crucial cyber capability that motivates the Dutch government to take an active role at the international negotiating table on cybersecurity. If the cyber norms and rules of responsible state behavior in cyberspace are formulated and respected by the widest range of states possible, states with critical infrastructure such as the "digital gateway" on its territory will be better prepared to protect it, which will in turn enhance their security. At the same time, having the "digital gateway" within its borders raises the Netherlands' image in the eyes of other states and gives the Dutch an excellent starting position to become a leader of international negotiations on the topic. Hence, an analysis of this cyber capability is indispensable here and also serves as the variable of control in this book.

I assess the variable of authority through Dutch activities in the international cyber arena. I examine the Dutch vision of its role, approach, and agenda in the international cyber community during the 2015 Global Conference on Cyberspace and in documentation of the Dutch international cyber strategy Building Digital Bridges. I discuss the Dutch role in new initiatives such as the Global Forum on Cyber Expertise, the Global Commission on the Stability of Cyberspace, and The Hague Process; look into the Dutch presidency of the Council of the European Union; and turn to Dutch activities in relation to traditional platforms like the United Nations Group of Governmental Experts on Advancing Responsible State Behavior in Cyberspace. Finally, I evaluate the relation of the two variables to see if their roles are in balance or if one prevails over the other.

At stake for the Netherlands is both a stronger international legal sovereignty that benefits the entire international community and a strengthening of its own international legal sovereignty, two interlinked objectives. The ultimate goal of the Dutch is to contribute to the process of formulating and clarifying cyber norms and the rules for responsible state behavior in cyberspace across the international community. Achieving this will help states better protect their critical infrastructure and could increase security domestically, regionally, and globally. To attain its goal, the Netherlands first needed to cultivate a reputation for being a distinguished negotiation partner and leader, which included strengthening its international legal sovereignty. By doing so, its voice in the international community has become stronger, and it is easier for the Dutch to influence negotiations in the direction they desire. Hence, one objective leads to the fulfillment of the other in the Dutch case.

Key Digital Infrastructure in the Netherlands

Traditionally, the Netherlands has been a much trafficked transport intersection. Because of its colonial history and its location near highly populated and industrialized centers for European business, since the Middle Ages staples and luxury goods have crossed its borders to reach Europe or be shipped to all corners of the world. Initially, maritime transport reigned, which led to the Port of Rotterdam becoming one of the oldest and largest ports of Europe. Building and maintaining its status as a maritime power remained a focal point in Dutch politics for centuries, bringing economic profit and strengthening the nation's international political rank. The supremacy of maritime transport was disrupted by the railway boom and then aviation in the twentieth century. To keep the status of being one of the largest European transport hubs, the Netherlands built Schiphol Airport, the busiest airport in terms of aircraft movement. The importance attached to the Port of Rotterdam and later Schiphol Airport shows that the Netherlands has been long aware of the wealth generated from its role as the international gateway to Europe, no matter what the transport mode is. Its actions in the twenty-first century reveal that the Dutch government intends to maintain this position and the international political status attached to it into the future.

The second half of the twentieth century and especially its last decade brought about a new phenomenon, cyberspace and the internet, and the Dutch were again prompted to seize an opportunity. The rapid expansion of the internet network from US territory to Europe and beyond required a resourceful and nimble reaction to the need to construct digital infrastructure. Again, thanks to its location between the strong economies of western and northern Europe and in the center of the EU's single market, the Netherlands was ready to react. Centrum Wiskunde & Informatica, the Dutch national research institute for mathematics and computer science, was the first non-US institution to gain access, in November 1988, to the network that is today known as the internet.[4] Currently, the Netherlands claims once again to be an international distribution hub: it is a frontrunner in digital infrastructure and the digital gateway to Europe. The significance of the digital infrastructure was nicely underlined by Bert Koenders, the Dutch minister of foreign affairs, who said, "The Dutch digital gateway to Europe is now more important to our economy than Amsterdam's Schiphol Airport and the Port of Rotterdam combined. So, for the Netherlands, bits and bytes outweigh Boeings and boats."[5]

The construction of this international digital hub, a cyber capability with a global reach, has two potentially crucial impacts on Dutch international legal sovereignty. First, the Dutch government must protect this digital gateway for the whole of the European continent, preferably not only technically but also on the basis of international law in cyberspace. This is a strong motivation to get involved in international negotiations on the establishment of cyber norms. Second, hosting such digital infrastructure on its territory raises the Dutch reputation in the eyes of the international community. The combination of the two is then a favorable starting point for the Netherlands to build its international legal sovereignty. That is also why the international digital hub on Dutch territory is a subject of study here, constituting the control variable for this chapter.

The Dutch international digital hub is one of the most important global hubs for the exchange of data and digital services. It comprises internet exchanges and backbone connectivity, data centers, cloud providers, and the accompanying ecosystems for support. All these components combine to form the digital gateway and have higher growth rates and a larger economic impact than the Port of Rotterdam and Schiphol Airport.[6] The Dutch government has added to these two *mainports*, the Dutch word for these huge physical distribution hubs and their economic ecosystem, a third *mainport*, the digital gateway, with a goal to develop policies and visions to strengthen it.[7] The digital gateway is why the Netherlands has become home to numerous tech companies and attracts large foreign investments and, most importantly, why the Dutch government has cultivated a forward-looking mindset with respect to cybersecurity and the need for an international dialogue on its enhancement worldwide.

Although the Dutch government is not necessarily the owner of this cyber capability, that capability is an important element of its political agenda, and the government provides the stakeholders of the digital infrastructure and accompanying services with favorable conditions for their growth. An example of this is the work of the Netherlands Foreign Investment Agency, an operational unit of the Dutch Ministry of Economic Affairs. The agency provides new companies and those with already-existing operations on the Dutch market with free assistance at all stages of business. Agency services include assisting with recruiting new talent, connecting companies with suitable partners, introducing them to public-private partnerships, and providing personalized guidance on tax, governmental, and permit procedures. The Netherlands Foreign Investment Agency, together with regional economic development agencies and large cities, has created a collaborative team, the Invest in Holland Network, for which the digital gateway to Europe entails a key agenda item given its economic potential.[8]

One of the pivotal components of the third *mainport* is the presence of several internet exchange points on its territory—in particular, the Amsterdam Internet Exchange (AMS-IX). The internet is a network of networks that are mutually interconnected. Exchange points allow the internet's networks to interconnect directly—that is, via the exchange point itself and not through other networks. Direct connection has several benefits. For example, it increases network redundancy and reduces latency because internet traffic can be redirected through a number of different routes while taking the fastest ones. Moreover, it reduces connectivity costs because of the direct exchange of internet traffic with multiple networks via a single exchange point.[9] Internet exchange points are thus used by internet service providers, content providers, enterprises, and anybody else whose goal is network optimization.

Although several internet exchange points are on Dutch territory, the AMS-IX is the most prominent one. The AMS-IX was established in the 1990s as a not-for-profit organization and developed into a neutral and independent peering point interconnecting several hundred communications networks. Since its foundation, it has grown immensely in both number of connected networks and traffic volume. When measured by number of peering networks and internet traffic exchanged, the AMS-IX was the second-largest internet exchange point in the world in 2020.[10] Hence, the

Netherlands' internet exchange points in general and the AMS-IX in particular, together with a large portion of the undersea optical cables that directly connect continental Europe and North America,[11] heavily contribute to the extraordinarily strong position of the Netherlands in global digital infrastructure.

The other crucial component of the Dutch digital gateway is the data center and cloud industry, which is supposedly the fastest-growing sector in the country.[12] Moreover, the Dutch data center market is one of the most advanced in the whole of Europe. It is estimated that one-third of all European data centers are in Amsterdam and its surrounding area.[13] Top commercial data centers and key hyperscale cloud organizations are in the Netherlands. Amsterdam, Groningen, Rotterdam, and Eindhoven are home to large data center campuses, and two hyperscale campuses are in Wieringerwerf and Eemshaven, respectively.[14]

This attractiveness of the Netherlands to data centers stems from several factors. First is the excellent internet connectivity via terrestrial and submarine cables and through the AMS-IX and other internet exchange points on Dutch territory. Second, huge data centers consume large amounts of energy. Thus, electricity capacity, reliable power supply, and favorable electricity prices are important advantages. Third, the stable political and economic climate also adds value. The Netherlands is a politically neutral country focused on international trade, and it provides favorable laws and taxes. The highly educated and multilingual workforce complete the list of favorable conditions in the Netherlands and its growing data center and cloud industry.[15]

The Dutch government is not passive in the Dutch data center industry. It actively and closely cooperates with the Dutch Data Center Association, for instance, a representative of the data center industry. The Ministry of the Interior and Kingdom Relations cooperated in the Implementation Program of the Spatial Economic Development Strategy, which coordinates the spatial layout of data centers. This close cooperation helps ensure that the regulations regarding data centers and their ecosystems work smoothly. The Data Center Association and the Dutch government also cooperate on energy efficiency, innovation, and sustainability. Finally, the government is active in education and employment to provide favorable conditions for the data center industry to have a sufficient pool of IT and technology-related talent.[16]

Over time, these cyber capabilities, the high standard of living, and favorable conditions created by the Dutch government have paid off. The Dutch cloud and hosting sector is one of the biggest globally, facilitating over 20 percent of the total e-commerce sales in Europe.[17] Moreover, the data center and cloud industry attracts approximately 20 percent of all foreign direct investment going into the Netherlands, heavily contributing to the Dutch digital gateway being the largest sector of foreign direct investment.[18] Overall, the strong digital ecosystem represented by the digital gateway is highly attractive for the innovative community of start-ups and international tech companies, such as Booking.com, Palo Alto Networks, and Netflix, that established European headquarters in the Netherlands.[19] This guarantees a healthy investment climate and economic growth. The total internet economy of the Netherlands is estimated to be €110 billion and accounts for 264,000 jobs in internet-related IT. The total value of the digital sector is estimated to be around one-quarter of the national gross domestic product.[20]

A globally significant digital infrastructure on Dutch territory has associated effects on modern technologies and cybersecurity with international reach. I discuss three important institutions and organizations based in the Netherlands and associated with the functioning of the internet, its security, or the development of modern technologies: the Réseaux IP Européens (European IP Networks) Network Coordination Center (RIPE NCC), The Hague Security Delta, and the European Cybercrime Center. Although their work is not cyber capabilities per se, they strongly contribute to the overall Dutch reputation in the international cyber community and thus prepare the ground for a strengthening of Dutch international legal sovereignty in cyberspace.

The organization whose work is most closely associated with the functioning of the internet is the RIPE NCC, a not-for-profit membership organization that is a regional internet registry. Each computer's IP address is assigned by its internet service provider (ISP). ISPs obtain allocations of these IP addresses directly from a regional internet registry. Thus, each regional registry coordinates the IP addressing system in its assigned region and maintains the registry of who holds the addresses, which makes them an integral component of the backbone of the internet. The RIPE NCC, which was established in 1992 in Amsterdam, is one of five registries, and it covers Europe, the Middle East, and the whole of central Asia, including the Russian Federation. With 23,224 members as of December 2021, it is the largest registry in the world, and also the oldest.[21]

Another organization created partly thanks to the digital infrastructure on Dutch territory and the Dutch government's interest in this area is The Hague Security Delta (HSD). It is a network of governmental, businesses, and knowledge institutions that cooperate on innovation and knowledge development in different areas of security such as cybersecurity, forensics, and protection of critical infrastructure. The HSD office provides partners with access to talent, knowledge, capital, and markets through opportunities and events such as the International Cybersecurity Summer School and a Cybersecurity Week. The heart of the Dutch security cluster is its HSD campus, the national innovation center for security in The Hague. The HSD is the largest security cluster in Europe.[22]

The third organization is the European Cybercrime Center (EC3), set up by Europol in 2013 in The Hague to "strengthen the law enforcement response to cybercrime in the EU and thus to help protect European citizens, businesses and governments from online crime."[23] EC3 covers the whole spectrum of cybercriminal activities of the dark web, from high-tech crimes to payment fraud. EC3 serves as an information hub on cybercrime, supports operations and investigations by EU member states, supports training and capacity building, provides highly specialized technical and digital forensic support, and represents the EU law-enforcement community.[24] Its reach is mainly regional but often goes beyond European borders.

The presence of such significant cyber capabilities as the third *mainport* on Dutch territory crucially influences both domestic and international developments. Domestically, it is an important enabler and engine of innovations in different sectors of the digital economy and society. The Dutch government is aware of this, and although it might not be the owner of such digital infrastructure itself, this situation creates favorable conditions for growth. On the international level, it increases the Netherlands' prestige in the eyes of the international cyber and tech community. The Netherlands is an attractive location for both international tech companies and international organizations dealing with the development and protection of cyberspace. The following section outlines how this motivates the government to take an active role in international negotiations on cyber norms to create a protective environment for itself, which simultaneously raises the Dutch reputation of being a skillful international negotiator.

The Dutch Role in International Cyber Negotiations

The Netherlands has a long history of active involvement in creating and shaping international law and formulating norms of state behavior. One of the earliest examples is the work of Hugo Grotius. Two masterpieces of this Dutch-born jurist, diplomat, and humanist of the seventeenth century have had an enduring impact. *De jure belli ac pacis* (*On the Law of War and Peace*) is a book on the legal status of war and considered a foundational building block of international law. In *Mare Liberum* (*The Freedom of the Seas*), Grotius argued that the sea was an international territory that could be freely used by all nations for seafaring trade. Grotius's work cemented the Dutch interest in shaping the field of international law and norms, which remains on the government's agenda today. The Hague hosted the first Peace Conference by the end of the nineteenth century, and The Hague Conventions of 1899 and 1907 followed. These events prepared the ground for The Hague to become home to international judicial bodies like the International Criminal Court and the International Court of Justice, the latter based in the Peace Palace, earning The Hague the moniker the City of Peace and Justice. To leave no room for doubt about the Dutch dedication to forming a lasting justice system and peace, the Constitution of the Kingdom of the Netherlands codifies in Article 90 that "the Government shall promote the development of the international legal order."[25]

Therefore, the Netherlands did not dawdle when cyberspace and its seemingly chaotic nature came to the attention of international relations and international law. Its long history of international legal development predestined the Netherlands to take an active role in forming platforms for debates on cyber norms creation and taking an active role in already-established forums. This section closely examines Dutch activities and initiatives in this regard because they catapulted the Netherlands into the frontrunner position on international legal sovereignty in cyberspace, and they constitute the authority variable in this chapter.

The apparent wake-up call for the Netherlands to develop national structures, procedures, and legislation for cybersecurity was the 2011 DigiNotar incident. DigiNotar was a Dutch certificate authority company whose digital certificates were used to access key services worldwide, such as all online tax returns filed in the Netherlands. In June 2011, it was revealed that hackers had compromised DigiNotar and issued hundreds of fake security certificates. These certificates could be used on websites of the US Central Intelligence Agency and Israel's Mossad and websites of companies like Microsoft, Google, and Twitter. The damage caused to the Dutch digital infrastructure was enormous. An expert even claimed in the aftermath of the hack that "the long-term effects of the DigiNotar hack could be more serious than Stuxnet," a computer worm uncovered in 2010 that attacked Iranian nuclear enrichment facilities and set back the Iranian nuclear program by several months.[26] Besides spurring development of the national cybersecurity capabilities, the hack revealed to the Dutch that cybersecurity is a collective responsibility of nations.[27]

This idea officially emerged two years later in the 2013 National Cybersecurity Strategy, subtitled From Awareness to Capability. The document states, "The Netherlands aims to develop into an 'international centre of cyber diplomacy' where diplomats, policymakers and cyber experts come together" to build stability in cyberspace by working on topics like the application of legal rules in the cyber domain.[28] The strategy defined this idea as one of five objectives: "The Netherlands builds coalitions for freedom, security and peace in the digital domain." This objective embraced actions such as developing standards and trust-inspiring measures to counter conflict escalation in cyberspace in cooperation with international partners (action 25), creating an expert hub in the field of international law and cybersecurity (action 26), and continuing to act as the international leader in internet freedom (action 27). Two more actions emphasized the Dutch government's need to increase its participation in multistakeholder events (action 28) and continue to support cybersecurity-capability building in third countries, or states beyond the EU borders, through both bilateral and regional initiatives (action 29).[29] These last two action points highlight the importance of including a broad variety of actors. Every additional actor that recognizes the Dutch initiative and leadership and participates in the negotiations strengthens the legitimacy of Dutch international legal sovereignty in cyberspace. This official proclamation of the plan to be a leader during international negotiations on pertinent cyber issues like the application of international law in the domain demonstrates the intent to build and maximally strengthen Dutch international legal sovereignty in cyberspace.

The true breakthrough in this direction was hosting the Global Conference on Cyberspace (GCCS),[30] jointly organized by the Dutch Ministries of Foreign Affairs, Security and Justice, Economic Affairs, and Defense and held in April 2015 in The Hague. The first GCCS was in London in 2011, others were in Budapest (2012), Seoul (2013), and New Delhi (2017). Being the host of such a prestigious event was the first opportunity for the Netherlands to showcase itself in front of the global cyber community as an active facilitator and negotiator. The conference gathers high-level representatives of governments, civil societies, and the private sector to discuss cooperation in cyberspace, cyber-capability building, and norms for responsible behavior in cyberspace, all topics related the Dutch strategy for international cooperation. The government of the Netherlands defined the objectives of GCCS 2015: "The goal of GCCS 2015 is to further enhance international cooperation in the digital arena. Another item on the agenda is the establishment of standards for responsible internet use. The Netherlands champions an open, free and secure internet. By investing in international cooperation between public and private parties, the Netherlands not only succeeds in improving its own digital security; it also creates opportunities for economic growth and innovation."[31]

Including as many actors as possible guarantees a larger global impact but makes the debate more difficult. In the words of Bert Koenders, the then-minister of foreign affairs, "The fact that the internet knows no boundaries means international cooperation is vital. At this conference we specifically want the debate to include countries whose views on the cyber domain differ from those of Western countries. That debate is crucial, because the internet is something we all share."[32] Indeed, GCCS 2015 attracted an impressive 1,500 attendees from over a hundred nations.[33] This inclusive multistakeholder approach proved successful here and has been used in other

Dutch initiatives in this field, attracting states that have not previously participated.[34] Further, the ability of involving a broad spectrum of actors, including those that have not been very active so far, raises the Dutch reputation as a skillful negotiator on cyber issues and contributes to the strengthening of its international legal sovereignty in cyberspace. By hosting GCCS 2015, the Netherlands firmly cemented itself in the global debate on cyberspace and has built on this foundation with its subsequent actions.

In March 2015, almost simultaneously with GCCS 2015, the Netherlands Scientific Council for Governance Policy presented to the Dutch Ministry of Foreign Affairs a report, "The Public Core of the Internet: An International Agenda for Internet Governance," subsequently published as a book. The report calls for an international norm stipulating that the public core of the internet must be protected against unwarranted intervention by states and other parties. The internet was created to operate internationally, no matter the user's nationality or status. Thus, states' efforts to fence off their cyberspace and increase their governance powers can potentially negatively affect internet infrastructure. The report's key argument is that the infrastructure of the internet and its core protocols should be considered a global public good because they benefit everyone in the world. An international standard should be agreed on to identify the infrastructure and core protocols as a neutral zone in which governments are forbidden to intervene. Every state whose economy and society depend on the functionality and integrity of the internet should aim to achieve this nonintervention norm.[35]

The exact parts of the internet infrastructure and core protocols that constitute the global public good must still be determined; however, what the Netherlands makes clear is that the public core "does not comprise the whole of the internet or even enter into the content layer of the internet but it is limited to the logical and physical infrastructural layers of the core internet. It is deliberately a 'lowest common denominator approach' that aims to keep the concept of the public core as close as possible to the minimum that is needed to protect the functionality of the internet."[36] This approach has a single goal: to secure the broadest possible international support for the norm. If content such as discussions on human rights was included under the public core of the internet, a consensus could never be reached.[37] Focusing on a less controversial topic of interest to all states helps involve as many stakeholders as possible.

Although the report advises the Dutch government to assign cyberspace and internet governance a high priority on its foreign policy agenda, its core message has a global appeal. It highlights that the international political arena of internet governance is changing as the internet experiences a demographic shift of its center of gravity from the Western and Northern Hemispheres to the Eastern and Southern Hemispheres. The next billion online users will originate from emerging economies with cultural and political backgrounds different from the currently dominant Western ones, which may erode Western nations' influence in favor of governments with different opinions about online security. The world may be split into two extremes: on one side, a camp wishing to strengthen the current multistakeholder, bottom-up model, on the other, a camp wishing to reinforce a top-down influence for nation-states. Between these two, many states have not articulated their position or clearly sided with either camp yet.[38] The report calls for expanding the negotiation table on cyber diplomacy and internet governance to include states whose technical and political cyber capabilities are still developing. Through this expansion, the Dutch government could achieve broader coalitions willing to enforce a nonintervention norm that protects the public core of the internet.[39] As a secondary effect, a multistakeholder coalition again contributes to profiling the Netherlands as a leader of international legal sovereignty.

The report on the public core of the internet and the hosting of GCCS 2015 defined where the Netherlands was standing and in what direction it would want to move on international negotiations on cyber issues. Together they helped cultivate lines of communication and build the networks, as well as the content. Above all, the report and the conference were the first indications of the Dutch efforts to enhance its cyber international legal sovereignty and become a leader in this regard.

To clearly set its goals and the modes for achieving them in the international cyber arena, the Netherlands, one of few countries to do this, published its international cyber strategy, Building Digital Bridges: Towards an Integrated International Cyber Policy, in 2017. The strategy defines several basic principles of the government's policy, one of them being the public core:

"The economic and social advantages associated with the internet require the 'public core' of the internet to function in a reliable, predictable, stable and safe way. This core possesses elements of an international public good that transcends individual sovereign and private interests. The Netherlands recognises that, given our dependence on the internet, it is necessary to exercise restraint when engaging in activities that can affect that public core."[40] The Netherlands is a competitive market positioned to profit from digitalization and is evolving into an information and digital knowledge society. Hence, it supports an open and nonfragmented internet where data can circulate without restrictions.

The strategy also notes the sharp division in the international debate on cyberspace between the camp favoring the multistakeholder model, the rule of international law, and protection of the internet's integrity and the camp of more state-oriented countries championing limited applicability of international law and more governmental control. Not forgetting the group of the undecided states, with their various economic, social, and political interests, it states, "The Netherlands is keen to convince them that a free, open and safe internet would serve those very interests."[41] The Dutch vision is that the government must take an integrated approach to international cooperation on cyber policy because the internet's transnational nature requires any challenge or threat to be resolved within an international forum. For the Netherlands to promote its domestic and foreign interests, the strategy advises the Dutch government to promote broad coalitions and partnerships on both bilateral and multilateral levels in international organizations such as the EU, NATO, UN, Organization for Economic Cooperation and Development, and Organization for Security and Cooperation in Europe. Multistakeholder and public-private platforms are used to engage the private sector, academia, and the nongovernmental sector. Transborder operational partnerships, especially in the field of security, have also been created on the basis of these bodies and coalitions.[42] The multistakeholder approach to broaden participants in public forums and negotiations on cyber issues is another element of the strategy.

To reaffirm its commitment to enhancing international cyber cooperation and playing a leading role in it, the Netherlands has launched new elements within its government's structures with this purpose. One example is the Cyber Task Force, within the Dutch Ministry of Foreign Affairs, which was introduced during GCCS 2015 to supervise diplomatic engagement in the digital domain.[43] Parallel to that, the Netherlands created a position for a special envoy for international cyber policy who represents the Dutch government during negotiations on the cybersecurity agenda abroad.[44] Uri Rosenthal, the first special envoy, organized GCCS 2015 and dissemination of its results. Rosenthal had previously served as the Dutch minister of foreign affairs, which underlines the importance the Dutch give to cybersecurity.[45] Most importantly, the government introduced the idea of deploying cyber diplomats at key embassies abroad to promote the Dutch cyber policy. The cyber diplomats "will act as liaisons for other governments and international organizations, provide information about trends and developments and offer substantive support for strategic priorities. To this end they will work with attachés from a number of ministries (security and justice, economic affairs, and defence), the business community, academia and NGOs."[46] Thus, the government's strategy enumerates the tools and platforms it plans to use. The following initiatives have attempted to turn the vision into reality.

One of the Dutch flagship projects to intensify its presence in the international cyber community, promote its goals and interests within the agenda, and potentially maximize its cyber international legal sovereignty is the Global Forum on Cyber Expertise (GFCE). The GFCE was launched by forty-two governments, intergovernmental organizations, and companies during GCCS 2015 as the conference's main outcome. The idea behind the GFCE is that societies have financial and human resources challenges when developing capacities to take full advantage of cyberspace. There is thus an urgent need to find smarter ways to cooperate with each other and establish best practices. "The GFCE will create a pragmatic, action-oriented and flexible forum. It will be consistent with, complement and reinforce existing bilateral, multilateral, multi-party, regional and international efforts to build cyber capacity and expertise and avoid duplication and overlap."[47]

In his speech at GCCS 2015, when speaking of the GFCE, Koenders emphasized the importance of the multistakeholder approach: "It is vital to include different stakeholders in a debate that could prove to be the next key dilemma in international security."[48] GFCE is a neutral, nonpolitical platform focused on building cyber capacity, not discussing norms and politics. GFCE starts where the policy stops, and so almost all countries, international organizations, or private companies can join the platform.[49] The Dutch thus initiated a platform that has the potential to encompass states from nearly the whole spectrum of opinions on cyber issues.

The first two years of the GFCE's existence were dedicated to the expansion of its network of members and partners from all over the world. The preliminary focus areas covered cybersecurity, cybercrime, data protection, and e-governance.[50] In 2017 the GFCE's focus shifted to positioning the platform as a global coordinating body for cyber-capacity building. This was initiated during GCCS 2017 in New Delhi, when the GFCE community endorsed the Delhi Communique on a GFCE Global Agenda for Cyber Capacity Building. This document called for joint action to strengthen global cyber capacities while emphasizing topics such as cyber incident management, critical infrastructure protection, and cybersecurity standards. Later, the GFCE would be dedicated to facilitating and coordinating sharing of knowledge and expertise for cyber-capacity building.[51]

From the beginning of the GFCE's existence, the Netherlands felt responsible for its success. The Dutch supported the GFCE financially and provided staff for its secretariat for the initial four years to secure continuity.[52] Furthermore, the cochair is Dutch and the secretariat is located in The Hague. Overall, however, the GFCE is independent from the Dutch government. The GFCE hopes for more international involvement and a more international secretariat,[53] but Dutch influence on the platform will probably remain.

A counterweight to the GFCE's prioritization of a bottom-up, hands-on approach was the Global Commission on the Stability of Cyberspace (GCSC), another platform coinitiated by the Dutch that focused on developing norms through policy. The GCSC's formation was another result of GCCS 2015 and was announced by Koenders at the Munich Security Conference in 2017. Its activities concluded in December 2021. The GCSC addressed the rising political and social instability stemming from malicious activities in cyberspace. The rising number and sophistication of cyber attacks is proof of the deteriorating situation. The GCSC's mission statement described the situation: "Cyber activities are likely to play a leading role in this newly volatile environment, thereby increasing the risk of undermining the peaceful use of cyberspace to facilitate the economic growth and the expansion of individual freedoms. In order to counter these developments, the Global Commission on the Stability of Cyberspace develops proposals for norms and policies to enhance international security and stability and guide responsible state and non-state behavior in cyberspace."[54] During its first full commission meeting in June 2017, the GCSC put protection of the public core of the internet at the top of its research agenda. In this way, the GCSC contributed to mutual understanding and awareness on issues related to international cybersecurity.

The GCSC's panel of twenty-eight commissioners represented a broad range of governments, civil societies, and the private sector. The commissioners were globally renowned experts such as Ilya Sachkov, a founder of Group-IB, a leader of the Russian threats intelligence services; Christopher Painter, a senior official at the US Department of Justice, FBI, National Security Council, and State Department; Isaac Ben-Israel, a former major general of the Israel Defense Forces; Joseph Nye, creator of the "soft power" concept in international politics; Jeff Moss, a founder of the hacking conference DEF CON; and Jonathan Zittrain, a professor of international law and computer science at Harvard University. The commission also had special advisors, including internet pioneer Vint Cerf and former Swedish prime minister Carl Bildt, as well as two cochairs, one from the United States and one from India.[55]

Out of twenty-eight commissioners, three were from the Netherlands, and the GCSC included other links to the Netherlands. For example, The Hague Center for Strategic Studies was with the GCSC from its creation, convening the core group of supporters and funders immediately after GCCS 2015 (including the Ministry of Foreign Affairs of the Netherlands), drafting a strategic plan, and convening a meeting of the GCSC Inception Group to develop the main requirements for the commission's operation, structure, and goals and its mission statement.[56] The center was one of two independent think-tanks that provided operational support to the GCSC's secretariat. Other examples were the government of the Netherlands as a GCSC partner and the Municipality of The Hague as a supporter.[57]

In November 2019, the GCSC released a comprehensive report, "Advancing Cyberstability," offering a cyber stability framework, principles and norms for state behavior, and recommendations for the international community. The report specifies what must be done to ameliorate the security of cyberspace. The hand of the Dutch is noticeable in it. For example, the report puts lot of emphasis on multistakeholder engagement. It points out that state and nonstate actors should not impair the stability of cyberspace, one of four principles crucial to norms of responsible state behavior. And the report lists protection of the public core of the internet as one of the critical norms formulated to improve cyberspace stability.[58] During the Paris Peace Forum, at the report's release, Stef Block, then the Dutch minister of foreign affairs, said, "Since stability in cyberspace is directly linked with stability in the 'real world,' such a cyberstability framework is more crucial than ever. The next step in this multilateral process is to collect evidence and hold those who break the rules responsible. Together we must increase accountability and combine all pieces of the puzzle, between governments, tech and security firms, and civil society."[59] Although the mandate of the commission was fulfilled, the goal of the GCSC community to advocate for their conclusions and work on their implementation in practice continues.

In addition to the GFCE and the GCSC, the Dutch government has seized numerous opportunities to shape the international cyber debate, thus adding visibility to its status of international legal sovereignty leader. The Hague Process that accompanied the drafting of *Tallinn Manual 2.0 on the International Law Applicable to Cyber Operation* was one occasion. *Tallinn Manual* is probably the most widely used handbook for legal advisors on cyber issues. Its creation was facilitated by the NATO Cooperative Cyber Defense Center of Excellence and it was published by Cambridge University Press to stress its impartiality. A previous *Tallinn Manual*, published in 2013, dealt with international law applicable to cyber warfare. *Tallinn Manual 2.0* was considerably expanded and updated, discussing the most common cyber incidents that states face almost daily. Both versions of the handbook were drafted by a group of approximately twenty renowned international legal and technical experts.[60] However, the first edition of the *Tallinn Manual* was subjected to lot of criticism for excluding states and their opinion from the drafting process. That was an excellent opportunity for the Dutch Ministry of Foreign Affairs to step in, and together with NATO CCDCoE, jointly organize The Hague Process.

The Dutch motivation to develop The Hague Process was apparently twofold. First, it was an opportunity to continue the Dutch history of involvement in the formation of international law, in particular the more-than-century-old tradition of The Hague Conventions dealing with the laws of war and the peaceful settlement of disputes. Second, the Netherlands is concerned that the strategic threat environment in cyberspace is starting to resemble a classic security dilemma, which could escalate into an arms race. Hence, there is an urgent need to build a normative framework to regulate cyber operations between states.[61]

The Hague Process for *Tallinn Manual 2.0* was three two-day meetings in The Hague attended by delegates from more than fifty states and international organizations. The purpose was to offer the states an opportunity to unofficially comment on the draft of *Tallinn Manual 2.0* under the Chatham House Rule.[62] Given that international law is created and interpreted by states, The Hague Process was an invaluable contribution to the draft.[63] Michael Schmitt, the general editor of *Tallinn Manual 2.0*, writes in its introduction, "This contribution by the Dutch Government helped ensure the Manual is grounded in state understandings of the law and that it addresses the practical challenges states face on a daily basis."[64] Nonetheless, although the group of experts drafting the manual did take the states' comments and views into account, Schmitt adds that the content of *Tallinn Manual 2.0* is purely what the group of experts consider customary international law.[65] That being said, the undoubted value of The Hague Process was not only the insight into state views shared with experts but also the exchange of opinions among states themselves. Above all, that the Netherlands was able to gather representatives of so many states from all over the world attests to the growing role of the Dutch in the cyber community and its international legal sovereignty. The Netherlands made a strong contribution to drafting the most influential handbook on the application of international law in cyberspace and moved closer to becoming a leader and key facilitator of international cyber negotiations. The contribution was recognized when Koenders was one of only two politicians who were asked to write a foreword to *Tallinn Manual 2.0*.[66]

The Netherlands had another opportunity to lead in strengthening an international normative framework for the regulation of cyberspace when its turn came to take the presidency of the Council of the EU from January 1 to June 30, 2016. Programme of the Netherlands Presidency of the Council of the European Union states, "The Netherlands firmly believes in taking an integrated approach to complex issues like the migration crisis, terrorism and cybersecurity. In this connection the Netherlands will also work to improve the EU institutions' working methods when it comes to external policy."[67] The Dutch vision was then formulated in Developing a Joint EU Diplomatic Response against Coercive Cyber Operations published during its presidency. According to the document, some coercive cyber operations require more than solely defense of the EU's and its member states' networks and improved resilience. Cyber diplomacy might deter potential aggressors by signaling the consequences of malicious operations. The document suggests several diplomatic instruments and encourages the European External Action Service to develop them into a framework.[68]

The suggestions led to two concrete outcomes that bring the EU and its member states closer in their responses to malicious cyber attacks. First, the Council of the EU adopted recommendations in Council Conclusions on a Framework for a Joint EU Diplomatic Response to Malicious Cyber Activities ("Cyber Diplomacy Toolbox") in June 2017. The framework of the Cyber Diplomacy Toolbox offers instruments of the EU's Common Foreign and Security Policy for holding to account malicious cyber actors. It also helps improve cooperation within the EU, mitigate potential cyber threats, and potentially prevent conflicts.[69] The second outcome was the Council of the EU's Decision Concerning Restrictive Measures against Cyber Attacks Threatening the Union or its Member States, adopted in May 2019, with measures strongly advocated by the Netherlands and in joint cooperation with the UK government.[70] With these, the Council of the EU established a sanction framework that gives the EU power to impose targeted restrictive measures "to deter and respond to cyber attacks which constitute an external threat to the EU or its member states, including cyber attacks against third states or international organizations where restricted measures are considered necessary to achieve the objectives of the Common Foreign and Security Policy."[71] Under this framework, the EU can impose sanctions on persons or entities found accountable for cyber attacks, intending to conduct a cyber attack, or rendering material, technical, or financial support for such activities. The sanctions include banning travel to the EU or freezing assets.[72] These restrictive measures are a powerful policy tool and an important addition to the Cyber Diplomacy Toolbox. The Cyber Diplomacy Toolbox and the EU sanction regime are proof of the success of the Dutch efforts to unify all member states and the EU as an institution in order to stabilize the increasingly volatile atmosphere in cyberspace. The accord of fellow EU member states following the Dutch initiative further establishes the Netherlands as a pioneer in the international cyber community, this time on the EU level.

The final platform mentioned here in which the Netherlands plays an important role is the UN, especially the UN Group of Governmental Experts (UN GGE) on Advancing Responsible State Behavior in Cyberspace in the Context of International Security (formerly known as Developments in the Field of Information and Telecommunications in the Context of International Security, mentioned in chapter 1) and the Open-Ended Working Group. Information and communications technology (ICT) in the context of international security first appeared before the UN in 1998 in a draft resolution by the Russian Federation submitted at the First Committee of the UN General Assembly. Later, in 2004, the first UN GGE on the use of ICTs in the context of international security was established and entrusted with the difficult task of exploring "the threats posed by the use of ICTs in the context of international security and how these threats should be addressed."[73] This started a tradition of UN GGE meetings, the most important and prestigious platform on the topic within the UN's structures. The UN GGE considered topics such as how international law applies in the use of ICT, confidence-building measures, capacity building, and the norms, rules, and principles of responsible state behavior.[74] Four UN GGEs (in 2009/2010, 2012/2013, 2014/2015, and 2019/2021) reached an agreement and published substantive reports that include recommendations and conclusions welcomed by all UN member states. Another two (in 2004/2005 and 2016/2017) did not reach a consensus.

Given that the work scope of a UN GGE was very close to the Dutch efforts in the international cyber community, the Netherlands was keen to become a member of the prestigious UN GGE club. The members (originally limited to fifteen, later twenty-five) were composed of the five permanent members of the Security Council, whose seats were guaranteed, and other states selected by geographic distribution. Usually, states had to send an official request for a membership and could lobby at the highest levels to get a seat at the table. The Netherlands gained membership twice (in 2016/2017 and 2019/2021) because of its strong interest in the matter, and it did not hesitate to play an active part.[75] The Netherlands, for example, presented a proposal for a norm on the protection of the public core of the internet, one of its core topics in the international cyber arena, to the 2016/2017 UN GGE.[76]

The Netherlands has also been very active in the Open-Ended Working Group that was created alongside the 2019/2021 UN GGE (the working group's second mandate was approved for 2021 to 2025) and is open to any interested member of the General Assembly.[77] The working group was "tasked to continue to develop the rules, norms, and principles of [the] responsible behaviour of states, discuss ways for their implementation, and to study the possibility of establishing regular institutional dialogue with broad participation under the auspices of the UN."[78] The Dutch have been active in working group sessions[79] while the GCSC also submitted its final report "Advancing Cyberstability," discussed earlier, at the beginning of the working group.[80] Having its voice recognized by such a broad and distinguished audience honors the Dutch vision of a multistakeholder approach to international cyber negotiations, while also fulfilling the Dutch quest for stretching its international legal sovereignty in cyberspace to the maximum.

The Dutch displays leadership in establishing the rules and norms of state behavior in cyberspace in its participation in the new and already existing platforms and initiatives. The GFCE and GCSC brought new thinking and ideas about the issues, but they do not have the force of the UN process.[81] The Netherlands recognizes that the UN GGE's work is very important, and so the new platforms are complementary to the original structures.[82] Therefore, the Netherlands, in pursuit of its leadership position, is active in the new and the more traditional platforms of international negotiations on cybersecurity issues.

Conclusion

International legal sovereignty revolves primarily around a state's recognition by other states and secondarily around a state's activities in the international arena, such as the state's acceptance as a juridical equal, its membership in international organizations, and the facilitation of treaty making. Activities of a state in cyberspace are usually directly connected to its recognition as an equal in the noncyber environment, and thus the international legal sovereignty of a state directly extends from the physical world to the cyber domain. The government can then decide whether to behave passively in the international cyber arena or be an agile actor, boosting its international legal sovereignty and using it as a powerful tool to enhance its security, economy, and interests. The Netherlands decided to take the latter path, extending its international legal sovereignty to the maximum possible extent by reaching out to as many actors as possible in its international negotiations, thereby establishing itself as a thought leader of global developments in international relations and law in cyberspace.

The Netherlands hosts on its territory a digital infrastructure that grants it the status of being the digital gateway to Europe. The digital infrastructure consists of internet exchange points like the AMS-IX, the highly advanced data center market, an expansive cloud industry, and an extensive network of submarine cables. Furthermore, the favorable conditions created by the government and the good Dutch reputation attract many international tech companies and international organizations like the RIPE NCC and the European Cybercrime Center. The international digital hub and its accompanying services are pivotal for the digital economy, not only in the Netherlands itself but for the whole of Europe and beyond. Although the Dutch government is not necessarily the owner of this infrastructure, it feels a keen responsibility for its protection and defense. This influences the political agenda of the Dutch government itself and how the Netherlands is regarded abroad. For this reason, digital infrastructure represents a cyber capability constituting the variable of control for this chapter.

The Netherlands is well aware that such key digital infrastructure must be protected not only technically but also by international law applicable in cyberspace. As intensity and sophistication of cyber attacks increase, international law in cyberspace is needed to deter malicious actors and make cyberspace a more predictable and secure place. This notion, together with the long tradition of the Dutch playing an active role in the development of international law, was an excellent starting point for establishing its leadership of international negotiations on norms of state behavior in cyberspace.

In the second half of the 2010s and in the early 2020s, the Netherlands has established new platforms for the negotiation of cyber issues, and has vigorously participated in already-established forums, seeking to engage as many stakeholders as possible while also setting agenda topics. This involvement indicates Dutch efforts to strengthen and stretch its international legal sovereignty in cyberspace to new limits. In doing so, the Netherlands has also strengthened its voice and influence during international negotiations and contributed to the clarification of norms and rules of responsible state behavior in cyberspace; ultimately, this helps states protect their critical infrastructure and further stabilizes the cyber domain.

The Dutch breakthrough for strengthening their international legal sovereignty was the GCCS organized by the Dutch authorities in 2015 in The Hague, followed by the publication of a report on the public core of the internet. These two events were the first indications of the Dutch efforts toward enhancing their cyber international legal sovereignty. GCCS 2015 and the report on the public core of the internet outlined where the Netherlands stood and the direction it would take on the international cyber scene: promotion of an open, free, and safe internet; defense of key infrastructure; and protection of the public core of the internet against unwanted intervention by state and nonstate actors, among other items. Furthermore, these two events clearly stressed the need for an inclusive multistakeholder approach during the negotiations. The more stakeholders and states that take part in a norm's negotiations, the stronger the norm. This is particularly important given the slowly changing equilibrium in favor of emerging economies. The Netherlands thus aims to involve the broadest possible range of actors in the international negotiations on cyber issues, in line with its success in negotiating other cybersecurity initiatives and activities.

The GFCE and GCSC are two examples of the multistakeholder approach of the following years. The GFCE addresses the urgent need of the international cyber community to find a smart way to cooperate with each other through capacity building and the establishment of best practices. The GFCE was initiated and supported by the Dutch government as a neutral and nonpolitical platform specializing in a bottom-up and hands-on approach. The GCSC acted as a counterpart to the GFCE and was a norm and politics-oriented platform to develop proposals to enhance international stability, security, and responsible state behavior in cyberspace. The Netherlands was not only an initiator and a promoter of these platforms but also provided financial and personnel support.

In addition to creating platforms, the Netherlands was active in existing processes. It was the main organizer and host of The Hague Process, which offered states a space to share their comments on the draft *Tallinn Manual 2.0*, the most influential handbook on the application of international law in cyberspace so far. During its 2016 presidency of the Council of the EU, the Netherlands set in motion the creation of the Cyber Diplomacy Toolbox and the sanction framework of the EU, offering different instruments of Common Foreign and Security Policy with which to hold perpetrators of malicious cyber activities responsible for their actions. Finally, the Netherlands has long been an active member of the UN GGE meetings and the Open-Ended Working Group on developing responsible state behavior in cyberspace. All these Dutch initiatives and activities, from the 2015 GCCS to the UN GGE, are elements of the authority variable of this research.

These initiatives and platforms confirm that the Netherlands has always tried to engage with a broad variety of actors who have consequently recognized the Dutch as an authority suitable to initiate or move forward negotiations. In many of these initiatives, the Netherlands succeeded in bringing stakeholders with different approaches to cybersecurity and cyberspace to a single negotiation table to discuss pertinent issues, from building cyber capabilities to developing norms of responsible state behavior. The Netherlands proved its leadership in closed platforms such as the EU and the UN GGE and in multistakeholder initiatives such as the GCSC, The Hague Process, and the GFCE. The success of this quest for broad recognition of its efforts by stakeholders from different opinion camps grants the Netherlands its leadership in international legal sovereignty in cyberspace.

The digital infrastructure of the Netherlands, thanks to which it is called the digital gateway to Europe, gives the Dutch government reason to be active in the international cyber arena. The digital hub does not, however, directly influence initiatives discussed in the chapter or the Dutch quest for stronger international legal sovereignty. In fact, a state does not need to possess similar key infrastructure within its borders in order to strengthen its international legal sovereignty. Thus, the variable of control is only a motivation for the state to get engaged and has a minor influence. Clarification of rules and norms of state behavior, a theme of the Dutch efforts, stabilizes cyberspace and contributes to the security of the digital hub located on Dutch territory. The vigorous efforts of the Dutch in supporting global endeavors to understand how international law applies to cyberspace while employing a multistakeholder approach heavily contribute to raising its status and recognition in the eyes of other states, which is instrumental to its international legal sovereignty in cyberspace. Thus, the variable of authority dominates in international legal sovereignty in cyberspace.

FIVE

Turkey and Domestic Sovereignty

Stephen Krasner defines domestic sovereignty as "the formal organization of political authority within the state and the ability of public authorities to exercise effective control within the borders of their own policy."[1] In the physical world, domestic sovereignty can be enforced, for example, through maintaining order, collecting taxes, fighting drug use, minimizing corruption, and controlling street crime.

As the life of society expands into the digital environment, so too do the government's authority and structures to exercise control there. In the cyber realm, the strength of domestic sovereignty, which is entirely determined by the organization and effectiveness of authority, is best observed in how governments approach life on the internet. Specifically, if governments want to regulate everyday life on the internet, which often mirrors developments in the physical world, they primarily regulate online content and exercise internet restrictions. Governments have been using legal, extralegal, and technical strategies and tools to do so since the global spread of the internet, but some governments have become quite masterful in such practices, especially since the 2010s.[2] Rigorous application of domestic sovereignty is not limited to authoritarian regimes such as China but is also frequently practiced by democracies.

Concentrating on the regulation of internet content does not suffice, however; to capture and potentially master the essence of domestic sovereignty in cyberspace, internet structures must be considered. Although the internet was originally developed as a governmental project in cooperation with academia, as soon as it opened up to the private sector in the late 1980s and early 1990s and began spreading across the globe, governments started to lose influence over it and the private sphere and the global community gained influence. As internet infrastructure grew, computerization expanded, and social media boomed, private companies began to drive internet development. Although most governments had minimal influence on the global internet's progress, they realized the internet's potential and tried to affect events in cyberspace within their borders through the application of domestic sovereignty. To do that, they had to build close relations with the private sector and other stakeholders on which the internet's structures and functioning depend. Governments' relations with interested stakeholders and their approach to internet content and its regulation are the focus of this chapter.

Within the pool of democratic constitutions of the transatlantic area, the Republic of Turkey stands out with respect to its approach to domestic sovereignty in cyberspace. Mustafa Kemal Atatürk founded modern Turkey as a parliamentary republic with a secular constitution in 1923. Since then, it has established itself as an integral part of the transatlantic community, becoming a member of NATO, Organization for Economic Cooperation and Development, Organization for Security and Cooperation in Europe, and Council of Europe; an EU member candidate; and a US ally. In 2002 the pious and populist AK Party (Justice and Development Party) rose to power. Its leader, Recep Tayyip Erdoğan, despite the party's official promises, started slowly transitioning from a secular policy toward religion having an ever-increasing role in the state. This political sway toward a "Muslim democracy" has caused the enactment of criticized policies restricting reproductive rights, education, individual expression, and access to information.[3] Furthermore, the security situation in neighboring countries has deteriorated, and terrorist attacks have increased within Turkey's borders. On top of that, Turkey is known for being highly sensitive to defamation; its penal code criminalizes speech that insults Turkish ethnicity, the Turkish nation, or the Turkish governing body.[4] These three factors—the change in the AK Party's policy direction, deteriorating security, sensitivity to defamation—have resulted in the Turkish government accumulating substantial legislative, judicial, and technical powers to block or filter activities on the internet on its territory over the years. Even though these powers were initially based on safety-related concerns following political and security developments in Turkey in 2013, national security started to override prioritization of freedoms online and human rights.[5] The online restrictions culminated during an unsuccessful coup attempt against the Turkish government on July 15, 2016. The coup was immediately followed by a two-year-long state of emergency, which had ramifications for the online restrictions debate. This chapter keeps in mind how the behavior of the state in cyberspace reflects the gradual erosion of human and civil rights in Turkey. It covers the years 2007–2016, especially the second half of the period.

The government's growing prioritization of security at the expense of online freedoms is reflected in Turkey's score in the Freedom on the Net Index, by Freedom House. In 2009, Turkey received forty-two out of one hundred points and was designated partly free, along with other countries generally perceived as democratic. In 2011, Turkey's score started to deteriorate, but the country still retained the position of a partly free country in terms of online freedoms until 2016, the year of the failed military coup, when it reached sixty-one points and was declared not free for the first time.[6] Turkey thus noticeably extended its domestic sovereignty into cyberspace, confining the limits of what is considered freedom. Although Turkey cannot be compared like-for-like with the democratic nations in this book's other chapters, I include it as an excellent demonstration of how easily and quickly governments slipping from democratic values to semiauthoritarian rule in the physical world can project these tendencies into cyberspace and enforce them. Turkey's story is a warning to democratically elected governments about their behavior in the cyber domain. This chapter excludes the years since 2016 because the book includes nonauthoritarian regimes only.

The study begins with the enactment of Law No. 5651, Regulation of Publications on the Internet and Combating Crimes Committed by Means of Such Publication, in May 2007. This law was the main legislation on the subject in Turkey preceding the military coup. Law No. 5651 sets the legislative framework for internet restrictions in Turkey and constitutes the variable of authority for this chapter. Before the law was enacted, no specific legal arrangement governed internet access in the country. The impulse to create Law No. 5651 in 2007 was purportedly to protect children and families from online crimes. The law defines and identifies internet actors, and it lays out administrative provisions designating roles and obligations of the internet actors and the responsible governmental authority. It lists a catalog of crimes and sets the legal framework and procedures for blocking access to websites or removing content online. Following political, social, and security turmoil in Turkey in 2013, the law was amended in 2014 and 2015. These two amendments tightened the legal framework and strengthened the powers of governmental authorities. Law No. 5651 and its two amendments are thus the core of the analysis of the authority variable here, in particular the responsibilities imposed on internet service providers and the powers given to the relevant governmental bodies by the law.

For the variable of control, I examine the effectiveness of the public authorities to exercise internet restrictions in Turkey between 2007 and 2016. In contrast to other democracies, Turkey opted for full state control, in which it asserts the legal framework and does not allow regulation by any other. Analysis of Turkey's control variable centers on the role and powers of the Information and Communications Technologies Authority (Bilgi Teknolojileri ve İletişim Kurumu, BTK) and the Presidency of Telecommunication and Communication (Telekomünikasyon İletişim Başkanlığı, TİB), regulators of the telecommunications sector in the country. The analysis also looks into the relations between these bodies and the internet service providers (ISPs), a key intermediary that connects users to the internet's backbone, and Türk Telekom, a company owning the vast majority of the internet infrastructure in Turkey. The study of these institutions and their mutual relations paints a comprehensive picture for assessing the variable of control.

Logic dictated splitting the analysis of control into two parts in this chapter, in contrast to the other chapters. The chapter first briefly introduces the

BTK and the TİB, as necessary to understand the context of Law No. 5651, its origins, and resulting developments, explained in the section studying the authority variable. For the second part of the analysis of control, I explore the internet restrictions in practice and evaluate how effective they were during the observed period.

Key Regulators of the Turkish Telecommunications Sector

The institutional architecture of the telecommunications sector in Turkey between 2007 and 2016 was firmly regulated by the BTK, the main regulatory body, and by the TİB, a BTK division. The BTK was founded as the Telecommunications Authority in January 2000, and in November 2008 it was transformed into the Information and Communications Technologies Authority (BTK). As the regulator, the BTK was tasked with "authorization, inspection, dispute resolution, protection of consumer rights, regulation of sectoral competition, issuing of technical regulations and spectrum management and inspection."[7] The BTK also oversaw information technologies, a task delegated to the TİB over time.

The TİB became the key actor in internet restrictions soon after its foundation within the BTK's structures in 2005 because of its strong mandate and gradually growing powers. Preceding Law No. 5651, the TİB was tasked with the surveillance and interception of communications in Turkey. After enactment of Law No. 5651 in 2007, it monitored internet content and enforced blocking decisions.[8] Law No. 5651 stipulated that blocking decisions issued by the judges, courts, and public prosecutors be sent to the TİB, which forwarded them to the respective ISPs for execution.[9] The TİB could also issue its own administrative orders for certain content. If it wanted to avoid a blocking order that would affect an entire website, it could compel content and hosting providers to remove certain offending content from servers. It also determined the minimum acceptable criteria for software and hardware used for screening, monitoring, and filtering. Because of these regulatory powers, which grew over time, the TİB was often criticized in debates about freedom of access and internet censorship.

Despite their clear division of competencies and labor, the TİB and the BTK were closely linked to each other and to the rest of the government.[10]

The BTK chairman was the direct superior of the TİB president, and both were members of the Turkish Cybersecurity Council, responsible for cybersecurity. Alongside its own staff, the TİB hosted representatives from the Turkish National Police, the National Intelligence Agency, and the Gendarmerie General Command.[11] The Ministry of Transportation would suggest BTK board members to the Cabinet of Ministers, and the cabinet would appoint them without consulting the telecommunications sector. That board members were governmental appointees was mentioned sometimes as a potential threat to the BTK's independence. Similarly, the TİB used to be criticized for an apparent lack of independence from the executive organs.[12] The ties of the TİB and the BTK and with other governmental institutions were thus close.

Legal Framework for Internet Restrictions Regime

The turbulent process of the creation of Law No. 5651 indicates the importance of the law and its provisions. Before Law No. 5651, no particular law governed internet access in Turkey, although there had been attempts to regulate the internet. Opinion was that existing acts such as the Press Law and Turkish Criminal Law sufficed to regulate access to internet content and crimes committed online.[13] The first attempt to formulate an internet law came in the aftermath of enactment of a new penal code in 2004, which included additional provisions for computer crime and internet regulation. To address gaps in criminal law and procedures, the Ministry of Justice gathered a commission consisting of members of public institutions and representatives of law schools and internet-oriented nongovernmental organizations in early 2006 to draft the Law on Network Services and Computer Crimes.[14] These efforts were not welcomed by the prime minister, who had a different agenda regarding internet law.

A watershed moment for internet law occurred in the autumn of 2006, when the news media was flooded by coverage of child abuse and pornography. The volume grew so large that child pornography seemed to be one of the most serious problems in Turkey. Mustafa Akgül and Melih Kırlıdoğ noted that "this came across as an orchestrated effort to pass the Internet Censorship Law."[15] Prime Minister Recep Tayyip Erdoğan asked the Ministry of Transportation, as the institution responsible for the BTK, to sort out the declared issue of child pornography. This led to introduction of internet restrictions. The Ministry of Justice and its efforts were bypassed.

The drafting of Law No. 5651 was the top priority for the Ministry of Transportation; however, the drafting process was very different from that at the Ministry of Justice for the 2006 bill. This time, the bill was drafted behind closed doors, and only state institutions could participate.[16] To influence public opinion in favor of the upcoming law, the government started to promise a "clean internet" to protect children from online abuse. The transportation minister, Binali Yıldırım, stated, "Turkey will be a model of providing a clean and safe internet."[17] Despite the attempts of nongovernmental organizations to alert Turkish society of the censorship potential of the upcoming law, Law No. 5651 entered into effect in May 2007. The law was fully in force by November of the same year, as soon as the required secondary regulations were passed.[18]

The justification of Law No. 5651 was built on two articles of Turkey's constitution. Article 41 states, "Family is the foundation of the Turkish society" and "the State shall take the necessary measures and establish the necessary organization to protect [the] peace and welfare of the family, especially [the] mother and children."[19] Article 58, "Protection of the Youth," states that "the State shall take necessary measures to protect youth from addiction to alcohol and drugs, crime, gambling, and similar vices, and ignorance."[20] Seizing its opportunity, when fear of child abuse and pornography filled the atmosphere, Turkey passed a law to protect the family and children from criminal activities committed on the internet.

Law No. 5651 was comprehensive from the beginning of its existence: It defined internet actors—such as access, hosting, and content providers—and mass-use providers, such as internet cafés. It spelled out administrative provisions, designating roles and obligations to these internet actors and to the TİB.[21] It also itself blocked access to websites and under related procedures covered in Articles 8 and 9. Article 8 and, to some extent, Article 9 were the key provisions governing internet restrictions in Turkey between 2007 and 2016, and the following discussion examines them to better understand the authority Law No. 5651 granted the Turkish government.

Article 8, "Access Blocking Decision and Execution of Such Decision," was the core of Law No. 5651 because it specified the blocking regime, including the crimes for which a website could be blocked and the procedures to do so. The first paragraph of Article 8 stated that access to internet broadcast could be blocked when sufficient suspicion existed that its content was criminal. Article 8 then cataloged nine crimes, referring to the Turkish penal code and other laws: incitement to suicide, sexual abuse of children, facilitation of the use of narcotics, provision of substances harmful to health, obscenity, prostitution, facilitation of gambling, crimes against Mustafa Kemal Atatürk, and betting and gambling.[22] The law had a strong emphasis on the protection of society, youth in particular, but also included crimes that could be broadly interpreted, such as crimes against Atatürk, the father of the nation.

Blocking decisions, according to Article 8, could be granted by a judge during an investigation or by a court during a prosecution.[23] In either case, a copy of the blocking decision issued by a court, a public prosecutor, or a judge was sent to the TİB for further action.[24] Law No. 5651 also stipulated that if sufficient suspicion existed that crimes listed in Article 8(1) were committed, regardless of whether a website's content or hosting provider resided inside Turkey, the TİB could also issue a blocking order. For such an administrative order, the TİB issued it ex officio, with no need for a judge, court, or public prosecutor order.[25] Hence, the TİB could unilaterally issue a blocking order purely on suspicion of a crime listed in Article 8(1) having been committed.[26]

Whether the blocking decision was a judicial or administrative order, it was collected by the TİB and sent immediately to the ISP for execution. That ISP had twenty-four hours to execute the order. If it did not comply with an order through precautionary injunction by a judge, a court, or a public prosecutor, its responsible person could be imprisoned for six months to two years.[27] Furthermore, if the ISP failed to execute an administrative blocking order issued by the TİB, it risked a fine of between 10,000 and 100,000 Turkish liras (approximately €5,700–€57,000 when the law entered fully into force at the end of 2007).[28] If the ISP did not comply with the administrative order within twenty-four hours of the issuance of the fine, its provider's activity license could be revoked by the BTK.[29]

Websites receiving blocking orders had two options. They could remove the harmful content, and if the TİB, a court, or a prosecutor verified the removal, the ban could be reversed. Alternatively, a website could challenge the blocking order. If it was an administrative blocking decision by the TİB, the order could be challenged under Article 11 of the Turkish Code of Administrative Procedure. According to Yaman Akdeniz, a recognized expert on the rights of internet users and a professor of law at Istanbul Bilgi University, the TİB would then need to review its decision within sixty days. If the TİB did not answer the challenge within that time or rejected it, the website could appeal to an administrative court for a judicial review and ask for a suspension of the execution order.[30]

Supplementing Article 8, Article 9 of Law No. 5651 covered online content removal with respect to individuals. Article 9 provided that individuals believing their personal rights were infringed through online content could ask the content or hosting provider to remove the content from a website. If the initial request was not addressed or was rejected, the individual could take the case to court. Article 9(1) specified that an individual had the right to a reply and could demand that the content or hosting provider display the reply alongside the contested material for a week, to achieve the same public impact.[31] In contrast to Article 8, Article 9 did not provide for blocking orders as a remedy for infringement of an individual's personal rights. The courts could order only that the contested material be taken down, not had access blocked.[32] Article 9 did not have the decisive role that Article 8 had for internet restrictions in its original version, although later amendments would soon change that.

The amendments of 2014 and 2015 were a consequence of two major crises in the second half of 2013, during which digital communications became a major source of information about unfolding events. The first public upheaval came in the summer of 2013, when a minor protest over environmental issues in Istanbul rapidly grew into one of the largest public movements in Turkish history, the Gezi Park protests. Social media spread images of police brutality against the first protesters, which mobilized society. Social media was also a source of information (or misinformation) and an organizing tool for demonstrations across Turkey.[33]

The other major crisis was a massive corruption scandal of the AK Party that was revealed in December 2013. Social media again played an important role in the dissemination of the scandal's impact. For example, the AK Party's opposition used social media to share audio files and transcripts of illegal wiretaps of Prime Minister Erdoğan, his cabinet ministers, and businessmen with close ties to the government.[34] These two major crises led to the AK Party government imposing further restrictions to suppress the perceived threat of digital communications like Twitter and YouTube by banning or throttling social media platforms. The long-term consequence was that the government started to prepare the two amendments to Law No. 5651, giving it more control over internet content.

The first amendment entered into force in February 2014, giving significantly more authority over internet content to the government. One of the most radical changes stemming from the first amendment to Law No. 5651 was the establishment of the Access Providers Association (Erişim Sağlayıcıları Birliği, ESB). According to Article 6/A of the law, the ESB's main goal was to ensure the enforcement of blocking orders issued on legal provisions other than Article 8 (the catalog of crimes) of Law No. 5651. The ESB consisted of all ISPs operating on Turkish territory. Membership was compulsory, and companies that did not join could not operate in Turkey. Furthermore, the ESB charter and future changes to it were subject to approval by the TİB. The ESB was established as a private legal entity, with its seat in Ankara.[35] But its status as a "government-controlled ISP union,"[36] with its compulsory industry-wide membership and close connection to and supervision by the TİB, made visible the government's authority over the part of the private sector engaged in the bestowment of online services.

Another major change in Law No. 5651 concerned procedures for content removal under Article 9, making it easier for individuals convinced that online content violated their personal rights to request an access ban. Under the amended provision, such persons could request content removal from a content provider, or from a hosting provider if the content provider could not be reached. Additionally, they could apply directly to a court and request an access ban on the offensive content. In either case, the providers or the court were obliged to evaluate the application within twenty-four hours. If a request was made to a court and was successful, an order for a partial or full blocking of access could be issued and forwarded to the ESB for further implementation. The ESB then had to execute the order within four hours of receiving it.[37]

A new article, Article 9A, "Access Ban due to Privacy of Private Life," addressed "violation of personal privacy." Anyone claiming a privacy violation from online content could directly contact the TİB and request an access ban. The TİB would then forward this request to the ESB for immediate enforcement, and ISPs had to execute it within four hours of receipt. However, if the president of the TİB deemed it necessary to act without delay, for privacy concerns, he could issue an order for the TİB to execute the access ban directly. Article 9A stated that the TİB's decision in these cases had to be sent to a judge within twenty-four hours for assessment, and that the judge had to make a decision on the matter within forty-eight hours or the decision was automatically withdrawn.[38]

The 2014 amendment placed much more pressure on the providers because of the newly imposed technical burden. The legislation did not specify the technical measures to use to ban access, but it removed the phrase "if technically possible" from the relevant article of Law No. 5651.[39] With the amending legislation, the burden of securing the needed software and hardware for executing blocking decisions fell on the access providers, no matter their size. Providers were also now required to keep a record of user traffic for two years, and if requested, share these details with the TİB to help it fulfill its statutory duties. According to the amended Article 6, the ISPs were obliged to hand over any information requested by the TİB, but it did not specify the extent of this requirement.[40] This, in the end, provided the TİB with broad discretion, and ISPs' duties and obligations became rather vague.[41] Having to acquire powerful technologies to comply with the new obligations was problematic for small- and medium-size providers, for whom it was a major investment.[42] The financial burden was so heavy that "only certain access providers [were] expected to survive and small and medium sized access providers [were] expected to be eliminated from the market."[43]

The 2014 amendment also adjusted the punishments and sanctions for not obeying the blocking orders. All criminal sanctions of imprisonment were abolished, which contributed to a delicate balancing between the rights and obligations of internet providers on Turkish territory. But ISPs that did not comply with blocking orders issued by the TİB could still be fined 10,000–100,000 Turkish liras (€3,500–€35,000 in 2014) by the authority. Furthermore, if the ISP failed to comply with the order within twenty-four hours, it risked revocation of its ISP license by the BTK.[44]

The 2014 amendment was clearly intended to allow the government to interfere with online content more easily and swiftly while pushing judicial mechanisms into the background.[45] The amendment received much criticism that it "impose[d] inordinate levels of state control over the use of the Internet and enable[d] streamlined mechanisms for state censorship of Internet-based content."[46] For example, according to some, Article 9A, creating the second administrative route of issuing blocking orders, "inappropriately extend[ed] the authority of an administrative body by granting it judicial powers, whereas it ought to be the duty of judicial bodies to evaluate whether content violates laws."[47] Another criticism related to the amendment's four hours for a blocking decision to be implemented but no mention of a time frame for lifting it, "meaning that even if they [were] nullified, blocking decisions may [have] remain[ed] in place."[48] Hence, passage of the 2014 amendment to Law No. 5651 suggests that there was "an undeniable element of central state control being imposed on the persons engaged in the provision of Internet content and Internet related services."[49]

The 2015 amendment of Law No. 5651 only confirmed the trend of tightening governmental authority over internet content. The most far-reaching provision of the new amendment in this regard was the introduction of Article 8/A, which further expanded the TİB's authority. The TİB was given control of content removal and prevention of access to websites "in cases where the delay of a decision could endanger the protection of the right to life, the protection of the life and private property of the people, the protection of national security and public order, prevention of crime or the preservation of the public health, upon demand by the Prime Ministry or ministries dealing with national security and the protection of the public order, prevention of crime or the preservation of public health."[50] In other words, the authority to issue blocking decisions was broadened to include cabinet ministers and the prime minister, who could justify their order by invoking the protection of public order, public health, national security, prevention of crime, and protection of life and property. In this case, ISPs were required to execute the orders immediately, no later than four hours from notification. If ISPs failed to comply with the TİB's request, they could face an administrative fine of up to 500,000 Turkish liras (€178,000 in March 2015).[51]

This history of the legislative framework governing internet content restrictions under Law No. 5651 chronicles the growing authority of the TİB as a representative of the Turkish government in the political-digital ecosystem between 2007 and 2016. The original version of Law No. 5651, passed in 2007, had already set out a comprehensive and rigorous system of judicial and administrative procedures for blocking access that granted the TİB certain decision powers. The climax of the government's authority over online content and restriction through the legal framework was reached in the two amendments of 2014 and 2015. At this point of legislative development, the Turkish government's regulation of access to online content became solely state-control oriented, and this approach was subsequently fully employed in practical terms.

Internet Restrictions in Practice

To paint a complete picture of online content restrictions in Turkey, two key actors in the telecommunications infrastructure and their relations need elaboration: Türk Telekom, the dominant telecom and broadband internet operator in the country, and ISPs, the key intermediaries connecting users with the internet backbone.

Türk Telekom had close ties with the government for all of 2007–2016. Established in 1994 as a public utility, Türk Telekom was a state company and a monopoly granted exclusive rights for all telecommunications infrastructure, except for mobile services.[52] After long national debate and international pressure, the government privatized the company in 2005 and sold 55 percent to Oger Telecom, a Dubai-based private investor. In 2008, another 15 percent started to be publicly traded on the stock market.[53] Yet the government did not want to lose its grip on the company entirely, so the remaining 30 percent remained in the possession of the Ministry of Treasury and Finance, the undersecretary of the Ministry of Transportation served as the vice-chair of Türk Telekom's board, and in March 2014 (at the time of the first amendment to Law No. 5651) the chief advisor to Prime Minister Erdoğan became an independent member of the board.[54] Despite privatization efforts and only one-third of Türk Telekom being owned by the state between 2007 and 2016, the company remained "very close to the government," and "the independence of the country's dominant internet provider [was] a matter of serious concern."[55] Freedom House notes that "these close relationships ensure[d] that Türk Telekom continue[d] to receive preferential treatment regardless of the legal obligation that should prevent favouritism."[56]

Türk Telekom remained dominant in the internet infrastructure and domestic market in Turkey. In 2016, the year of the attempted coup, it owned 214,395 kilometers of fiber-optic infrastructure in Turkey, whereas other operators had a combined total of only 58,155 kilometers. Around 124,374 kilometers of this infrastructure constituted the internet backbone of Turkey, and the rest was used for access distribution.[57] On top of that, the internet backbone was run by TTNET, Türk Telekom's wholly owned subsidiary, founded in 2006, and the largest ISP in Turkey. The total number of ISPs in the country in 2016 was approximately 359; however, the great majority of them acted as resellers for Türk Telekom. At that time, a decade after the privatization, TTNET had around 71 percent of the market share, dominating the ISP market.[58] This was a unique opportunity for the government and its internet restrictions regime; "Most of the filtering of international traffic [took] place on the Türk Telekom network, which link[ed] to other commercial ISPs within the country."[59] Similarly, "all internet traffic passe[d] through Türk Telekom's infrastructure, thereby allowing centralized control over online content and facilitating the implementation of shutdown decision[s]."[60] Türk Telekom dominated the internet infrastructure and services between 2007 and 2016, and although it was a privatized entity, it behaved "as a state-owned company."[61]

ISPs also played a key role as another enabler of governmental restrictions. In Turkey, governmental authorities had considerable influence over ISPs. For example, the government's licensing regime required ISPs to obtain a certificate of authorization for their services from the BTK. To restrict access to illegal content, in 2008 the TİB requested that all ISPs install domain name system servers and synchronize them with the TİB's central server. This measure facilitated automatic updating of a list of websites ordered to be banned under the catalog of crimes.[62] However, this restriction had the significant drawback of being disproportional. It had a substantial impact on freedom of speech and access to information. During domain name system tampering, an ISP does not respond with the corresponding IP address when an internet user attempts to access a website by entering the domain name. The ISP either does not resolve the domain name, replies with an incorrect IP address, or redirects the user to a website with a restriction explanation. Websites such as YouTube, Google, and Twitter were at times subject to this restriction method.[63] Later, during the first amendment to Law No. 5651 in 2014, a method more respectful of freedom of expression was introduced into the Turkish system. The URL (uniform resource locator) restriction method allowed ISPs to restrict access to only the specific content, not the entire website. The URL method still required the ISPs to implement a large upgrade of hardware and software, because the ISP must control and examine all traffic to assess whether the web page a user is trying to open is banned. To do that, the ISP must maintain detailed traffic logs of the user with the help of deep packet inspection technologies. Through this, the ISP could restrict access to individual URL addresses instead of blocking the whole domain.[64] Hence, the TİB and the government had considerable power to influence the restriction methods in practice and how the ISPs executed the judicial and administrative orders.

The TİB's appetite for internet restrictions has grown exponentially over the years since Law No. 5651 passed. By May 11, 2009, less than two years after its enactment, 2,601 websites were blocked under Law No. 5651. Of those, judicial orders blocked 18 percent and administrative orders issued by the TİB blocked 82 percent.[65] The TİB stopped publishing statistics for blocking activities in 2009, and so Engelliweb (Blocked Web, in Turkish), an interactive online database anonymously launched in 2007, took up the role of statistics keeper. Engelliweb collects, verifies, and organizes data about blocked websites and has developed over the years into the only comprehensive monitoring database and analytic tool of blocking in Turkey.[66] Engelliweb observed exponential growth in the number of blocked websites and the percentage the TİB ordered to be blocked compared with judicial orders. For example, in May 2014, Engelliweb reported roughly 40,800 blocked websites in Turkey, of which 89.4 percent were blocked by the TİB (without a court order) and 7.3 percent by courts and prosecutors.[67] Two years later, in May 2016, the number of blocked websites grew to 111,000 in total. The proportion remained about the same: the TİB ordered 94.1 percent; judges and courts, 4.2 percent.[68]

The real numbers of blocked websites were likely well above those published by Engelliweb, because the database included only websites reported as blocked by online users. Website owners were not informed of blocking decisions and were usually surprised to find their websites not accessible within Turkey. Furthermore, it was difficult for website owners to learn what triggered the blocking order, making an appeal difficult.[69] This opacity prohibited tracing the real number of blocked websites.

Another demonstration of the government's grip on internet restrictions was its proactive manner in requesting content removal. The treatment of social media platforms is an example; they either had to comply with the court and administrative orders or they faced blocking themselves. The transparency reports issued regularly by some of these platforms showed that the pressure on them by state authorities was significant and growing. For example, Turkey has regularly ranked among the states with the highest number of removal requests in Twitter transparency reports since mid-2012, when it first published those statistics. Between January 2014 and June 2016 Turkey filed the most removal requests with Twitter out of all monitored countries. Similarly, Turkey accounted for approximately 90 percent of all tweets withheld by the platform worldwide in July–December 2015.[70] Some experts highlight the compliance of certain companies, such as Twitter or Facebook, with Turkish authorities' requests so as to avert a total ban and the subsequent loss of users and revenue from the growing Turkish market.[71] For example, Twitter has implemented its "country withheld content" tool on Turkish territory since March 2014, which allows "content to be withheld in a specific jurisdiction while remaining visible to the rest of the world."[72]

Compliance with the government's requirements did not necessarily allow the companies and their websites to evade fines or even a complete ban on Turkish territory, which often became the subject of appeals. Taking Twitter as an example again, Turkey banned the platform several times after its refusal to comply with orders to remove supposedly damaging content. Erdoğan vowed to "wipe out Twitter" after the platform published tweets with allegations of corruption in the prime minister's closest circle in March 2014.[73] According to Erdoğan's office, Twitter did not comply with a Turkish court's order to remove the links, which forced the authorities to ban the social media site on its territory. The controversial ban, which was broadly circumvented by users across Turkey in the end,[74] was even criticized by Turkey's President Abdullah Gül.[75] After two weeks of blocking, the Constitutional Court of Turkey ruled that the TİB had to lift the ban: "Even though TIB acted pursuant to the court judgments on [the] just and pressing social need of protecting the right of privacy, its complete blockage of Twitter, rather than banning a specific URL address went beyond the scope of its authority given by the judgements."[76] The ban violated the freedom of expression protected under Article 26 of Turkey's constitution.[77] On another occasion, the BTK fined Twitter 150,000 Turkish liras (€48,400), punishing the platform under Law No. 5651 for noncompliance with its request to remove content that was evaluated by the body as "terrorist propaganda" in December 2015. Apparently, most of the content in question was connected to the Kurdistan Workers Party, which Turkey, as well as the EU and United States, designates a terrorist organization.[78]

Other social media platforms were also often banned on Turkish territory because of noncompliance with local authorities' requests. Most typical was the two-year ban of YouTube. In 2007, Greek users posted a video clip that dubbed Mustafa Kemal Atatürk and Turks homosexuals. Following a storm of complaints from Turkish users, YouTube was banned in May 2008 for the crime of insulting Atatürk and Turkishness. The ban was lifted by the Ankara court in October 2010, after the video was removed.[79]

In addition to blocking online content, the government used filtering as a control mechanism. In February 2011, the BTK publicly introduced the Safer Internet initiative. Articles 41 and 58 of the constitution, the protection of children and families from harmful online content, were the justification for the new proposal.[80] All internet users in Turkey would be obliged to pick one of four predefined profiles to access the internet: standard, family, children, or domestic. The proposal was met with heavy criticism and even major protests across the country, which forced the BTK to modify its initial plans. The softened version of the Safer Internet initiative had only two profiles, family and child, and these were voluntary. The profiles functioned as filters that blocked undesired content. The family profile blocked access to blacklisted websites. The child profile allowed access to only a whitelist of websites.[81] The BTK created both lists and sent them to ISPs, where the filtering took place. The ISPs had to apply list updates immediately and also bear all costs associated with upgrading their systems to comply with the Safer Internet initiative while offering the filtering service for free.[82]

Although selecting a profile was voluntary, the initiative raised serious concerns, especially regarding the blacklist and whitelist design: The BTK's lists of restricted and allowed websites were not publicized. The only option was to search for each website's URL on the dedicated BTK website. Even this was restricted, however; after five searches, visitors were required by the BTK website to wait fifteen minutes before checking another one. This procedure massively reduced the chances of knowing what websites were in the blacklist and whitelist.[83] Another concern was about the content that put websites on the lists. The selection criteria were criticized as "arbitrary" and "discriminatory."[84] For example, the child profile blocked access to social media platforms like YouTube and Facebook and to the Armenian minority newspaper *Argos*. It also did not allow access to websites that advocated the theory of evolution but did allow websites with antievolution themes. The government continued to maintain the filtering database without much transparency or clear public criteria.[85] A number of users, nevertheless, selected profiles and voluntarily limited their access to the internet. By mid-2013, one and a half years after the Safe Internet initiative's implementation, it had 1.4 million subscribers.[86]

To conclude, it is apparent that the Turkish government was determined to exercise a strict state-centric approach toward internet restrictions between 2007 and mid-2016. The government was gradually tightening up its control over online content accessible on its territory. Initially, it based these powers on Law No. 5651 but later put progressively more emphasis on its administrative capabilities and their hierarchical influence over other actors in the country. The Turkish government was not swayed by the criticism of the European Court of Human Rights,[87] the Venice Commission,[88] and other human rights organizations or by their blocking attempts often being easily circumvented by more skillful users using tools such as proxies, VPNs, or onion routing.[89] In the end, the situation escalated to its peak in the events accompanying and following the attempted coup in July 2016, in which social media and the internet played an absolutely crucial role.[90]

Conclusion

Stephen Krasner defines domestic sovereignty as the formal organization of political authority within a state's borders and the ability of public institutions to exercise effective control. In cyberspace, that can be translated into how governments approach life on the internet. In other words, domestic sovereignty in cyberspace can be defined through how governments regulate online content and practice internet restrictions.

Turkey stands out as a democracy that has accumulated substantive legislative, judicial, and technical powers over the years to block and filter online content. In contrast to most other democracies that rely on industry-led initiatives, the Turkish government has opted for a completely state-controlled approach toward regulating access to online content. The initiative to protect families and children gradually developed into a security-driven regime of online restrictions that culminated during and in the aftermath of the attempted military coup of mid-2016.

Human and civil rights gradually eroded in Turkey, and my inclusion of Turkey among democratic case studies might surprise some. But within my defined time frame, Turkey was still considered a free or partially free and democratic country, and it is an example of a country that stretched its state sovereignty into cyberspace to the very limits of what is considered freedom and continued beyond that fragile border. Turkey should serve as a lesson and a warning for other democratically elected governments for how easily and quickly governments backsliding toward authoritarianism in the physical world can project these tendencies into cyberspace, which is why I have included it in this book. This is also the reason why this chapter examined only the period from the enactment of Law No. 5651 in 2007 (a key legislative framework for internet regulations in Turkey) to the unsuccessful military coup.

The state-centric hierarchy and Law No. 5651 at the center of the analysis represent the variables of control and authority, respectively. The authority variable is based on the legislative framework that provided the legal justification for the regulation regime of online content. The variable of control is based on the ability and effectiveness of public authorities, the BTK and TİB, to exercise internet regulation on Turkish territory in practice, through hierarchical relations with the other actors, such as Türk Telekom, ISPs, and the ESB.

Law No. 5651, passed in 2007 and representing the variable of authority, is a comprehensive piece of legislation that evolved over the years from a measure protecting families and children to a powerful tool helping build the hierarchical regime of regulation. When the law entered into force, it defined key internet actors and their roles and obligations. The core of the legislation was laid out in Articles 8 and 9, which specified the rules and procedures of blocking access to online content. Article 8 outlined the blocking regime, including the crimes for which a website could be blocked and the procedures to do so. It also specified who could issue blocking orders, a judge and a court or the TİB. In an administrative decision by the TİB, a judge or court order was not needed, giving fairly significant powers to the governmental body. Article 9 gave individuals a method for online content removal.

As a consequence of two major political crises in Turkish society in 2013, the government amended Law No. 5651 in 2014 and 2015, which tightened the regulation regime. The first amendment gave significantly more power over internet content to the government. It also established the ESB, to streamline the enforcement of blocking orders. The amendment added Article 9A, which allowed even tougher application of blocking orders. Finally, the amendment put the heavy burden of the cost of acquiring the software and hardware necessary for the execution of the blocking orders on the access providers. The 2014 amendment thus contributed to the growing central-state control over internet-related services and allowed the government to interfere with online content more easily and swiftly while pushing the judicial mechanisms into the background. The second amendment passed in 2015 and continued the trend of tightening governmental power over internet content through its Article 8/A, expanding the TİB's authority to issue blocking decisions. Law No. 5651 and its amendments, representing the variable of authority, have helped develop and strengthen the state-controlled system of online content regulation and its hierarchical structure.

The state-centric approach of the Turkish government constitutes the variable of control and is embodied by the hierarchical system and its effective exercise of the regulation regime in practice. The government's BTK and TİB were two powerful regulators of the hierarchical system. The dominant telecom and broadband internet operator Türk Telekom played another key role. Even after privatization, the company retained close and enduring relations with the government. Türk Telekom's subsidiary TTNET, the largest ISP in Turkey, also ran the country's internet backbone. Other ISPs also enabled the governmental restrictions. A licensing regime that required ISPs to obtain a certificate of authorization from the BTK gave profound power to governmental authorities over the ISPs. This was further potentiated by the establishment of the ESB in the first amendment to Law No. 5651. The compulsory membership of ISPs in the ESB together with the close connection to and supervision by the TİB extended governmental power over a crucial part of the private sector engaged in online services. The TİB and the government, respectively, have created a system in which they could swiftly influence restriction methods in practice and the modes by which the ISPs executed the judicial and administrative orders.

The TİB's appetite for internet restrictions grew exponentially over the years, and its implementation of the restrictions exemplify the efficiency of the growing hierarchical system. The number of blocked websites grew as well as the percentage of websites blocked by the TİB's administrative orders rather than judicial orders. Turkey, compared with other countries, was proactive in requesting content removal from social media platforms. These requests were often successful because the social platforms wanted to avoid blocking orders. But a certain level of compliance did not always guarantee that the social media platforms escaped fines or even total bans on Turkish territory. The government also implemented a filtering system. Despite some initial resistance to the Safer Internet initiative, Turkish society voluntarily accepted the initiative.

Although the variables of authority and control in the Turkish approach were equal at the beginning of the examined period, in 2007, the variable of control prevailed over authority by mid-2016. In 2007, Law No. 5651 paved the way for the regulation regime by setting blocking procedures and powers and obligations of stakeholders. At that time, authority and control were in close cooperation. However, with the gradual construction of the state-centric approach, which tightened control over online content, Law No. 5651 became a tool of the government to exercise effective control by introducing administrative capabilities and setting out their hierarchical influence over other actors. Therefore, at the end of the examined period, even though authority retained a certain importance in the regulation regime, control prevailed over it in Turkey.

Inclusion of this case study might be debatable, due to the authoritative tendencies of the Turkish government later in the examined period. The result of this case study is influenced by the Turkish government becoming inclined toward authoritative rule both inside and outside cyberspace, especially closer to 2016. On one hand, this might have had a strong effect on control prevailing over authority in the end. On the other hand, the Turkish government was still elected by the will of the people, and the Freedom on the Net Index by Freedom House classified it as "partly free" in that time frame. This was a transitional period for Turkey, in which it was inclining toward authoritarian rule but still considered a democracy. This is a good reason to include Turkey in the analysis but also a motive to study it deeper as a warning for other democratic governments.

SIX

The United States and Interdependence Sovereignty

Stephen Krasner describes interdependence sovereignty as "the ability of public authorities to regulate the flow of information, ideas, goods, people, pollutants, or capital across the borders of their state."[1] This type of state sovereignty deals with a state's ability to regulate transborder movements, a topic that has not lost its relevance in today's globalized and mutually interdependent world. Despite the globalization trend, states retain their national policy agendas and do not give up their sovereignty. Therefore, interdependence sovereignty remains a pertinent concept that gained even more momentum with the growing tension between certain states escalating into trade wars and concerns over supply chains at the end of 2010s and beginning of 2020s.

Interdependence sovereignty does not lose its significance in cyberspace either. Although cyberspace is often thought of as being borderless, certain authoritarian regimes have proved that national borders do indeed exist in this domain. The Great Firewall of China, a combination of technologies and legislative measures to regulate cross-border internet traffic and block access to selected foreign websites from Chinese territory, is the most notorious example. Free access to information is one of the cornerstones of any democracy, which is the primary subject of this book, but the transborder movement of free information in cyberspace has not much preoccupied the transatlantic democracies. What has been the center of concern for many of them at the end of the 2010s and beginning of the 2020s is the security and integrity of a supply chain that supports the development of their national critical infrastructure, a concern heightened by the threats of espionage and sabotage. No single state in today's globalized world is capable of building its critical infrastructure using technologies developed purely on its own territory by its national trusted producers and manufacturers. States depend on components whose basic elements are manufactured in one country and shipped to another for assembly and then ultimately become part of a complex system of critical infrastructure in a third country, their final destination. This creates multiple security risks because it gives opportunity for adversaries to implant malicious technology in the components, which can later be exploited for espionage or data theft, for example. Any government concerned for the security of its critical infrastructure should thus have as much control as possible over its supply chain and have a network of trustworthy suppliers. Coming back to Krasner's definition of interdependence sovereignty, to maximally increase the security of their critical infrastructure, governments should be cautious and regulate what kinds of components with what history they let across their borders to become part of their critical systems. This is even more topical with the approaching age of the powerful 5G technology standard for broadband cellular networks.

The United States, with its strong stand regarding Chinese tech companies in general, and Huawei Technologies in particular, has been the frontrunner in this quest for a secure and trustworthy supply chain and clean critical infrastructure throughout the 2010s and early 2020s. The United States is aware that if it wants to maintain its role of world superpower, it must also retain its position as a global leader in modern technologies. Because China has aspired to become the United States's counterbalance in world politics, it has recognized the importance of also being a technology leader while using economic policies and espionage to gain an advantage.[2] For instance, between 2011 and 2018, China was involved in or benefited from more than 90 percent of the US Department of Justice cases of economic espionage.[3] This power competition has reached a climax with the arrival of

5G. US manufacturing has been in decline for several decades, leaving its telecom industry, as in so many other nations, dependent on foreign manufacturers.[4] Although Cisco Systems is still an important player, the majority of companies are foreign—for example, Swedish Ericsson, Finnish Nokia, and Chinese Huawei. Given the competitive nature of US-Chinese relations and the Chinese espionage attempts, it is no surprise that Huawei is conspicuous to US eyes for being a champion of the Chinese regime. Ericsson and Nokia come from friendly, trustworthy countries, and they have become a preferred alternative. Despite much effort, Huawei has failed to persuade the United States of its trustworthiness, and President Donald Trump's administration did not hesitate to call the company "an arm of the Chinese Communist Party's surveillance state."[5]

Huawei's history, its relationship with the Chinese government, and the domestic legislation that it must obey lend credence to the security concerns of the United States and other pro-Western countries. After its establishment in the late 1980s, Huawei built its early success by servicing rural areas of China. Within ten years it had success in Chinese urban markets, setting the basis for a rapid international expansion in the first decade of the twenty-first century. The Shenzhen-based company has been particularly successful in emerging markets in Africa and Asia but has also found its way into the markets of Europe, India, and Japan. Its growth was so rapid that by 2013 it had become the second-largest supplier of IT equipment by revenue worldwide, after Ericsson.[6] Even more crucially, Huawei was the first company that could offer all the elements of a 5G network, leaving its closest competitors Nokia and Ericsson lagging.[7] Its ambitions to dominate the market of 5G wireless communications combined with its low-cost products and its investments into research and development positioned Huawei to become the largest producer of 5G equipment worldwide and expand its market share. This fast expansion and success created serious security concerns for various reasons.

I do not comprehensively analyze why Huawei is perceived as a security risk in some countries, only mentioning the most often cited concerns. Huawei has always been reluctant to share information regarding its internal management structures and decision-making, which has led to the question of the exact role of the internal party committee deployed by the Chinese

Communist Party within the company's structures. Similarly, the ties of Huawei's top management with the Chinese government, Communist Party, and People's Liberation Army are not clear. For example, Ren Zhengfei, the company's founder, is suspected to have close ties with the army thanks to his former military career, which might have boosted the company's growth and gotten it contracts overseas. Furthermore, Huawei has been criticized several times because of its questionable attention to international legal obligations, undermining the company's image as a respectable business partner. An illustrative example is the contracts Huawei made with the Iranian government at a time when Iran was subject to international sanctions.[8] A serious security concern about Huawei is Chinese cybersecurity and intelligence legislation that Huawei is obliged to obey. Since Xi Jinping's election as general secretary of the Chinese Communist Party in 2012, an interrelated package of national security laws and regulations has been drafted to enforce the legal basis for Chinese security operations, demanding that both Chinese and foreign companies, organizations and citizens cooperate with China. For example, the National Intelligence Law of 2017 raises significant concerns, because it requires citizens and companies operating in China to provide access, cooperation, assistance, and support for China's intelligence-gathering activities, which shifts the balance from intelligence "defense" to "offense."[9] Chinese laws that oblige companies and individuals to potentially assist Chinese officials in intelligence activities, together with Huawei's record and unclear ties with China's government and Communist Party, alarm the United States and allied countries. They are afraid that Huawei equipment in their critical infrastructure could give the Chinese government access to sensitive computer systems through secret backdoors, potentially exploiting them for espionage or disruption of key services.

Huawei is not the only Chinese company targeted by restrictions abroad; others are the ZTE Corporation, Hikvision, Dahua, and many more. Most efforts target Chinese entities, but other foreign companies have been banned from important infrastructure because of security concerns too. For example, Kaspersky Lab, a Russian antivirus company, was banned from use in US federal agencies in December 2017.[10] This fear of intrusion into domestic critical infrastructure by foreign vendors exists in many countries, and Huawei dominates in the lists of banned entities. The greatest and loudest proponent of denying Huawei access to its national critical infrastructure has been the US government, which is also why the United States is at the center of the analysis here, as a pioneer of interdependence sovereignty in cyberspace.

I assess the variable of control through the study of the strong US interest in and approach to building a secure critical infrastructure, in particular telecommunications infrastructure and the new fifth generation of the technology standard (5G). Such cyber capabilities are a crucial building block in the US effort to maintain its position as a world tech leader and a superpower. Telecommunications systems are at the heart of multiple modern critical infrastructures that depend on the reliable and safe transmission of information. Furthermore, the close interdependence of critical infrastructure systems means that failure in one system can cause disruptions in multiple other systems. The disruption of the telecommunications infrastructure, crucial for the reliable functioning of critical infrastructure, could have serious consequences for the whole of modern society and a state's economy. This is why the US government so carefully scrutinizes these systems' security. This chapter first explores the US perception of the security of critical infrastructure, 5G, and supply chain policy, illustrating these with concrete examples like the 5G FAST Plan by the Federal Communications Commission (FCC) and the National Strategy to Secure 5G.

In today's interdependent world, not a single state is self-sufficient for tech components manufactured on its own territory, and a government with such a strong interest in its domestic cyber capabilities and their security as the United States must be vigilant regarding critical infrastructure suppliers. Hence, the variable of authority in this chapter is the administrative and legislative actions the US government has taken to first minimize Huawei's presence in its critical infrastructure and then completely remove it. Although the first concerns about the security of Huawei's components can be traced back to 2012 or even earlier in the United States, the coordinated campaign against the Chinese telecom vendor started in 2018. At that time, the US administration began not only implementing measures aimed at removing Huawei from its key infrastructure at a national level but also orchestrating a global effort to bar the Chinese company from supplying 5G system gear. The US government prohibited US-based companies from providing software and hardware to Huawei, targeting its supply chain network and seriously crippling the company's business. When the US did not stop at its national level but implemented measures that influenced the company's operations and its allies' operations, the United States went further than any other nation-state in enforcing its interdependence sovereignty in cyberspace.

The goal of this chapter is not to compile a comprehensive list of all legal and administrative measures ever issued by the US government directly or indirectly targeted against Huawei but to map out the most significant ones forming the US approach. It analyzes the years from 2012 to 2016, a period covering the congressional report on Huawei and ZTE, which triggered these events, up until the end of President Trump's administration, when the efforts culminated.

US Critical Infrastructure, 5G, and Supply Chain

Different definitions of critical infrastructure exist. I use the one in Executive Order No. 13,636, Improving Critical Infrastructure Cybersecurity, signed by President Barack Obama in February 2013, which is also used by the National Institute of Standards and Technology, a nonregulatory agency of the US Department of Commerce. It defines critical infrastructure as "systems and assets, whether physical or virtual, so vital to the United States that the incapacity or destruction of such systems and assets would have a debilitating impact on security, national economic security, national public health or safety, or any combination of those matters."[11] In other words, the critical infrastructure community is composed of public and private operators and owners with the crucial task of securing national infrastructure. All these functions are supported by industrial control systems and information technologies, which have a heavy dependence on reliable technologies and telecommunications systems. These critical infrastructures include banking and financial systems, electric power grids, mass transit systems, and gas, oil, and water systems.

Furthermore, modern critical infrastructure typically has strong interdependence among these systems, which augments the risk that failure of one network will cause disruptions in multiple others. This can potentially have a devastating effect on all aspects of modern society, especially where online dependency is high, as it is in the United States. The security vulnerabilities of such critical systems are broad and range from sophisticated cyber attacks perpetrated by another nation-state to cyber espionage. However, a vulnerability in the spotlight in the United States in the 2010s and early 2020s stems from telecommunications supply chains from potentially adversarial foreign sources.

The supply chain nowadays is profoundly globalized, and its security is an incredibly complex problem. Throughout product development, there are multiple opportunities to tamper with telecommunications systems and components by inserting malicious hardware or software implants that can cause the shutdown or degradation of a system of national critical infrastructure in a crisis or even during a war. A state must thus have as much trust and confidence in these networks as possible. Because of the international interdependence of the tech world, it is impossible for any state, including the United States, to rely on only its own national design and manufacturing. Hence, governments have no choice but to trust the companies that produce the individual components of their critical infrastructure. For example, if Huawei technology were deployed in the US backbone communications systems, it would become part of the core national infrastructure that essential socioeconomic services and functions depend on. Huawei would then be an integral component of strategically significant systems critical for US society, including the military and security services of the country. The importance of fundamental infrastructure to society makes the development of communications systems a strategic decision for not only the operators themselves but the whole nation. On top of that, the relative permanence of such infrastructure and the cost of withdrawing potentially dangerous components from existing systems can have long-term effects at the national level, as well as on cooperation with international allies and partners.

Having equipment from a potentially dangerous vendor in national critical infrastructure came to the fore with the arrival of 5G, which is expected to cause an immense growth of Internet-of-Things-enabled services and subsequently the digital dependency of modern society. Industrially developed states have nationwide coverage of three generations of broadband mobile network technology, 2G, 3G, and 4G. Phone calls and text messages can fluctuate among the three generations, and more demanding services that require an internet connection are restricted to 3G and 4G.[12] The next generation, 5G, has the "potential of becoming the digital nervous system of the contemporary societies."[13] Contrary to older generations, which focused on advancing network speed to improve internet access, 5G supports three major functions. First, 5G enables enhanced mobile broadband, allowing higher data speeds and faster downloads. Second, it secures low-latency communication, which is crucial for devices such as autonomous vehicles that require uninterrupted communication. Finally, 5G allows machine-to-machine communications in which billions of devices continuously communicate with each other.[14] These characteristics will accelerate development in the research and implementation of automation, robotics, virtual reality, artificial intelligence, and machine learning, eventually ushering in the transformation of digital societies as we know them today. 5G will influence a broad spectrum of activities, from factory automation, smart cities, and driverless cars to telemedicine, smart electric grids, public safety, and the armed forces, having immense implications for critical civilian and defense aspects of life.

The new 5G networks will inevitably also expand the scale of possible vulnerabilities, increase the possibilities for malicious actors to exploit these vulnerabilities, and make it more difficult to track adversarial cyber activity. It will be more important than ever for states to have the highest assurances possible that their critical networks and data will be safe from malicious meddling. The 5G rollout should be recognized as a strategic choice rather than merely a technological one in which cost and speed are the only determining parameters.[15] This is even more imperative considering that 5G technology blurs the boundaries between the core and the edge of communications networks, which is the basic technical characteristic distinguishing it from the previous generations of networks. In the old 4G systems, the edge and core of the networks were separated, and so if the core was protected, users' data were safe as well; 5G technology is different. It boosts the processing power across the whole network, which makes it faster, but the blurring of borders between the edge and core of the network means the whole network must have as much protection as the core in the 4G networks. Distinctions between critical and noncritical elements are also blurred.[16] This means that limiting certain vendors to only the edge of networks does not dispel the threat, because a security threat anywhere in the 5G network structure is a threat to the whole system.[17] Given the overwhelming complexity of 5G architecture, states must carefully choose who will be involved in the development of their national 5G networks from the very beginning.

Therefore, it is almost impossible to separate what is critical and noncritical in 5G network infrastructure, and it all must be recognized as what the US government calls a "national critical function."[18] The United States knows very well the importance of 5G for its future as a world tech superpower and for its national security,[19] and it has consequently adopted a broader strategy to secure its position that includes regulatory adjustments, a legal liability regime, and technical measures. The US quest for 5G superiority is displayed in two documents in this chapter: the 5G FAST (Facilitate America's Superiority in 5G Technology) Plan of the FCC and the National Strategy to Secure 5G issued by the Trump administration. The FCC's comprehensive strategy was introduced by the FCC chairman Ajit Pai in September 2018. The strategy involves three key elements. First, it attempts to push more spectrum into the market to make additional spectrum available for 5G services. Second, it updates the current infrastructure policy and encourages the private sector to invest more in the development of 5G networks. Finally, it modernizes outdated regulations to promote the wired backbone of 5G. Interestingly, part of the last point is supply chain integrity, within which the FCC has, for instance, adopted a ban on the use of taxpayer money for services or technologies from vendors that threaten the integrity of US national communications networks or its supply chain.[20]

The National Strategy to Secure 5G is more security and strategy oriented, complementing the 5G FAST Plan and legislation on the security of 5G networks such as the Secure and Trusted Communications Networks Act, discussed later. The strategy, published in March 2020, formally introduces the United States' desire to safeguard 5G infrastructure on the national and international levels, setting forth a "vision for America to lead the development, deployment, and management of secure and reliable 5G communications infrastructure worldwide, arm-in-arm with [its] closest partners and allies."[21] The strategy outlines four aims: (1) facilitate the domestic rollout of 5G, (2) assess the risks and identify the core security principles of 5G infrastructure, (3) manage the risks to economic and national security from the use of 5G infrastructure, and (4) promote responsible global development and deployment of 5G infrastructure.[22] Three features of the strategy are particularly relevant for this chapter. The document highlights cooperation with the private sector on the identification, development, and application of core security principles to US 5G infrastructure, management of supply chain risks in the US governmental infrastructure, and promotion of responsible global development and deployment of 5G, including US leadership in international standards development and adoption.[23] The strategy, together with the FCC's 5G FAST Plan, illustrates the importance of 5G security for the well-being of the US nation and society.

As a result of these reflections, securing its supply chain for critical infrastructure has become a top priority for the United States, achieved by banning providers posing a potential security risk. Banning is a radical but effective way to make sure that all the components in critical infrastructure come from trusted vendors, although bans will inevitably have repercussions in terms of trade policy, the economy, and international relations. Given the far-reaching consequences, such decisions must be made with caution, as a last resort when all the other preventive actions are unsatisfactory. This applies to any state in the world, and even more so to the United States, which is a global superpower with a broad sphere of influence, meaning any of its decisions in this regard will inevitably invoke disarray and disputes. If a state with global powers similar to the United States' decides to take this path, the impact will reach beyond its own supply chain to influence the global supply chain, realigning it to reflect the new geopolitical realities. Ultimately, it can shift the level of international tech interdependence, influencing the volatility of the international system.[24]

US Administrative and Legislative Actions against Huawei Technologies

Although the massive anti-Huawei campaign led by the US government reached full strength only at the end of the 2010s and in the early 2020s, the first signs of the US government's security concerns over Chinese telecom companies, and Huawei in particular, trace back to 2008–2011. The US government's representatives had already thwarted Huawei's plans to obtain deals with US companies such as AT&T and Verizon Communications and to acquire US start-ups, justifying the action by saying even a minor deal "could pose a serious risk to America's national and economic security," as Senators Jim Webb (D-Va.) and Jon Kyi (R-Ariz.) phrased it in their statement in February 2011.[25] For example, Huawei had to give up its plan to acquire the networking company 3Com in 2008 over these concerns. Two years later, the company had to withdraw from a contract bid with the US company Sprint for similar reasons. The most visible example was the failed attempt to acquire the Silicon Valley software start-up 3Leaf Systems in 2011, a deal worth $2 million. 3Leaf Systems was bankrupt and searching for a buyer. Huawei stepped in and offered jobs to its employees, but the US government saw that as a ploy to circumvent governmental approval procedures for an acquisition. In the end, Huawei withdrew from the deal before it reached President Obama for review.[26]

Following up on the preceding obstacles in conducting business in the US market, Huawei published an open letter addressed to the US government in February 2011 in which it denied posing any security concerns and demanded a full investigation into its operations.[27] The letter triggered a yearlong investigation into the counterintelligence and security threat posed by Huawei as well as ZTE, another Chinese telecommunications company doing business in the United States, conducted by the House Permanent Select Committee on Intelligence. The committee aspired to better comprehend the level of risk posed to the United States by these two top Chinese telecommunications equipment manufacturers.[28] Because the final report concluding the investigation was the first comprehensive statement of the US government formulating its opinion on Huawei's presence in its critical infrastructure, and hence a key milestone in their relations, it is worth paying attention to the report's conclusions and recommendations.

The committee found that neither of the investigated companies responded sufficiently or clearly to their lines of inquiry and, despite repeated requests, provided little or no internal documentation supporting their answers. Neither company explained its formal relationship or regulatory interaction with the Chinese Communist Party, Chinese government, or Chinese authorities. The precise role of the Chinese Communist Party Committee within the companies' structures, and thus the Chinese state's influence on company operations, was not explained. Huawei in particular did not provide clear and complete information about its history, ownership, decision-making processes, corporate structure, financial arrangements, or operations. Furthermore, the investigation concluded that Huawei likely depended on the support of the Chinese government.[29] The report found that "the risks associated with Huawei's and ZTE's provision of equipment to U.S. critical infrastructure could undermine core U.S. national-security interests" and that "Chinese telecommunications companies provide an opportunity for the Chinese government to tamper with the United States telecommunications supply chain."[30]

The committee also formulated recommendations, the most relevant of which I mention here. First, the committee stressed that the US authorities ought to view the expansion of the two Chinese companies into the US telecommunications market with suspicion. It appealed to the US intelligence community to keep the private sector as informed of the threats and risks as possible and urged the Committee on Foreign Investment in the United States, an interagency committee, to block acquisitions and similar operations involving the investigated companies. It stated that US government systems should avoid Huawei's and ZTE's equipment. The same advice was also addressed to governmental contractors, especially those with contracts involving sensitive US programs. Second, the committee recommended that private companies in the United States carefully consider whether to do business with the investigated Chinese companies because of the associated long-term security risks. US systems developers and network providers were strongly advised to opt for other vendors for their operations. Finally, the committees on jurisdiction within the US Congress were encouraged to discuss potential legislation to better manage the threats posed by private telecommunications entities with ties to nation-states that could not be trusted to build sensitive infrastructure.[31]

Although the general public had access to only the unclassified report and not the classified appendix, which provided significantly more detail justifying the committee's security concerns, the unclassified part sufficed to set Huawei's position in the United States. Already in March 2013, as a condition for the approval of Softbank's acquisition of Sprint Nextel, valued at $20 billion, the US government had sought oversight of the network equipment purchases to prevent gear manufactured by Huawei and ZTE becoming part of the US infrastructure. Representatives of the two US companies traveled to Capitol Hill and pledged not to use gear from either of the Chinese telecommunications providers in Sprint's network core.[32] Furthermore, at approximately the same time, President Obama signed into law an appropriations act that essentially prohibited federal agencies from buying IT systems from entities owned, directed, or subsidized by China without prior permission from the Federal Bureau of Investigation or another appropriate federal agency.[33] These events brought about a more or less stable period, during which Huawei and ZTE were unofficially blacklisted by the US government in the eyes of the US public and the professional community. This lasted for five years, until the US administration opted for a more radical position in 2018.

That year marked the beginning of a harsh campaign by the United States against Huawei and other Chinese tech companies that might be a security risk for US infrastructure and society. In May 2018, the US Defense Department published a directive forbidding the purchase of ZTE and Huawei mobile phones on US military bases, citing security risks posed by such devices. Internet modems and other wireless devices were also included in the ban. Although the directive did not prevent US service members from bringing the devices to work, the Pentagon sent a clear message to its employees: "Service members should be mindful of the security risks posed by the use of Huawei devices, regardless of where they were purchased."[34] In August 2018, President Trump signed into law a bill banning Huawei and ZTE technology from use by the federal government and governmental contractors as part of the much larger National Defense Authorization Act 2019. The ban covered the use of equipment or services that were "critical" or "essential" to systems, with the exception of components that could not be used to route or view data.[35] Huawei filed an unsuccessful legal motion seeking to pronounce the act unconstitutional,[36] and the company was pushed out of the US market in the following two years.

In May 2019, the US government's intention to ban Huawei in the United States became crystal clear. President Trump signed the executive order Securing the Information and Communications Technology and Services Supply Chain on May 15, 2019, invoking the International Emergency

Economic Powers Act, which bestows on the president the authority to regulate commerce in reaction to a national emergency.[37] The order essentially prohibits the purchase or use of communications technology manufactured by entities "owned by, controlled by, or subject to the jurisdiction or direction of foreign adversaries," thereby possibly creating an "undue risk of sabotage" of US communications systems or "catastrophic effects" for infrastructure. The order defines "foreign adversary" as "any foreign government or foreign non-government person engaged in a long-term pattern or serious instances of conduct significantly adverse to the national security of the United States or security and safety of United States persons."[38] On the basis of the order, the US Commerce Department was directed to create a plan to identify particular persons and countries posing a threat and enforce the order within 150 days. Commerce Secretary Wilbur Ross noted that the law would shield against "foreign adversaries [accessing] the nation's information and communications technology and services supply chain, [and now] under President Trump's leadership, Americans will be able to trust that our data and infrastructure are secure."[39]

At the same time, the Bureau of Industry and Security, an integral part of the US Department of Commerce, took a separate but related action. It added Huawei and its affiliates to its Entity List, which effectively prohibits US companies from doing business with this Chinese telecommunications giant.[40] The transfer or sale of US technology to a company on the Entity List requires a license issued by the bureau, which could be denied if the transfer or sale would damage US foreign policy interests or national security.[41] This went far beyond a simple ban on products and services by potentially dangerous foreign vendors deployed in the US infrastructure. This step, in fact, also regulated the transfer of goods and services of US entities abroad, meaning in the opposite direction. It soon turned out to have far-reaching implications directly affecting Huawei and its business not only in the United States but all over the world.

US companies reacted immediately to the Trump administration's order. For example, Google suspended business with Huawei and cut off support to the company for many Android software and hardware services. Google also limited access to applications like Gmail, Google Maps, and the Google Play store in new handsets produced by Huawei.[42] The most devastating effect the order had was on the supply of microchips, which were absolutely essential for Huawei, then the second-largest smartphone producer worldwide after South Korean Samsung.[43] Right after the signing of the order into law, US companies Intel, Qualcomm, Xilinx, and Broadcom, some of the world's largest chipmakers, suspended their cooperation with Huawei.[44] In the aftermath, Huawei relied on certain exemptions in the US ban while attempting to reduce its reliance on US chip manufacturers. This was mainly achieved through a strong, rapid boost of its in-house production by Huawei's chip unit, HiSilicon.

Another heavy blow by the US administration came in mid-May 2020, when it issued a new rule barring Huawei and its suppliers from using US technology and software. Despite the hopes for independence from US technology, HiSilicon still depended on outside manufacturers like the Taiwan Semiconductor Manufacturing Company (TSMC) and the Shanghai-based Semiconductor Manufacturing International Corporation (SMIC) to mass produce chips to its specifications. Many of these operations, however, depended to some extent on technology refined and developed in the United States. The US Department of Commerce saw this as a loophole allowing Huawei to undermine its status as a blacklisted entity.[45] US Commerce Secretary Ross noted in relation to the previous ban that "there has been a very highly technical loophole through which Huawei has been able, in effect, to use U.S. technology with foreign fab producers," and he called the rule change a "highly tailored thing to try to correct that loophole."[46] The new rule expanded US authority so that suppliers of US-made technology must request a US governmental license before the sale, including semiconductors made abroad with US technology. The rule entered into effect in September 2020, granting a 120-day grace period.[47] As a consequence of the rule change, Richard Yu, president of Huawei's consumer unit announced that production of Huawei's Kirin chips would close on September 15, 2020. Although the Kirin chips were designed by the company's own engineers, they depended on contractors that required US technology. Because of the second round of US restrictions, the chip producers accepted orders only until May 15, 2020.[48] The US pressure caused Huawei growing damage while also having a heavy impact on the global supply chain.

By the same token, the radical US restrictions and campaign against Huawei inevitably had implications for US companies and the development of US infrastructure, in particular in preparation for 5G deployment. The major US carriers did not include Huawei components in their networks, but some smaller, rural carriers did. Huawei is renowned for the low cost of its products and services, which smaller entities find hard to ignore. Rural areas hence received significant attention from the US administration. The FCC identified over fifty mostly small telecommunications entities using either the equipment or the services of Huawei and other Chinese companies in their networks, and US rural telecommunications networks estimated a cost of $1.837 billion to replace all Huawei and ZTE switches and routers in their networks.[49] To avoid disruption to the services of rural US telecommunications network operators, as well as major US tech companies, the US Department of Commerce had to grant temporary licenses for doing business with Huawei in May 2019. This reprieve was extended several times, for 90 days in August and November 2019 and for 45 days in February 2020.[50] The US Commerce Department said, "The department is issuing these narrow licences to authorise limited and specific activities which do not pose a significant risk to the national security or foreign policy interests of the United States."[51] On the occasion of the reprieve in February 2020, the department also noted that "the 45-day extension is necessary to allow existing telecommunication providers—particularly those in rural US communities—the ability to continue to temporarily and securely operate existing networks while they identify alternatives to Huawei for future operation."[52] Nevertheless, despite the repeated reprieves, Huawei remained on the Entity List.

In the meantime, the US administration continued with the implementation of further restrictive measures against Huawei, intensifying its crusade against the company. In August 2019, the US government banned all its agencies, including the National Aeronautics and Space Administration and the Pentagon, from purchasing equipment made by Huawei and other Chinese companies perceived as a national security threat such as ZTE, Dahua, and Hikvision.[53] Three months later, the FCC banned telecommunications companies from buying Huawei and ZTE components and services from its Universal Service Fund.[54] In March 2020, the Secure and Trusted

Communications Networks Act was passed, effectively prohibiting US companies from using federal funds to purchase equipment from companies deemed a threat to national security, Huawei and others like them.[55] Simultaneously, a $1 billion reimbursement program called the Secure and Trusted Communications Networks Reimbursement Program was established to aid smaller providers with the cost of substituting the prohibited equipment manufactured by Huawei and ZTE.[56] In May 2020, President Trump extended the executive order Securing the Information and Communications Technology and Services Supply Chain, which barred US companies from using telecommunications components provided by companies perceived as a national security threat, for another year.[57] Two months later, the Pentagon listed Huawei among companies it says are controlled or owned by China's military, claiming that "this list will be a useful tool for the U.S. government, companies, investors, academic institutions, and like-minded partners to conduct due diligence with regard to partnerships with these entities."[58] This announcement was followed less than a week later by the FCC's announcement designating Huawei and ZTE as "national security threats."[59] On this subject, FCC chairman Ajit Pai said, "We cannot and will not allow the Chinese Communist Party to exploit network vulnerabilities and compromise our critical communications infrastructure."[60] Not long after, the US administration set in place a regulation that barred the government from purchasing products and services from any company using products from five listed Chinese companies, including Huawei. A company wanting to use products or services from the five companies and to sell its products to the US government would need a US government waiver.[61] The last major rule regulating the US-Huawei relationship introduced before President Trump left the White House was the ban on US investments in companies linked to the Chinese military from November 2020. This executive order aimed to deter in particular US investment companies, pension funds, and individuals from buying shares of thirty-one Chinese companies, including Huawei, that the US Department of Defense claimed to be controlled or owned by the People's Liberation Army.[62] This was the final major step in a series of domestic regulations restricting Huawei's presence in the US market and critical infrastructure, which culminated during the last year of Donald Trump's administration.

The US administration did not limit itself to its own domestic market in its crusade against Huawei's goods crossing its borders. It also tried to influence foreign allies. The logic behind this move was simple: to trust its closest allies and partners and to safely exchange information with them, the United States required all to be free from the potential security threats embodied by Huawei and similar companies. Before 2018, only a few countries, among them the UK, Australia, India, and Germany, viewed Chinese technologies as a potential threat to their national security. In 2018 the US government initiated a powerful outreach campaign to dissuade their foreign allies' governments and their own internet and wireless providers from using Huawei's equipment in their government and commercial networks. At the time, Huawei was popular among carriers in several allied countries, including some of the United States' closest military allies.[63] The United States went so far as to threaten to reassess its information-sharing policy with allied countries that used Huawei network components, highlighting that they could not see any difference between the core and the edge regions of the 5G networks. Robert Strayer, the deputy assistant secretary for cyber, international communications, and information policy at the State Department said, "If other countries insert and allow untrusted vendors to build out and become the vendors for their 5G networks we will have to reassess the ability for us to share information and be connected with them in the ways that we are today."[64] The US government even considered reexamination of its relations and information sharing with the UK, its closest political and military ally.[65] Up until 2020, these US efforts to persuade like-minded countries to avoid Huawei's products seemed to work on an almost bilateral basis.

In 2020 the US government launched a comprehensive and systematic initiative, coined the Clean Network, an umbrella term for multiple lines of effort. For instance, the 5G Clean Path initiative requires that all 5G network traffic entering and exiting US diplomatic facilities must be "clean"—that is, not "use any transmission, control, computing, or storage equipment from untrusted IT vendors, such as Huawei and ZTE."[66] The Clean Carrier initiative exists to "ensure untrusted People's Republic of China . . . carriers are not connected with U.S. telecommunications networks" because such companies "should not provide international telecommunications services to and from the United States."[67] The Clean Store initiative was launched to "remove untrusted applications from U.S. mobile app stores," and the Clean Apps initiative "prevent[s] untrusted [Chinese] smartphone manufacturers from pre-installing . . . trusted apps on their apps store."[68] The Clean Network initiative was launched as a "comprehensive effort by a coalition of like-minded countries and companies to secure their critical telecommunications, cloud, data analytics, mobile apps, Internet of Things, and 5G technologies from malign actors by relying on only trusted vendors who are not subject to unjust or extra-judicial control by authoritarian governments, such as the Chinese Communist Party."[69] The Clean Network initiative complements the Digital Trust Standards and the Prague Proposals. The Digital Trust Standards were developed by a group of international experts at the request of the US Department of State and offer governments and network owners and operators criteria for assessing the trustworthiness and security of telecommunications equipment suppliers.[70] The Prague Proposals on 5G Security is a set of principles and recommendations for states to consider when designing, constructing, and administrating their 5G infrastructure.[71] As of December 2020, the Clean Network initiative has been joined by 180 telecommunications companies and 50 national governments, which together represent two-thirds of the global gross domestic product.[72] Although not all the participating states have fully committed to the principles set out in the Clean Network initiative, the numbers clearly suggest that the United States has strong support in its campaign against the Chinese telecommunications dominance of Huawei Technologies and ultimate goal of ensuring its national security.

When considering the immediate impact of the US campaign against Huawei and other Chinese companies accused of having close ties with Chinese governmental structures, the United States has achieved its goal. Huawei failed to establish itself in the US market and had to partially or completely withdraw from many governmental business deals in other countries too. It was quickly replaced by industry competitors. For example, in early 2020, executives from Nokia and Ericsson, Huawei's largest competitors in the telecom equipment market for 5G gear, visited Capitol Hill to reassure US lawmakers that their components and services are secure and safe, and hence trustworthy to supply the US wireless carriers constructing 5G networks.[73] Keith Krach, the undersecretary for economic growth, energy, and the environment in the US State Department, in an op-ed for *Daily Telegraph* wrote, "US telecom providers have chosen wisely. They are successfully deploying Ericsson and Nokia throughout their 5G systems, and are working with other trusted firms for further expansion. They understand that a secure 'edge' is just as important as a secure 'core,' because it's all part of an integrated system."[74] The United States has expelled Huawei elements from its domestic critical infrastructure, opting for the safer alternative of Nokia and Ericsson, coming from trustworthy allied countries. The United States advanced and stretched its interdependence sovereignty in cyberspace to the maximum degree possible when it successfully regulated the transborder movement of Huawei's products and services and influenced its acceptance in other, allied countries.

Conclusion

Krasner interprets interdependence sovereignty as a state's ability to regulate transborder movement of information, ideas, people, or goods. Applying interdependence sovereignty to cyberspace, the democracies of the transatlantic area have mainly focused their attention on the movement of goods over their borders—more specifically, technical components and services manufactured abroad and destined to become part of the domestic critical infrastructure. Because no state of today's interconnected world can build its infrastructure with technologies developed solely on its own territory, they must rely on a complicated globalized supply chain. The comprehensive supply chain, however, offers multiple opportunities for adversaries to insert malicious components that can be exploited for a cyber attack or espionage. Therefore, any government concerned about the security of critical infrastructure should seek to have as much control as possible over the supply chain and develop a network of trustworthy suppliers.

The United States has been campaigning to prevent Huawei Technologies and similar Chinese companies from entering its market and infrastructure. The United States has maintained its position as a tech superpower but still must rely on foreign telecommunications companies for its infrastructure. China aspires to become the United States' counterbalance in world politics, and so it attempts to keep up with the speed of tech development and even become a global tech leader. This power struggle between these two actors has only intensified with the arrival of 5G, the powerful next generation of technology standard. Huawei has been one of the biggest providers of 5G gear, but because of its close ties to the Chinese government, many pro-Western countries perceive it as a threat to their national security.

These countries, encouraged by the United States, have realized the importance of a secure supply chain, especially with respect to 5G and its potential impact on critical infrastructure and modern society. With its enhanced mobile broadband, low latency, and massive machine-to-machine communication, 5G will immensely boost the growth of the Internet of Things in various sectors, from energy, health, and transportation to smart cities and the military. Naturally, this creates a new variety of potential vulnerabilities that, if exploited, could have a dire impact. Given that there is no major difference between the core and the edge of the network in 5G, states will need to have the highest assurance possible that their critical infrastructure is safe from malicious meddling. Therefore, states must perceive the 5G rollout as a strategic choice more than a technological one (in which money and speed play the decisive roles). The United States is well aware of the potential of 5G and has made the maximum effort to build 5G superiority. To help with this task, the US government has put forward two key documents: the FCC's 5G FAST Plan sets out a comprehensive strategy for the United States to facilitate the development and spread of 5G technology, and the National Strategy to Secure 5G of the United States is a security- and strategy-oriented document complementing the 5G FAST Plan. These documents illustrate the importance of 5G and its security for the well-being of US society and the consequent need to secure the supply chain for critical infrastructure.

To maximize its supply chain security and protect it from adversarial meddling, the United States began a broad domestic campaign against Huawei and similar Chinese telecommunications companies. Although the first sign of US protectionism in this regard can be traced back to 2008–2011, the true breakthrough came in 2012. After a yearlong investigation into the alleged threats posed to the United States by Huawei and ZTE, the House Permanent Select Committee on Intelligence concluded that the two Chinese companies could indeed present a risk to US critical infrastructure and in doing so undermine US national security. This outcome unofficially blacklisted Huawei and ZTE in the eyes of the US public and significantly slowed their expansion into the US market for the following few years.

The campaign against Huawei's presence in US infrastructure strengthened in 2018, when President Trump signed a bill into law banning the use of Huawei and ZTE technology by the federal government and governmental contractors as a part of the National Defense Authorization Act 2019. In the spring of 2019, Trump signed an executive order, Securing the Information and Communications Technology and Services Supply Chain, that prohibited the purchase and use of communications technology manufactured by entities controlled by, owned by, or subject to the jurisdiction of foreign adversaries. At the same time, the US Department of Commerce added Huawei and its affiliates to its Entity List, which essentially prohibits US companies from doing business with these Chinese companies. The situation then culminated in 2020. In mid-May of 2020, the US administration issued a new rule, barring Huawei and its suppliers from using US technology and software. This decision disrupted Huawei's own supply chain, especially for indispensable semiconductors. In the summer, the Pentagon added Huawei to the list of companies controlled or owned by the Chinese military, and the FCC proclaimed Huawei and ZTE national security threats. The final significant move came in November, when US investment in companies linked to the Chinese military was banned.

The US administration also started an outreach campaign to persuade other states to remove technologies in their infrastructure provided by Huawei and other potentially dangerous entities. The motivation for this was that, even if the United States freed itself of potentially dangerous Chinese technologies, it was still vulnerable if foreign partners and allies used that technology. Thus, the United States started a comprehensive umbrella initiative, the Clean Network, comprising several lines of effort, such as the 5G Clean Path, Clean Carrier, and Clean Apps initiatives. This was a significant and truly unprecedented step because it signified a shift in the strategy of the United States in the fight against Huawei from an America-first approach to collective efforts to guarantee US national security beyond its borders.

All in all, the US quest against Huawei's presence in its domestic critical infrastructure and also in certain instances abroad has been a success. This is visible in the growing number of signed 5G contracts held with Nokia and Ericsson compared with the slowing rate of new contracts signed with Huawei.[75] Huawei's chief executive and founder, Ren Zhengfei, confirmed this trend, citing the US blacklisting as a cause.[76] Despite claiming to be "the most audited technology company in the world,"[77] Huawei executives could not persuade the US government or many others of its trustworthiness. The US government under Joe Biden's administration has pursued the same path and implemented legislation and policies to bring the supply chains back from China.

The US exercise of interdependence sovereignty toward the Chinese company Huawei reveals an important limitation to this type of sovereignty in cyberspace. By banning certain allegedly dangerous vendors from the design and construction of critical infrastructure, governments all around the world try to minimize security risks. At the same time, however, they have to accept that they cannot get rid of all foreign vendors. The global supply chain is too complex, mainly owing to globalization, and no single state is absolutely self-sustaining and independent from the system. Therefore, it is impossible for a state to reach complete interdependence sovereignty in cyberspace. It can exercise it to only a certain degree, by banning one vendor or a limited group of vendors seen as potential security threats, for example, so as to minimize security concerns while remaining part of the modern tech-dependent society. This inherent characteristic of interdependence sovereignty in cyberspace, however, does not undermine its relevance compared with the other three sovereignty types examined in the book.

When examining interdependence sovereignty in terms of the variables of authority and control, the United States and its protective approach toward Huawei's presence in its critical infrastructure demonstrates that, although control is present, authority plays the superior role. For the United States to maintain its position as a tech superpower, it must develop a strong and powerful critical infrastructure, which depends on 5G technologies. These systems need to be as secure as possible, which means that the state must have trust in its supply chain. That is the moment when authority becomes relevant, by defining the conditions under which the infrastructure can be built. This is embodied in the administrative and legislative actions of the US government in regulating the transborder movement of goods, targeting

Huawei's business in both the domestic and the international markets. The variable of control is thus a motivational tool for enhancing the variable of authority. Authority would not be so strongly enforced if control were not perceived as important. In other words, the variable of control justifies the need for the activities under the variable of authority. Therefore, control is indeed present, but authority prevails over it in the case of interdependence sovereignty and the United States.

SEVEN
Implications for State Sovereignty

State sovereignty has existed for centuries as a concept, and this book illustrates its relevance even in today's globalized world. The understanding and interpretation of the concept has continually evolved in order to assimilate contemporary political developments and the international environment. Across history, the actions of states in the practice of sovereignty have always determined the course of the concept's development. The flexibility of state sovereignty has given it utility across different ideologies, political systems, and styles of governance. Cyberspace, the latest challenge to its existence, is no exception. States are not willing to give up their sovereignty in the cyber domain, and we must examine their practice of sovereignty in cyberspace. Cyberspace is a domain created by humans that has characteristics distinctly different from the tangible physical domains of land, sea, air, and space in which sovereignty has traditionally been applied. Hence, the question arises of whether and how cyberspace changes our understanding of state sovereignty. The scant research done so far has not examined how democratic states exercise their sovereignty in cyberspace in an in-depth and complex manner and, more importantly, what impact this state practice has on our traditional perception of the concept of state sovereignty. I contribute to filling in that gap in this book.

Theoretical Implications for State Sovereignty

The first overall conclusion that I draw from the case studies is that authority and control are strongly present in cyberspace and that their distribution in this unique environment indeed differs substantially from the one described by Stephen Krasner in the noncyber domains. I discuss the variables' distribution according to Krasner and lay out their binary distribution in table 1.1. The case studies of sovereignty in cyberspace that I present reveal the need for an approach in the cyber domain different from the binary distribution. The peculiar nature of the space often requires a combination of the two variables, although their employment is not always equal. I suggest a distribution of variables that better describes the minor and major influences of authority and control in each sovereignty type. My more nuanced matrix better visualizes the fragile balance of authority and control in cyberspace.

The matrix assigns the value 0, 1, or 2 to each variable within a sovereignty type, representing the relevance of the variable in question. Hence, a value of 0 indicates that the variable is absent or that it does not play a decisive role. In practice, it means that either a legal framework or cyber capabilities are irrelevant for the state to reach its desired goal. A value of 1 indicates that the variable is present but not dominant in relation to the other variable. In other words, a government uses either its existing cyber capabilities or a legal framework to reach its goal, but the variable's role is not decisive over the other variable's role. A value of 2 signifies that one variable predominates, and the other is either absent or present but not decisive. In such instances, the exercise of state sovereignty depends on either a legal framework or cyber capabilities to reach the desired goal.

Table 7.1 applies the matrix to the relations between authority and control in the case-studies of sovereignty types in cyberspace in the book. Westphalian sovereignty balances authority and control, with both a legal framework and cyber capabilities playing crucial roles. International legal sovereignty predominantly depends on authority, and control is insignificant

TABLE 7.1. Distribution of authority and control in cyberspace

Sovereignty type	Authority	Control
Westphalian	1	1
International legal	2	0
Domestic	1	2
Interdependence	2	1

Source: The author, inspired by the typology of state sovereignty by Stephen Krasner.

for the ultimate goal of the government. In domestic and interdependence sovereignty, both variables are present, but one endorses the other, dominant one. In domestic sovereignty, authority seconds the predominant control variable. In interdependence sovereignty, control motivates the government to promote the dominant variable of authority to achieve its aims.

Comparing the distribution in table 7.1 to the distribution of authority and control described by Stephen Krasner (table 1.1), I make two major observations. First, the distribution of authority and control inside and outside cyberspace is much different in each type, except for international legal sovereignty. In this sovereignty type, authority (i.e., international law) is always a determinant, and control plays a minor role in both distributions. According to Krasner, Westphalian sovereignty depends on authority; however, Estonia and its data embassies prove that control—that is, cyber capabilities—is equally important for securing this sovereignty type in cyberspace. Moving to domestic sovereignty, Krasner claims authority and control to be equally significant. The Turkish approach to internet restrictions confirms that both variables are present in cyberspace, but control prevails over authority, especially in the final years of the examined period. Interdependence sovereignty reveals probably the most significant difference between the two distributions. Krasner claims the type depends on control, but the US approach to Huawei shows that, although both variables are present, authority significantly dominates, being motivated by control, which is represented by critical infrastructure. Thus, the distribution of authority and control in cyberspace widely differs from that outside the cyber domain, and it is necessary to approach it in a much more nuanced manner.

Second, I observe the overall presence of the variables across the four types of sovereignty. According to Krasner, two types (domestic sovereignty and interdependence sovereignty) are determined by control. In cyberspace, control (represented by cyber capabilities) contributes to fulfilling the government's goal to a certain degree in all types, except for international legal sovereignty. Even more striking, however, is the presence of authority. Krasner claims that authority is important for all the sovereignty types, aside from interdependence sovereignty. The four case studies, however, prove that authority is present and contributes to the governments' ultimate goals in all four sovereignty types. Overall, authority seems to play a slightly more crucial role than control in cyberspace. This conclusion must be interpreted with caution, because it is derived from four case studies of democratic governments, based on the rule of law. The will of the people, expressed through democratic elections, gives these governments the legitimacy to act, and consequently their behavior in cyberspace must be supported and within the limits of the law, so that they can maintain the trust of their citizens. The reality of and reliance on authority in cyberspace in nondemocratic regimes is highly probable to be diametrically different.

This analysis of the variables' distribution among the sovereignty types in cyberspace and their comparison to Krasner's interpretation leads to answers to the research questions. The first working question relates to the practice of authority and control: *In what way is the exercise of authority and control by states in cyberspace different from the traditional domains?* As the preceding detailed analysis of the different distributions of authority and control in cyberspace compared with the noncyber environment make apparent, the methods (defined through the practice of authority and control) by which state sovereignty is exercised by democratic governments in cyberspace are different from those used in the traditional domains. Governments in cyberspace must work carefully with the legal frameworks and cyber capabilities available to them and in most cases rely not on one but rather balance both. This is most likely due to the different characteristic features of cyberspace; it is a man-made domain with blurred borders and a heavy information potential that is crucial for any digital society, and it stands in contrast to the tangible physical natural domains of the air, sea, and land on which state sovereignty has traditionally been built.

The methods of sovereignty exercised in cyberspace directly relate to the tools that governments use in the second working question: *What kinds of tools do states employ to exercise their sovereignty in cyberspace?* I operationalize authority and control through legal frameworks and cyber capabilities, respectively, which facilitates the definition and exploration of the two main types of tools (legal and technical) that states use to achieve their sovereignty goals. In terms of legal tools, governments have both domestic and international law at their disposal. Westphalian and international legal sovereignty show a heavy dependency on international law. Estonia could not have established its data embassy in Luxembourg without a specific dedicated bilateral agreement with the grand duchy, because the existing international law on diplomatic relations was insufficient to meet the particular characteristics of cyberspace. The Netherlands relied on multilateral negotiations related to international law to enhance its international legal sovereignty. Turkey, in contrast, worked solely with internal regulations and its domestic legal framework to reach the full potential of its domestic sovereignty. Interdependence sovereignty turned out to be the most complex type in terms of the use of legal tools. The US administration not only enforced domestic legislation, with an ultimately transborder impact, but also used its influence in international negotiations to persuade other nation-states to support its cause. Hence, governments reach their sovereignty goals using legal tools on both the domestic and the international levels, and the latter is enforced through both international multilateral negotiations and bilateral agreements.

The technical tools used by governments prove to be more miscellaneous than the legal ones. They encompass a full range of cyber capabilities available in cyberspace, from (critical) infrastructure itself, including an internet backbone or the newly arriving 5G, to modern technologies such as blockchain and data centers with their security standards. What is intriguing beyond such variability is that all these cyber capabilities do not need to be owned solely by the state to enforce a particular sovereignty type. Estonia relies on its state-owned infrastructure, but it needs a data center with the highest security standard and owned by a foreign government. Similarly, Turkey and the United States work with infrastructure partially owned by the government itself and partially by the private sector. The Dutch case is also noteworthy here; although the digital gateway (including cyber capabilities) is owned by mainly nonstate actors and serves to motivate the government, it does not have a direct impact on the enforcement of international legal sovereignty as such. Therefore, the technical tools not only cover the whole spectrum of technologies available in cyberspace but, even more importantly, do not necessarily need to be owned by a government.

The differences in the exercise of authority and control inside and outside cyberspace and the analysis of the legal and technical tools resonate with my principal research question: *How does state practice of sovereignty in cyberspace change the traditional understanding of the concept?* The analysis of the four case studies confirms that the classical concept of state sovereignty does indeed exist in cyberspace, but we must accept certain modifications in our understanding of it for it to fit the cyber domain. The behavior of states in the four case studies suggests that governments are slowly realizing this and testing the limits of sovereignty in this new and challenging environment. Cyberspace does not possess the same characteristics as the other natural domains (sea, air, land, and space), in which the concept of state sovereignty has its origins, and hence the international community must take a more adaptive approach.

I have revealed here two concrete modifications of how the state practice of sovereignty in cyberspace changes the traditional understanding of the concept. First, authority and control are much more interconnected in cyberspace, as shown in three of the four case studies. The two factors strongly depend on each other and often influence each other in cyberspace, a reality not that strongly obvious in the four natural domains. Therefore, when considering any of the sovereignty types in cyberspace, a more comprehensive approach is called for to cover both authority and control and their potential dependencies and interactions. Second, much more flexible, open-minded, and creative thinking about sovereignty is required in cyberspace compared with the traditional four domains. The state practices in the four empirical chapters confirm that governments cannot rely solely on their own resources but must also cooperate with nonstate actors; this phenomenon is especially apparent with respect to cyber capabilities. Governments must be creative in the legal frameworks they use, because current laws and norms might not sufficiently cover the new realities of the modern technology-dependent landscape. After all, the constructed domain of cyberspace is far from static, as demonstrated by its rapid and continuous evolution. Hence, states must be ready for all the current and future developments. If governments want to retain their sovereignty in cyberspace, they must have a creative and flexible understanding of the concept. Although this contrasts with the more stable traditional four domains, where states have more time to consider and develop their behavior, it seems that they are realizing the need for flexibility in cyberspace.

The findings in this book have important implications also for the wider debate about sovereignty. States are clearly not willing to give up their sovereignty in cyberspace and are ready to defend their legitimacy and powers despite the unpredictable character of the cyber domain. At this moment in time, we have entered a crucial phase in which the concept of sovereignty is being established in cyberspace but has yet to gain a concrete universal shape recognized by consensus and globally exercised by states. The future will reveal if this is even possible. One thing, however, is certain: even in the new domain of cyberspace, sovereignty remains a living concept that can adapt to any political regime in any environment at any point of the modern era.

Practical Implications for State Sovereignty

The theory of state sovereignty and how cyberspace has transformed our perception of it on the basis of states' practices is at the core of this book. Yet, throughout the book, practical implications for the state practice of sovereignty have come up many times. Each empirical chapter represents one of four long-term trends in states' approaches to cyberspace. These are the efforts to preserve the confidentiality, integrity, and accessibility of governmental data in the digital era; international negotiations on norms of behavior in cyberspace; the push toward state control of the internet; and protection of national infrastructure. Besides affecting the theory of state sovereignty in cyberspace, this study of pioneering approaches also reveals policy implications that must not be overlooked, especially in the context of the evolving systemic and strategic competition over the future of cyber governance and the fragility of certain policy areas. In the following section, I make a few practical observations that go beyond the research framework and the theory of state sovereignty.

The globally recognized need to preserve the confidentiality, integrity, and accessibility of governmental data in cyberspace stems from a simple fact: every modern society inevitably moves its life into the cyber realm as part of its evolution. This move brings all the benefits of a digital society but also risks and threats to the digital continuity of a state. Estonia, a relatively small country with a Soviet heritage and long borders with its Russian neighbor, is well aware of perils to its highly digitalized society and the importance of maintaining its digital continuity under any security circumstances. Consequently, Tallinn is an innovator in technologies and cybersecurity and explores creative solutions; its data embassy is a shining example.

The Estonian data embassy is an unprecedented project. It uses existing resources but with an innovative twist. We can draw valuable lessons from this concept that was born of necessity. First, the bilateral treaty between Estonia and Luxembourg shows us that when we talk about innovations in cyberspace, we do not necessarily mean only technological innovations. Both sides of the deal identified and formulated their needs and conditions, which did not necessarily fit the existing international legal framework. After all, "data embassy" is more of a PR term, and it does not come under the umbrella of the Vienna Conventions on Diplomatic Relations and Consular Relations. Therefore, the two open-minded governments crafted a bilateral treaty that would accommodate their needs while creating an innovative tool that helps Estonia strengthen its Westphalian sovereignty in cyberspace. Estonia and Luxembourg show us that when thinking about innovations, we need to look beyond the horizon of technologies and consider other aspects such as international law and international relations.

Second, the Estonian case study demonstrates how important it is for any digitally mature state to think about how to secure its digital continuity with a ready, effective, and secure contingency plan in place for times of crisis. Estonia considered multiple solutions, including storing governmental data with private companies, and chose data embassies as the most suitable solution to meet its needs and secure its digital continuity. Expeditiously establishing systems for digital continuity is particularly relevant for digitalized states in unstable parts of the world. An example of a state that had to deal with its digital continuity contingency plans at the last minute is Ukraine in February 2022. When the Ukrainian government received intelligence that Russia was about to invade, it quickly prepared and executed contingency plans for the preservation of its critical infrastructure and prevention of governmental data falling into Russian hands. Among other actions, just a week into the invasion, the Ukrainian parliament passed a new law enabling the transfer of governmental data into the cloud. The government then asked cloud companies for help. The Ukrainian government decided to partner with Amazon Web Services to migrate its state systems into the cloud and outside Ukrainian borders. This was done with the help of Snowball, special devices that are secure and damage resistant, even to explosions. The devices upload data, encrypt it, transfer it, and then migrate it into the cloud. Snowball devices have been used across Ukraine since the first days of the invasion. As the minister of digital transformation of Ukraine, Mykhailo Fedorov, said, the migration includes state registries, databases, and other critical IT infrastructure for operating the economy, the tax system, banks, and governmental business.[1] Ukraine thus ensured the preservation of its governmental data and its digital continuity. However, because the government was unprepared for this kind of situation, it had to forgo its usual stringent security standards when it entrusted governmental data at the very last minute to a private company. Revisiting the case of Estonia and its data embassy, it becomes very clear that it is critically important for a state to have its crisis management and contingency planning in cyberspace in place before similar crises occur.

Third, beyond its creativity and innovation, Estonia is highly transparent in terms of the feasibility analysis of the solutions considered for securing its digital continuity. Like-minded governments commonly share know-how; however, Estonian policy goes further and publicly shares knowledge and experience with building a digital society with other countries, perhaps even unprecedentedly. The publicly run debate on the feasibility of the data embassy initiative is an example. In fact, Estonia has built its national brand around this transparency, coining the term "e-Estonia." The website https://e-estonia.com relates the story of how the state became cyber resilient and paperless and promotes the skills and services of Estonia's businesses and citizens, so building the brand abroad. The e-Estonia Briefing Center, a showroom of e-Estonia, advertises its services as follows: "We inspire global policy makers, political leaders, corporate executives, investors, and international media with the success story of e-Estonia, guide them on the digitalisation paths and build links to leading IT-service providers."[2] This transparency helps build the Estonian reputation as one of the most digitally mature states in the world and significantly raises its profile in the eyes of allies and other nations.

Finally, the Estonian data embassy being located on Luxembourgian territory teaches us that boosting one's sovereignty does not necessarily mean another's sovereignty is endangered or weakened. Luxembourg allows Estonia to operate with limited immunity in its data centers (and therefore on its territory). By carefully crafting the conditions of the deal, Luxembourg has preserved its own sovereignty. Hence, Estonian Westphalian sovereignty was not enforced at Luxembourgian expense.

Turning our attention to the international negotiations on norms of behavior in cyberspace, the vast majority of states today recognize that it is in their best interests to have a seat at the negotiating table. States do not need to seek international legal sovereignty in cyberspace because it extends from the physical world, and they enter the cyber domain as already-recognized actors. Nevertheless, they can then choose to either be passive observers that accept that the norms of behavior in cyberspace will be negotiated without their engagement or, as most governments do today, join the negotiating table to try to shape the norms in their best interests. When governments do join the negotiations, their negotiation position will reflect the state's politics outside cyberspace.

The Dutch efforts toward international negotiations show that the territorial or population size of a country does not much matter in cyberspace; even small states can have a big influence and become a leader in the cyber community. What really matters in international negotiations is a government's reputation and acceptance by others. To have a strong impact, a government needs to secure recognition as broadly as possible and diversify its activities on the topic; this is because different negotiating tables attract different stakeholders. Broad recognition and diverse activities are even more crucial today as the global balance of power shifts southward and toward emerging economies. The true art of norm shaping is to bring to the table states and nonstate actors covering the spectrum of interests and opinions and to run sustainable multistakeholder negotiations. The nonstate actors should include academia, the private sector, and civil society because they play highly important roles, whether because of their know-how or ownership of key infrastructure. The private sector and civil society, however, might be unwanted negotiating partners for some. For example, countries that promote greater control of online content will not want to sit at the same table as civil rights defenders. Similarly, others might dislike powerful private Western tech companies such as Google and Microsoft, which have considerable negotiating leverage, being involved.[3] When confronted with such cases, the leader of the initiative might find it a good idea to start with discussions on the basic, less controversial topics and build on that. After all, the logic behind this approach is very simple: the bigger and more diverse the group of participants at the negotiating table, the stronger the final agreed norm is.

Concurrent with and complementary to negotiations on the international stage are efforts of states to unilaterally formulate their positions on the applicability of international law. The majority of negotiations on the rules of international law applicable in cyberspace have taken place in past years at the multilateral level within the UN—for example, in its Group of Governmental Experts and Open-Ended Working Group. Initially successful, these initiatives have lately yielded limited results that lack major impact. Nonetheless, it remains of utmost importance for states to meet at these platforms to continue the debate and exchange opinions. At the same time, it is also important for governments to unilaterally formulate and publish their own views on the application of international law in cyberspace. This has been a trend only since the late 2010s, but there is an urgent need for it to continue; by publishing statements explaining how governments understand the application of international law in the context of cyberspace (including state sovereignty), state practice and *opinio juris* are formulated, which brings us a step closer to clarifying the application of international law in cyberspace and creating customary international law in the domain. Combining the multistakeholder negotiations with such unilateral actions is thus the most effective way to obtain a more stable cyberspace governed by the rules of international law.

In the lessons learned from the Dutch chapter, cyber diplomacy proved to be an efficient way to facilitate negotiations on cyberspace matters at the international level. The time when such topics could be handled purely by career diplomats with a broad spectrum of agendas is long gone. Nowadays, there is an urgent need to establish specialized cyber diplomacy departments in ministries of foreign affairs and to deploy diplomats with particular knowledge of cyberspace to the destinations most relevant to a government's interests. The emergence of cyber diplomacy shows that there is certainly no need to deploy a cyber attaché to every region or even continent; rather it is up to the state to decide what its national priorities in cyberspace are—security, business development, or representation in international organizations—and on that basis deploy its cyber diplomats to Silicon Valley, NATO, the EU in Brussels, or the most allied and cyber strategic countries. This practice yields countless benefits, including building trust and information-sharing channels, exchanging precious know-how, and constructing new business opportunities, which makes it an efficient tool for promoting national interests during international negotiations, as in the case of the Netherlands.

Nevertheless, not all the state practices discussed in the empirical chapters have positive practical implications—for example, Turkey's push toward strict state control of the internet. The behavior of the Turkish government should serve as a warning of the fragility of democratic values and how states slipping from democratic values to semiauthoritarian rule in the physical world can easily and quickly enforce these tendencies in cyberspace.

Every modern state, including democracies, that moves its life online will ultimately need to regulate and restrict the internet at some point. The overarching motivation is the protection of a state's citizens, especially the vulnerable ones, from harmful activities such as extremism, disinformation, hate speech, and terrorism. After all, protection of its people is one of the primary reasons for a state's existence. This behavior is justified up to the point where the system is governed by checks and balances that prevent the government from abusing its powers. However, when a government accumulates enough legislative, judicial, and technical power to block or filter online content, the system of checks and balances can be undermined, leading eventually to the erosion of civil and human rights. This is but a short step from a semiauthoritarian or authoritarian regime. By definition, governments that opt for a state-controlled or state-centric approach to online regulation are usually more inclined toward the accumulation of legislative, judicial, and technical power. In such cases, a government creates a hierarchical system of mutually interconnected bodies that ultimately depend on and are under the strict scrutiny of the government itself, potentially without the necessary checks and balances of power. That can result in a dangerous situation in which the government is able to exploit its powers, justifying such behavior, for example, through national security concerns, as happened in Turkey. To avoid such a state of affairs, it is safer to opt for a multistakeholder system in which other actors play their factual roles in supervising the government and preventing it from potential abuses of power.

The final practical implications that I draw relate to the protection of critical infrastructure and supply chains. For a state to be as sure as possible about the security of its national critical infrastructure, all the components that enter the network need to be manufactured and assembled within its borders in the best-case scenario. In the globalized world of today, it is impossible for any nation, even the United States or China, to contain the whole manufacturing process and the supply chain of any critical industry to its own soil. No single country is self-sufficient in this regard. Hence, the most secure way forward while minimizing the security risks is to develop a network of trustworthy (international) suppliers. The Clean Network is an example in this direction. States that are part of this initiative allow only trusted vendors into their 5G networks; some of the largest telecommunications companies strive to gain the label of being a "Clean Telco."[4]

It is also reasonable to consider a risk-based approach to the supply chain, in which the state identifies the cyber risks and their probability for the most valuable assets and then evaluates their possible impact on the cybersecurity of national critical infrastructure. The assessment gives the state a range of measures for limiting the activity of potentially dangerous supply chain manufacturers, ranging from warnings and restrictions to blacklisting and bans. This approach is a practical and realistic one while also being flexible enough for political maneuvering. Banning a supply chain manufacturer that potentially represents a security threat on the state's territory is, of course, the most serious and consequential decision and one that requires careful consideration of its national security and economic impact. National security is a fundamental factor of state sovereignty, and thus, governments should prioritize it. Yes, politicians might argue that banning a supply chain manufacturer is costly. The private sector might argue the same, having, for instance, already implemented components provided by a banned manufacturer. They would both be absolutely correct; such ban is an economically demanding decision but also not a decision in which financial cost should have a decisive influence. The cost of successful espionage or sabotage by foreign agents can go far beyond mere financial losses.

The last practical implication is the relationship between government and the private sector in the digital era. Governments need to secure their critical infrastructure to the maximum extent, including by opting to use only reliable and trustworthy suppliers. Governments might, however, find that challenging to do in today's world of big tech and national champion companies, which other companies find difficult to compete against and which thereby reduces the number of alternatives for customers. Having just a handful of companies, driven by high global demand and innovation, specialize in crucial products or services, such as semiconductors, adds to the challenge. In such cases, domestic and international outreach campaigns such as those described in the US chapter can have an unprecedented impact on the global supply chain as well as global business in general. The actions of the US government heavily influenced the semiconductor industry, affecting not only its allies' approach to critical infrastructure supply chains but also the private sector and its thinking about the role of geopolitics in business.

A possible solution has two elements: first, place more emphasis on diversification of supply chain vendors and, second, support companies that might be alternative suppliers, especially when the number of companies in the world capable of providing specialized products or services is limited. In the first element, by finding suppliers from a variety of different countries and continents, and outside the umbrella of the biggest technology corporations, governments reduce reliance on the narrow bottleneck of just a few private companies and are less affected if any of these suppliers become a possible security threat. Furthermore, if governments have more alternatives from which to choose, they gain more maneuvering space in domestic negotiations on construction of critical infrastructure and its subsequent political and economic impact. In the second element, the market simply might not offer many alternative suppliers. States need to take a long-term perspective and think strategically about how to create a more favorable situation through investments designed to support the diversification of market options. For example, governments might consider politically or economically supporting the growth of relevant companies in their own country if possible.

Alternatively, they can support investments of foreign companies from allied countries in their domestic markets and create favorable conditions for the companies to build manufacturing plants on their territory. Ultimately, both of these steps would decrease a state's vulnerability in terms of supply chain security, thereby supporting the government's strategic autonomy.

Finally, what we learned in the US chapter (but was present to some extent also in the other cases) is the importance of cherishing close cooperation between the government and the private sector in a public-private partnership in cyberspace. The state is not the only actor on the domestic stage or in international affairs in cyberspace; it needs to work hand in hand with the private sector. Governments can opt to cultivate close ties with private companies—for example, when they work together on solutions that benefit the state's business and functioning, as in Estonia. Or to avoid being accused of bias, governments might choose to behave neutrally toward the private sector, taking the role of a disinterested actor with whom it is hard to establish a closer connection for private companies. Luckily, states seem to realize that if they do not quickly partner up with private sector forces, they will lag in the international community, and so they are abandoning the neutral approach in favor of closer cooperation with the private sector and showing more trust in public-private partnerships.

Limitations and Avenues for Future Research

The analysis I present in this book has limitations, and the findings should not be understood as fully universal. First, I centered the research solely on democratic states in the transatlantic area that I consider pioneers of their respective sovereignty types in cyberspace and representing the outer limits of sovereignty in cyberspace as it is understood today. This helps us discern the direction that sovereignty in cyberspace is heading and how it is transforming. However, it does not necessarily mean that all other states behave in the same way or even desire to exercise a particular type of sovereignty so strongly that they reach the limits that I have described in the book.

Second, the case studies are all democracies (bearing in mind potential objections to including Turkey). Democratic governments in the transatlantic area arguably have very similar or identical perceptions of numerous cybersecurity issues owing to their comparative political, economic, social, and cultural alignment and through having membership in the same international organizations. I intentionally omit how sovereignty is exercised by authoritarian regimes. Authoritarian states have a different source of sovereignty: although they may claim that their legitimacy comes from the will of the people, the election of their governments is not necessarily free or democratic. Hence, their sovereignty limits are set differently, more intrusively, which can affect the application of their sovereignty in cyberspace and in turn would have distorted the outcome of the analysis.

Third, each case study focuses on one type of state sovereignty, ignoring that states usually implement multiple sovereignty types at once. Similar to their actions in the traditional domains, states usually cultivate several sovereignty types at the same time depending on their needs and interests. If the situation requires it, governments can direct their attention and efforts to developing one sovereignty type; this does not necessarily come at the expense of the other types. They can exist alongside each other and can influence each other too. For example, to build a data embassy abroad and so boost its Westphalian sovereignty in cyberspace, Estonia negotiated and signed an unprecedented treaty with Luxembourg; in doing so, Estonia also contributed to its international legal sovereignty because it set an important precedent for other states to follow in terms of international law in cyberspace. The principality of Monaco was the first state to follow this example.

Finally, I limited the research by time and types of technologies. I investigated how states have dealt with the arrival of modern technologies in the 2010s and early 2020s, during which they realized the potential of cyberspace and started to fully exploit that potential. Because new and more powerful technologies are continually being invented, however, states will need to deal with them continuously as they arise for the foreseeable future. For instance, it is only a matter of time until artificial intelligence, the metaverse, and quantum computing will become an integral part of the everyday agenda. This rapidly changing landscape is going to bring new challenges for states and their sovereignty.

Although these research limitations have an impact on the universality of the presented findings, they could be overcome by further research, possibly confirming the presented findings; broadening their applicability beyond the time frame, technology, and geographic limitations; and exploring new aspects of state sovereignty in cyberspace. I believe that future research can help governments further explore the concept of sovereignty in cyberspace and find new ways to react to technological innovations while adhering to democratic values.

Future research could explore how other democracies, outside the transatlantic area with a slightly different perception of cybersecurity issues, as well as those not aiming to stretch sovereignty to its limits, understand and approach the execution of their sovereignty in cyberspace. Are there any differences? If so, what are the reasons for them?

Another area for future research is the behavior of states with a state-centric approach to sovereignty in cyberspace. Turkey went from democratic to semidemocratic rule in the time frame. It has chosen a state-centric approach to its domestic sovereignty in cyberspace, and it remains a question whether states that have, in contrast, opted for a multistakeholder approach could also reach similar boundaries of their sovereignty in cyberspace or whether it is the approach that limits them. Similarly, it would be beneficial to study more examples of democracies with a state-centric approach to sovereignty in cyberspace to understand whether and how it influences their practice of democratic values.

Each case study was the most illustrative example I could find of the application of each sovereignty type in cyberspace. I intentionally focused on only one type of state sovereignty per case study, omitting the other types that might be cultivated by the respective governments, to better elucidate the observed phenomena. In reality, however, it is typical for governments to harness multiple types of sovereignty in cyberspace, as in the traditional domains, depending on factors such as their domestic and international political situation, economic interests, regional security, and stability. Future studies could explore the interactions between different sovereignty types exercised by a government. What is the dynamic among the four sovereignty types in cyberspace? How do they influence each other in the domain? Is any sovereignty type preferred in cyberspace over the others? If so, why?

Future research could explore the fundamental differences between the approach toward sovereignty in cyberspace of democratic and nondemocratic regimes and how this influences international negotiations. This would be particularly interesting to observe in global forums like the first World Conference on International Telecommunications, which took place in December 2012 in Dubai and during which states reviewed and revised the International Telecommunication Regulations.[5] In these international arenas states with different political regimes and distinct approaches to sovereignty in cyberspace encounter each other, negotiate, and attempt to achieve agreement. This type of interaction might be fertile ground for further revelations in the study of sovereignty in cyberspace.

Above all, there is the question of a state's ability to obtain the necessary cyber capabilities, and hence the control, to exercise a particular sovereignty type in cyberspace. I assumed in advance that the case studies in question had already developed the required cyber capabilities. This is not always the case, however, especially with regard to underdeveloped countries with fewer disposable resources. Some governments cannot invest enough into their cyber capabilities; consequently, their ability to exercise control, and by extension any particular type of sovereignty in cyberspace, is limited. Future research could explore how states that desire to exercise a particular sovereignty type in cyberspace but do not possess the necessary resources to obtain enough control to do so deal with such problems.

Finally, given that cyberspace is an ever-changing domain, future research should explore how the arrival of new technologies, such as the metaverse, artificial intelligence, quantum computing, and those as yet unknown, will influence the concept of state sovereignty in cyberspace. I am confident that regardless of the challenges brought about by tech inventions, states will persist in their desire to enforce their sovereignty in cyberspace in the future.

Conclusion

States do desire and will desire to retain their sovereignty in cyberspace and are willing to adjust their behavior inside and outside cyberspace accordingly to fit the characteristics of the domain. Cyberspace mirrors developments in the physical world as we move our lives online. Whatever happens outside cyberspace will most likely also be projected into cyberspace, be it related to politics, business, diplomacy, or one's personal life. This logic also works in reverse: actions in cyberspace often influence events in the physical world. Cyberspace has become an inseparable part of governments' agendas, and governments must follow the trends to keep up with the fast developments and innovations in the domain to retain their sovereignty in cyberspace.

Notes

Introduction

1. John Perry Barlow, "A Declaration of the Independence of Cyberspace," Electronic Frontier Foundation, February 8, 1996, https://www.eff.org/cyberspace-independence.

2. Ronald J. Deibert, Rafal Rohozinski, and Masashi Crete-Nishihata, "Cyclones in Cyberspace: Information Shaping and Denial in the 2008 Russia-Georgia War," *Security Dialogue* 43, no. 3 (2012): 5–6.

3. Hedley Bull, *The Anarchical Society* (New York: Palgrave, 1977).

4. Stephen Krasner, *Sovereignty: Organized Hypocrisy* (Princeton, NJ: Princeton University Press, 1999), 3–4.

5. Krasner, *Sovereignty*, 10.

Chapter One

1. Jean Bodin, *Six Books of the Commonwealth* (Lexington, KY: Seven Treasures, 2009); Thomas Hobbes, *Leviathan* (Oxford: Oxford University Press, 2014); John Locke, *Two Treatises of Government* (New Haven, CT: Yale University Press, 2003); Jean-Jacques Rousseau, *The Social Contract and Discourses* (London: Dant, 1988).

2. K. J. Holsti, *International Politics: A Framework for Analysis* (Englewood Cliffs, NJ: Prentice Hall, 1988), 80–81.

3. Robert Jackson, *Sovereignty: The Evolution of an Idea* (Cambridge, UK: Polity Press, 2007), 35.

4. Andreas Osiander, "Sovereignty, International Relations, and the Westphalian Myth," *International Organization* 55, no. 2 (2001): 251–287.

5. Leo Gross, "The Peace of Westphalia," *American Journal of International Law* 42, no. 1 (January 1948): 22–29.

6. Gross, 28–29.

7. Jackson, *Sovereignty*, 56–58; and see Edgar Grande and Louis W. Pauly, eds., *Complex Sovereignty: Reconstituting Political Authority in the Twenty-first Century* (Toronto: University of Toronto Press, 2005), 12.

8. Bodin, *Six Books of the Commonwealth*.

9. Jackson, *Sovereignty*, 62.

10. Hobbes, *Leviathan*.

11. Jackson, *Sovereignty*, 77.

12. Jackson, 74–75.

13. Jackson, 78.

14. Declaration of Independence, US Congress, July 4, 1776.

15. Locke, *Two Treatises of Government*.

16. Rousseau, *The Social Contract and Discourses*.

17. Immanuel Kant, *Toward Perpetual Peace and Other Writings on Politics, Peace, and History* (New Haven, CT: Yale University Press, 2006).

18. Jackson, *Sovereignty*, 82–86.

19. Max Weber, "Politics as a Vocation," in *Max Weber: Essays in Sociology*, ed. Hans Heinrich Gerth and Charles Wright Mills (New York: Oxford University Press, 1946), 78.

20. Weber, 78.

21. Weber, 77–78.

22. Markus Virgil Hoehne, "Somaliland: 30 Years of De Facto Statehood, and No End in Sight," Italian Institute for International Political Studies, May 7, 2021, https://www.ispionline.it/en/publication/somaliland-30-years-de-facto-statehood-and-no-end-sight-30363.

23. Barry Bartmann, "Between *De Jure* and *De Facto* Statehood: Revisiting the Status Issue for Taiwan," *Island Studies Journal* 3, no. 1 (2008): 113–128; Lev Nachman and Brian Hioe, "No, Taiwan's President Isn't 'Pro-Independence,'" *Diplomat*, April 23, 2020, https://thediplomat.com/2020/04/no-taiwans-president-isnt-pro-independence/.

24. Jackson, *Sovereignty*.

25. Grande and Pauly, *Complex Sovereignty*, 12.

26. Joseph A. Camilleri and Jim Falk, *The End of Sovereignty? The Politics of a Shrinking and Fragmenting World* (Hants, UK: Edward Elgar, 1992); Susan Strange, *The Retreat of the State: The Diffusion of Power in the World Economy* (Cambridge:

Cambridge University Press, 1996); Richard Rosecrance, *The Rise of the Virtual State: Wealth and Power in the Coming Century* (New York: Basic Books, 1999).

27. Camilleri and Falk, *The End of Sovereignty?*, 3.

28. Strange, *The Retreat of the State*, 4.

29. Strange, 7–8.

30. Rosecrance, *The Rise of the Virtual State*.

31. Rosecrance, 4–23.

32. Jackson, *Sovereignty*.

33. Daniel Philpott, *Revolutions in Sovereignty: How Ideas Shaped Modern International Relations* (Princeton, NJ: Princeton University Press, 2001), 4.

34. Philpott, 31.

35. Grande and Pauly, *Complex Sovereignty*, 4.

36. Grande and Pauly, *Complex Sovereignty*.

37. Grande and Pauly, 5–6.

38. Rodney Bruce Hall and Thomas J. Biersteker, eds., *The Emergence of Private Authority in Global Governance* (Cambridge: Cambridge University Press, 2002), 5.

39. Hall and Biersteker, 203.

40. Jean L. Cohen, *Globalization and Sovereignty: Rethinking Legality, Legitimacy and Constitutionalism* (Cambridge: Cambridge University Press, 2012), 4.

41. Jackson, *Sovereignty*, 141–142.

42. Jackson, 143.

43. John Agnew, *Globalization and Sovereignty* (Lanham, MD: Rowman & Littlefield, 2009), 8–9.

44. Agnew, 30.

45. Deibert, Rohozinski, and Crete-Nishihata, "Cyclones in Cyberspace," 5–6.

46. Geoffrey L. Herrera, "Cyberspace and Sovereignty: Thoughts on Physical Space and Digital Space," paper presented at the 1st International CISS/ETH Conference on the Information Revolution and the Changing Face of International Relations and Security, Lucerne, Switzerland, May 2005, p. 5.

47. Herrera, 10.

48. Herrera, 23.

49. Herrera, 30.

50. Forrest Hare, "Borders in Cyberspace: Can Sovereignty Adapt to the Challenges of Cybersecurity?," in *The Virtual Battlefield: Perspectives on Cyber Warfare*, ed. Christian Czosseck and Kenneth Geers (Amsterdam: IOS Press, 2009), 89–106.

51. Hare, 96–97.

52. Hare, 103.

53. Chris C. Demchak and Peter Dombrowski, "Rise of a Cybered Westphalian Age," *Strategic Studies Quarterly* 5, no. 1 (Spring 2011): 32–61.

54. Demchak and Dombrowski, 35.

55. The Stuxnet computer worm, uncovered in 2010, is supposedly responsible for significant damage to Iranian nuclear centrifuges, which substantially delayed Tehran's nuclear program. Although its creator is officially unknown, it is believed to be a joint effort by the United States and Israel.

56. Demchak and Dombrowski, "Rise of a Cybered Westphalian Age," 40.

57. Chris C. Demchak and Peter Dombrowski, "Cyber Westphalia: Asserting State Prerogatives in Cyberspace," *Georgetown Journal of International Affairs*, no. 20 (2014): 30.

58. Demchak and Dombrowski, 30.

59. Demchak and Dombrowski, 36–37.

60. Benedikt Pirker, "Territorial Sovereignty and Integrity and the Challenges of Cyberspace," in *Peacetime Regime for State Activities in Cyberspace*, ed. Katharina Ziolkowski (Tallinn: NATO CCDCoE, 2013).

61. Pirker, 191.

62. Wolff Heintschel von Heinegg, "Legal Implications of Territorial Sovereignty in Cyberspace," in *4th International Conference on Cyber Conflict*, ed. Christian Czosseck, Rain Ottis, and Katharina Ziolkowski (Tallinn: NATO CCDCoE, 2012), 8.

63. Heintschel von Heinegg, 19.

64. This UN GGE was later renamed Group of Governmental Experts on Advancing Responsible State Behavior in Cyberspace in the Context of International Security.

65. "Report of the Group of Governmental Experts on Developments in the Field of Information and Telecommunications in the Context of International Security," UN General Assembly, A/68/98, June 24, 2013, para. 20, https://dig.watch/wp-content/uploads/A_68_98_E.pdf.

66. "Report of the Group of Governmental Experts on Developments in the Field of Information and Telecommunications in the Context of International Security," UN General Assembly, A/70/174, July 22, 2015, paras. 27, 28b, https://documents-dds-ny.un.org/doc/UNDOC/GEN/N15/228/35/PDF/N1522835.pdf?OpenElement.

67. "Report of the Group of Governmental Experts on Advancing Responsible State Behavior in Cyberspace in the Context of International Security," UN General Assembly, A/76/135, July 14, 2021, https://dig.watch/wp-content/uploads/2022/08/UN-GGE-Report-2021.pdf.

68. Michael N. Schmitt, ed., *Tallinn Manual on the International Law Applicable to Cyber Warfare* (Cambridge: Cambridge University Press, 2013).

69. Michael N. Schmitt, ed., *Tallinn Manual 2.0 on the International Law Applicable to Cyber Operations* (Cambridge: Cambridge University Press, 2017).

70. Schmitt, *Tallinn Manual on the International Law*, 15.

71. Schmitt, *Tallinn Manual 2.0 on the International Law*, 11.

72. Schmitt, *Tallinn Manual 2.0 on the International Law*, 11–13.

73. Schmitt, *Tallinn Manual 2.0 on the International Law*, 23.

74. Schmitt, *Tallinn Manual 2.0 on the International Law*, 27–29.

75. See, for example, Harriet Moynihan, "The Application of International Law to Cyberattacks: Sovereignty and Non-Intervention," Chatham House, December 2, 2019, https://www.chathamhouse.org/2019/12/application-international-law-state-cyberattacks/2-application-sovereignty-cyberspace; and Andrea Leiter, "Cyber Sovereignty: A Snapshot from a Field in Motion," *Harvard International Law Journal Frontiers* 61 (2020), https://journals.law.harvard.edu/ilj/2020/04/cyber-sovereignty-a-snapshot-from-a-field-in-motion/.

76. See, for example, Luke Chircop, "Territorial Sovereignty in Cyberspace after 'Tallinn Manual 2.0,'" *Melbourne Journal of International Law* 20, no. 2 (December 2019): 349–377; and Fleur Johns, "Data Territories: Changing Architectures of Association in International Law," *Netherlands Yearbook of International Law*, July 20, 2016, https://papers.ssrn.com/sol3/papers.cfm?abstract_id=2810897.

77. See, for example, Yu Hong and Thomas Goodnight, "How to Think about Cyber Sovereignty: The Case of China," *Chinese Journal of Communication* 13, no. 1 (2020): 8–26; and Andrei Soldatov and Irina Borogan, "The New Iron Curtain Part 4: Russia's Sovereign Internet Takes Root," CEPA, April 5, 2022, https://cepa.org/article/the-new-iron-curtain-part-4-russias-sovereign-internet-takes-root/. Russia, and to some extent China, focuses on information security rather than cybersecurity, which aids in understanding their security posture in cyberspace. For more details, see, for example, Lora Saalman, Fei Su, and Larisa Saveleva Dovgal, "Cyber Posture Trends in China, Russia, the United States and the European Union," SIPRI, Stockholm, December 2022, https://www.sipri.org/publications/2022/other-publications/cyber-posture-trends-china-russia-united-states-and-european-union.

78. "Developments in the Field of Information and Telecommunications in the Context of International Security," UN Office for Disarmament Affairs, accessed July 5, 2022, https://www.un.org/disarmament/ict-security/.

79. Florian Kriener, "Cyber Space, Sovereignty and the Intricacies of International Law-Making," Völkerrechtsblog, April 16, 2021, https://voelkerrechtsblog.org/cyber-space-sovereignty-and-the-intricacies-of-international-law-making/.

80. "Cyber Law Toolkit: Sovereignty," NATO CCDCoE, last updated May 2, 2023, https://cyberlaw.ccdcoe.org/wiki/Sovereignty.

81. "Letter to the Parliament on the International Legal Order in Cyberspace," Netherlands Ministry of Foreign Affairs, July 5, 2019, https://www.government.nl/ministries/ministry-of-foreign-affairs/documents/parliamentary-documents/2019/09/26/letter-to-the-parliament-on-the-international-legal-order-in-cyberspace; "Official Compendium of Voluntary National Contributions on the Subject of How International Law Applies to the Use of Information and Communications

Technologies by States," A/76/136, UN Office for Disarmament Affairs, August 2021, https://front.un-arm.org/wp-content/uploads/2021/08/A-76-136-EN.pdf, p. 25; Jeremy Wright, "Cyber and International Law in the 21st Century," speech, May 23, 2018, https://www.gov.uk/government/speeches/cyber-and-international-law-in-the-21st-century.

82. Kriener, "Cyber Space, Sovereignty and the Intricacies of International Law-Making."

83. Patrick W. Franzese, "Sovereignty in Cyberspace: Can It Exist?," *Air Force Law Review* 64 (2009), 6–7.

84. Franzese, 11–14.

85. Franzese, 18.

86. Andrew Liaropoulos, "Exercising State Sovereignty in Cyberspace: An International Cyber-Order under Construction?," in *Proceedings of the 8th International Conference on Information Warfare and Security*, ed. Douglas Hart (Denver, CO: Regis University, 2013).

87. Liaropoulos, "Exercising State Sovereignty in Cyberspace."

88. Stephen Krasner, *Sovereignty: Organized Hypocrisy* (Princeton, NJ: Princeton University Press, 1999), 11–22.

89. Liaropoulos, "Exercising State Sovereignty in Cyberspace," 138–139.

90. Ben Buchanan, "Cryptography and Sovereignty," *Survival* 58, no. 5 (October–November 2016), 105.

91. Buchanan, 111–112.

92. Buchanan, 112–113.

93. Buchanan, 97.

94. David Betz and Tim Stevens, *Cyberspace and the State: Toward a Strategy for Cyber-power* (Abingdon, UK: Routledge, 2011), 55–74.

95. Betz and Stevens, 58.

96. Betz and Stevens, 60–63.

97. Betz and Stevens, 70–72.

98. Betz and Stevens, 64–66.

99. For further reading on authoritarian approaches to sovereignty in cyberspace, specifically Chinese and Russian, see, for example, Binxing Fang, *Cyberspace Sovereignty: Reflections on Building a Community of Common Future in Cyberspace* (Berlin: Springer, 2018); Rogier Creemers, *China's Approach to Cyber Sovereignty* (Berlin: Konrad Adenauer Stiftung, 2020), https://www.kas.de/documents/252038/7995358/China%E2%80%99s+Approach+to+Cyber+Sovereignty.pdf/2c6916a6-164c-fb0c-4e29-f933f472ac3f?version=1.0&t=1606143361537; Hong and Goodnight, "How to Think about Cyber Sovereignty"; Michael Kolton, "Interpreting China's Pursuit of Cyber Sovereignty and Its Views on Cyber Deterrence," *Cyber Defense Review* 2, no. 1 (Winter 2017): 119–154; Carolina Vendil Pallin and Mattias Hjelm, "Moscow's

Digital Offensive: Building Sovereignty in Cyberspace," Swedish Defense Research Agency, 2021, https://www.foi.se/rapportsammanfattning?reportNo=FOI%20Memo%207521; Eva Claessen, "Reshaping the Internet—the Impact of the Securitisation of Internet Infrastructure on Approaches to Internet Governance: The Case of Russia and the EU," *Journal of Cyber Policy* 5, no. 1 (2020): 140–157; and Valentin Weber, "The Sinicization of Russia's Cyber Sovereignty Model," Council on Foreign Relations, April 1, 2020, https://www.cfr.org/blog/sinicization-russias-cyber-sovereignty-model.

100. Stephen Krasner, "Think Again: Sovereignty," *Foreign Policy*, November 20, 2009, https://foreignpolicy.com/2009/11/20/think-again-sovereignty/.

101. Krasner, "Think Again."

102. Krasner, "Think Again."

103. Krasner, *Sovereignty: Organized Hypocrisy*, 3–4.

104. Krasner, 20.

105. Krasner, 20.

106. Krasner, 22.

107. Krasner, 14.

108. Krasner, 16–17.

109. Krasner, 14–16.

110. Krasner, 11.

111. Krasner, 12.

112. Krasner, 12.

113. Krasner, 12.

114. Krasner, 223.

115. Krasner, 4.

116. Krasner, 10.

117. Krasner, 4, 10.

118. Krasner, 7.

119. Krasner, 24.

120. Krasner, 69.

121. Krasner, 69.

122. Krasner, 71.

Chapter Two

1. Taavi Kotka and Innar Liiv, "Concept of Estonian Government Cloud and Data Embassies," in *Electronic Government and the Information Systems Perspective*, ed. Andrea Kő and Enrico Francesconi (Heidelberg: Springer, 2015), 151.

2. Translations of the title of this law differ. I use the translation by the Venice Commission, Council of Europe. See, for example, Turkey: Opinion on Law No. 5651 on Regulation of Publications on the Internet and Combating Crimes Committed by Means of Such Publication, Venice Commission, 107th Plenary Session,

Venice, June 10–11, 2016, https://www.venice.coe.int/webforms/documents/default.aspx?pdffile=CDL-AD(2016)011-e.

3. Mehmet Bedii Kaya, "The Regulation of Internet Intermediaries under Turkish Law: Is There a Delicate Balance between Rights and Obligations?," *Computer Law and Security Review* 32 (2016): 762.

4. Mike Rogers and Dutch Ruppersberger, "Investigative Report on the US National Security Issues Posed by Chinese Telecommunications Companies Huawei and ZTE," *US House of Representatives*, October 8, 2012, p. 45, http://intelligence.house.gov/sites/intelligence.house.gov/files/documents/Huawei-ZTE%20Investigative%20Report%20(FINAL).pdf.

5. Stephen Krasner, *Sovereignty: Organized Hypocrisy* (Princeton, NJ: Princeton University Press, 1999), 10.

6. Krasner, 10.

Chapter Three

1. Stephen Krasner, *Sovereignty: Organized Hypocrisy* (Princeton, NJ: Princeton University Press, 1999), 20.

2. Government of the Grand Duchy of Luxembourg, "E-Embassies in Luxembourg," Luxembourg: Let's Make It Happen, last updated October 1, 2021, https://luxembourg.public.lu/en/invest/innovation/e-embassies-in-luxembourg.html.

3. "How Did Estonia Become a Leader in Technology?," *Economist*, July 31, 2013, https://www.economist.com/the-economist-explains/2013/07/30/how-did-estonia-become-a-leader-in-technology?fsrc=scn/fb/te/bl/ed/howdidestoniabecomealeaderintechnology?fsrc=scn/fb/te/bl/ed/howdidestoniabecomealeaderintechnology.

4. "From Submarines to Cyber: Estonia's Innovation Journey," Microsoft Corporate Blogs, November 29, 2017, https://blogs.microsoft.com/eupolicy/2017/11/29/submarines-cyber-estonias-innovation-journey/.

5. "How Did Estonia Become a Leader in Technology?," *Economist*.

6. Vivienne Walt, "Welcome to Tomorrow Land," *Fortune*, May 1, 2017.

7. "Statistics," ID, Information System Authority, accessed November 8, 2019, https://www.id.ee/?lang=en&id=.

8. "E-identity," e-Estonia, accessed November 8, 2019, https://e-estonia.com/solutions/e-identity/id-card.

9. Taavi Kotka, Carlos Ivan Vargas Alvarez del Castillo, and Kaspar Korjus, "Estonian e-Residency: Redefining the Nation-State in the Digital Era," Working Paper Series, No. 3, Cyber Studies Program, University of Oxford, September 2015, p. 4.

10. Walt, "Welcome to Tomorrow Land," 67.

11. "Transforming Digital Continuity: Enhancing IT Resilience through Cloud Computing," Estonian Ministry of Economic Affairs and Communications and

Microsoft, May 2016, p. 11, https://query.prod.cms.rt.microsoft.com/cms/api/am/binary/REVtZY.

12. Joshua Davis, "Hackers Take Down the Most Wired Country in Europe," *Wired*, August 21, 2007, https://www.wired.com/2007/08/ff-estonia/.

13. "Population," Statistics Estonia, updated 2021, https://www.stat.ee/en/find-statistics/statistics-theme/population.

14. "A Cyber-Riot," *Economist*, May 10, 2007, https://www.economist.com/europe/2007/05/10/a-cyber-riot.

15. Damien McGuiness, "How a Cyber Attack Transformed Estonia," *BBC*, April 27, 2017, https://www.bbc.com/news/39655415.

16. "Transforming Digital Continuity," Ministry of Economic Affairs and Communications and Microsoft.

17. "Transforming Digital Continuity," Ministry of Economic Affairs and Communications and Microsoft; and see "Implementation of the Virtual Data Embassy Solution: Summary Report of the Research Project on Public Cloud Usage for Government," Estonian Ministry of Economic Affairs and Communications and Microsoft, 2015, https://www.microsoft.com/en-us/cybersecurity/content-hub/implementation-of-the-virtual-data-embassy-solution.

18. "Implementation of the Virtual Data Embassy Solution," Estonian Ministry of Economic Affairs and Communications and Microsoft, 7.

19. "Implementation of the Virtual Data Embassy Solution," Estonian Ministry of Economic Affairs and Communications and Microsoft, 7.

20. Taavi Kotka and Innar Liiv, "Concept of Estonian Government Cloud and Data Embassies," in *Electronic Government and the Information Systems Perspective*, ed. Andrea Kő and Enrico Francesconi (Switzerland: Springer, 2015), 150.

21. Kotka and Liiv, 151–154.

22. "Implementation of the Virtual Data Embassy Solution," Estonian Ministry of Economic Affairs and Communications and Microsoft, 1.

23. "Implementation of the Virtual Data Embassy Solution," Estonian Ministry of Economic Affairs and Communications and Microsoft, 8.

24. Interview with an employee of the Ministry of Economic Affairs and Communications of Estonia, Tallinn, May 30, 2018.

25. "Estonia to Open the World's First Data Embassy in Luxembourg," e-Estonia, June 14, 2017, https://e-estonia.com/estonia-to-open-the-worlds-first-data-embassy-in-luxembourg/.

26. Interview, May 30, 2018.

27. Kotka and Liiv, "Concept of Estonian Government Cloud and Data Embassies," 157.

28. "Digital Agenda 2020 for Estonia," Ministry of Economic Affairs and Communications, 2014, foreword, https://wp.itl.ee/files/DigitalAgenda2020_Estonia_ENG.pdf.

29. "Digital Agenda 2020 for Estonia," Ministry of Economic Affairs and Communications, Action line 1.

30. "Digital Agenda 2020 for Estonia," Ministry of Economic Affairs and Communications, Action line 1d. I use the term "data embassies"; some sources use "digital embassies."

31. "Implementation of the Virtual Data Embassy Solution," Estonian Ministry of Economic Affairs and Communications and Microsoft, 7–8.

32. Kotka and Liiv, "Concept of Estonian Government Cloud and Data Embassies," 157.

33. "Implementation of the Virtual Data Embassy Solution," Estonian Ministry of Economic Affairs and Communications and Microsoft, 7–8.

34. Kotka and Liiv, "Concept of Estonian Government Cloud and Data Embassies," 157–158.

35. "Estonia to Open the World's First Data Embassy in Luxembourg," e-Estonia.

36. Riigikogu Press Service, "The Riigikogu Approved Establishing of Luxembourg Data Embassy," press release, March 21, 2018, https://www.riigikogu.ee/en/press-releases/plenary-assembly/riigikogu-approved-establishing-luxembourg-data-embassy/.

37. "Implementation of the Virtual Data Embassy Solution," Estonian Ministry of Economic Affairs and Communications and Microsoft, 16.

38. "Implementation of the Virtual Data Embassy Solution," Estonian Ministry of Economic Affairs and Communications and Microsoft, 17.

39. Interview, May 30, 2018.

40. Vienna Convention on Diplomatic Relations, UN, April 18, 1961, https://legal.un.org/ilc/texts/instruments/english/conventions/9_1_1961.pdf.

41. Vienna Convention on Consular Relations, UN, April 24, 1963, https://legal.un.org/ilc/texts/instruments/english/conventions/9_2_1963.pdf.

42. Bartołomiej Sierzputowski, "The Data Embassy under Public International Law," *International and Comparative Law Quarterly* 68 (January 2019): 233–234.

43. Interview with an employee of the Ministry of Foreign Affairs of Estonia, Tallinn, May 28, 2018.

44. Interview with an employee of the Ministry of Foreign and European Affairs of Luxembourg, online, September 2, 2022; interview with an employee of the Government IT Center of Luxembourg, online, September 2, 2022.

45. "Diplomatic Immunity for Data: Estonia Creates a Virtual Embassy," Microsoft Corporate Blogs, December 14, 2017, https://blogs.microsoft.com/eupolicy/2017/12/14/diplomatic-immunity-data-estonia-creates-virtual-embassy/.

46. "Diplomatic Immunity for Data," Microsoft Corporate Blogs.

47. "Diplomatic Immunity for Data," Microsoft Corporate Blogs; Riigikogu Press Service, "The Riigikogu Approved Establishing of Luxembourg Data Embassy."

48. Agreement between the Republic of Estonia and the Grand Duchy of Luxembourg on the Hosting of Data and Information Systems, June 20, 2017, https://www.riigiteataja.ee/aktilisa/2280/3201/8002/Lux_Info_Agreement.pdf.

49. Interview, May 28, 2018.

50. Interview, May 28, 2018.

51. Vienna Convention on Diplomatic Relations, 1961, art. 1(i).

52. Agreement between the Republic of Estonia and the Grand Duchy of Luxembourg, June 20, 2017, arts. 1(a) and 1(b).

53. Vienna Convention on Diplomatic Relations, 1961, art. 22(1).

54. Vienna Convention on Diplomatic Relations, 1961, art. 22(3).

55. Vienna Convention on Diplomatic Relations, 1961, art. 24.

56. Agreement between the Republic of Estonia and the Grand Duchy of Luxembourg, art. 3(1).

57. Agreement between the Republic of Estonia and the Grand Duchy of Luxembourg, art. 6(2).

58. Agreement between the Republic of Estonia and the Grand Duchy of Luxembourg, art. 3(2).

59. Agreement between the Republic of Estonia and the Grand Duchy of Luxembourg, art. 5.

60. Sierzputowski, "The Data Embassy under Public International Law," 237.

61. Sierzputowski, 237.

62. Interview, May 28, 2018.

63. Interview with an employee of the Ministry of Foreign and European Affairs of Luxembourg, online, September 2, 2022.

64. Sierzputowski, "The Data Embassy under Public International Law," 241.

65. Interview, May 30, 2018.

66. "Embracing Innovation in Government: Global Trends 2018," World Government Summit, Organization for Economic Cooperation and Development, 2018, https://www.oecd.org/innovation/innovative-government/innovation2018.htm,p. 44.

67. All this book's sources use "X-Road," but it is also known as "X-tee." "Until 2018, it was named X-Road in English. Since 2018, however, X-Road is only used to refer to the technology developed together by Estonia and Finland through MTÜ Nordic Institute for Interoperability Solutions. The Estonian X-tee is now also called X-tee in English." "Data Exchange Layer X-tee," Information System Authority, Republic of Estonia, accessed May 14, 2022, https://www.ria.ee/en/state-information-system/x-tee.html.

68. "From Submarines to Cyber," Microsoft Corporate Blogs.

69. "Data Exchange Layer X-tee," Information System Authority.

70. "X-Road," E-Estonia, accessed May 14, 2022, https://e-estonia.com/solutions/interoperability-services/x-road/.

71. "Factsheet," X-Tee, accessed May 14, 2022, https://www.x-tee.ee/factsheets/EE/#eng.

72. "Factsheet," X-Tee.

73. "A blockchain is a distributed public record of events; an append-only record of events where each new event is cryptographically linked to the previous. New entries are created using a distributed consensus protocol." "Keyless Signature Infrastructure," Guardtime, accessed May 14, 2022, https://m.guardtime.com/files/KSI_data_sheet_201509.pdf.

74. "KSI Blockchain in Estonia," e-Estonia, accessed May 14, 2022, https://e-estonia.com/wp-content/uploads/2019sept-faq-ksi-blockchain-1-1.pdf.

75. "KSI Blockchain," e-Estonia, accessed May 14, 2022, https://e-estonia.com/solutions/cyber-security/ksi-blockchain/.

76. "KSI Blockchain in Estonia," e-Estonia.

77. "Tier Certification Overview," Uptime Institute, accessed May 13, 2022, https://uptimeinstitute.com/tier-certification.

78. Interview, May 30, 2018; and see Riigikogu Press Service, "The Riigikogu Approved Establishing of Luxembourg Data Embassy."

79. Interview, May 30, 2018.

80. Interview, Ministry of Foreign and European Affairs of Luxembourg, September 2, 2022; Interview, Government IT Center of Luxembourg, September 2, 2022.

81. Jonas Mercier and Jess Bauldry, "2nd Data Embassy for Lux," *Delano*, March 16, 2019, https://delano.lu/d/detail/news/2nd-data-embassy-lux/172985.

82. Complementary Agreement between the State of the Grand Duchy of Luxembourg and the European Patent Organisation concerning the inviolability of the archives of the European Patent Organisation, March 5, 2018, https://treaties.un.org/doc/Publication/UNTS/No%20Volume/55331/Part/I-55331-0800000280518e98.pdf.

83. Mercier and Bauldry, "2nd Data Embassy for Lux."

84. "E-Embassies in Luxembourg," Luxembourg: Let's Make It Happen.

Chapter Four

1. Stephen Krasner, *Sovereignty: Organized Hypocrisy* (Princeton, NJ: Princeton University Press, 1999), 4, 14–16.

2. Krasner, *Sovereignty*, 14.

3. "Digital Gateway to Europe," Digital Gateway to Europe, accessed October 22, 2023, https://www.digitalgateway.eu/.

4. "CWI History: First European Internet Connection," Centrum Wiskunde & Informatica, accessed June 5, 2022, https://www.cwi.nl/about/history/cwi-achievements-details.

5. Bert Koenders, "Tallinn Manual 2.0" (speech, The Hague, February 13, 2017).

6. "Positions: Digital Economy and Gateway," Dutch Data Center Association, accessed June 5, 2022, https://www.dutchdatacenters.nl/en/positions/digital-economy-gateway/.

7. Deloitte Consulting, *Dutch Digital Infrastructure 2016: Enabling the Digital Economy and Society* (Netherlands: Deloitte, November 2016).

8. "Invest in Holland," Digital Gateway to Europe, accessed April 27, 2020, http://www.digitalgateway.eu/invest-in-holland.html.

9. "Internet Peering," Amsterdam Internet Exchange, accessed January 13, 2020, https://www.ams-ix.net/ams/service/internet-peering.

10. "Internet Peering," Amsterdam Internet Exchange.

11. "Submarine Cable Map," TeleGeography, accessed June 3, 2022, https://www.submarinecablemap.com/.

12. "Positions," Dutch Data Center Association.

13. "Europe's Top Location for Data Centers," Invest in Holland, accessed January 13, 2020, https://investinholland.com/business-operations/data-centers/.

14. "Data Centers," Digital Gateway to Europe, accessed June 4, 2022, http://www.digitalgateway.eu/data-centers.html.

15. Deloitte Consulting, *Digital Infrastructure in the Netherlands: Driver for the Online Ecosystem* (Netherlands: Deloitte, November 2014).

16. "Collaborations," Dutch Data Center Association, accessed April 27, 2020, https://www.dutchdatacenters.nl/en/about-us/collaborations/.

17. "Cloud," Digital Gateway to Europe, accessed June 4, 2022, http://www.digitalgateway.eu/cloud.html.

18. "Data Centers: What Is the Economic Impact of Data Centers?," Dutch Data Center Association, accessed June 5, 2022, https://www.dutchdatacenters.nl/en/data-centers/what-is-the-economic-impact-of-data-centers/.

19. "Data Centers," Dutch Data Center Association.

20. "Data Centers," Dutch Data Center Association.

21. "Regional Internet Registries," Number Resource Organization, accessed July 2, 2022, https://www.nro.net/about/rirs/; "RIPE Network Coordination Centre," RIPE NCC, accessed July 2, 2022, https://www.ripe.net/.

22. "About HSD," Hague Security Delta, accessed July 2, 2022, https://securitydelta.nl/about/about-hsd; "Join the Largest Security Cluster in Europe: Factsheet," Hague Security Delta, accessed July 2, 2022, https://securitydelta.nl/images/HSD_Factsheet_International_DEF.pdf.

23. "About," European Cybercrime Center, accessed July 2, 2022, https://www.europol.europa.eu/about-europol/european-cybercrime-centre-ec3.

24. "About," European Cybercrime Center.

25. "The Constitution of the Kingdom of the Netherlands 2008," Government of the Netherlands, Ministry of the Interior and Kingdom Relations, published September 22, 2008, https://www.government.nl/documents/regulations/2012/10/18/the-constitution-of-the-kingdom-of-the-netherlands-2008.

26. Charles Arthur and agencies, "DigiNotar SSL Certificate Hack Amounts to Cyberwar, Says Expert," *Guardian*, September 5, 2011, https://www.theguardian.com/technology/2011/sep/05/diginotar-certificate-hack-cyberwar.

27. Interview with an employee of the Ministry of Security and Justice of the Netherlands, The Hague, November 8, 2017.

28. "National Cybersecurity Strategy 2: From Awareness to Capability," Ministry of Security and Justice, 2013, p. 21, https://www.enisa.europa.eu/topics/national-cyber-security-strategies/ncss-map/NCSS2Engelseversie.pdf.

29. "National Cybersecurity Strategy 2," Ministry of Security and Justice, 32.

30. Interview with an employee of The Netherlands Scientific Council for Government Policy, The Hague, November 9, 2017; interview with employee no. 1 of the Ministry of Foreign Affairs of the Netherlands, The Hague, November 8, 2017.

31. "Koenders Kicks Off Cyber Conference," Government of the Netherlands, April 16, 2015, https://www.government.nl/latest/news/2015/04/16/koenders-kicks-off-cyber-conference.

32. "'Free, Open and Secure Internet' Focus of Global Conference on CyberSpace 2015 in The Hague," Government of the Netherlands, March 27, 2015, https://www.government.nl/latest/news/2015/03/27/free-open-and-secure-internet-focus-of-global-conference-on-cyberspace-2015-in-the-hague.

33. "Free, Open and Secure Internet," Government of the Netherlands.

34. Interview, November 9, 2017.

35. Dennis Broeders, *The Public Core of the Internet: An International Agenda for Internet Governance* (Amsterdam: Amsterdam University Press, 2015), 7–9.

36. Dennis Broeders, "Aligning the International Protection of 'the Public Core of the Internet' with State Sovereignty and National Security," *Journal of Cyber Policy* 2, no. 3 (2017): 367.

37. Interview, November 9, 2017.

38. Broeders, *The Public Core of the Internet*, 12, 21–23.

39. Broeders, 100.

40. "International Cyber Strategy: Building Digital Bridges," Ministry of Foreign Affairs, February 12, 2017, p. 5, https://www.centruminternationaalrecht.nl/documents/1304248/1494823/11-DC-International%2BCyber%2BStrategy.pdf/270fa5da-b942-80e2-8461-f1ec9248e038.

41. "International Cyber Strategy," 5.

42. "International Cyber Strategy," 6.

43. Interview, employee no. 1, November 8, 2017.

44. "International Cyber Strategy," Ministry of Foreign Affairs, 7.

45. Interview, employee no. 1, November 8, 2017.

46. Interview, employee no. 1, November 8, 2017; and see "International Cyber Strategy," Ministry of Foreign Affairs, 8.

47. "The Hague Declaration on the GFCE," GFCE, April 16, 2015, https://thegfce.org/wp-content/uploads/2020/04/the-hague-declaration-on-the-gfce.pdf.

48. "Global Forum on Cyber Expertise Stationed in The Hague," *Cybersecurity Week*, April 20, 2015, https://www.cybersecurityweek.nl/2015/pressroom/news/24-global-forum-on-cyber-expertise-stationed-in-the-hague.

49. Interview with an employee of the GFCE, The Hague, November 10, 2017.

50. "Framework Document GFCE," GFCE, April 16, 2015, https://thegfce.org/wp-content/uploads/2020/04/framework-document-gfce.pdf.

51. "Delhi Communiqué on a GFCE Global Agenda for Cyber Capacity Building," GFCE, November 24, 2017, https://thegfce.org/wp-content/uploads/2020/04/DelhiCommunique.pdf; "History of the GFCE," GFCE, accessed July 3, 2022, https://thegfce.org/about-the-gfce/.

52. Interview, November 10, 2017; "Framework Document GFCE," GFCE.

53. Interview, November 10, 2017.

54. "Mission Statement," GCSC, accessed July 3, 2022, https://cyberstability.org/.

55. "Commissioner," GCSC, accessed July 3, 2022, https://cyberstability.org/commissioner/.

56. "Advancing Cyberstability," final report, GCSC, November 2019, p. 46, https://cyberstability.org/wp-content/uploads/2020/02/GCSC-Advancing-Cyberstability.pdf.

57. "About," GCSC, accessed July 3, 2022, https://cyberstability.org/about/.

58. "Advancing Cyberstability," GCSC.

59. "A Call to Action on Advancing Cyber Stability: Global Commission Launches Final Report," GCSC, accessed July 3, 2022, https://cyberstability.org/news/a-call-to-action-on-advancing-cyberstability-global-commission-launches-final-report/.

60. Interestingly, two members of the international group of experts for *Tallinn Manual 2.0* were Dutch, representing the Netherlands Defense Academy and the University of Amsterdam. In the first edition, one was Dutch.

61. Koenders, "Tallinn Manual 2.0"; Rutger van Marissing, panel "International Law and Cyber Operations: Launch of the Tallinn Manual 2.0," Atlantic Council, February 8, 2017, https://www.atlanticcouncil.org/unused/webcasts/international-law-and-cyber-operations-launch-of-the-tallinn-manual-2-0/.

62. Used to "create a trusted environment to understand and resolve complex problems," the Chatham House Rule states, "When a meeting, or part thereof, is held under the Chatham House Rule, participants are free to use the information received, but neither the identity nor the affiliation of the speaker(s), nor that of any other participant, may be revealed." "Chatham House Rule," Chatham House, accessed September 10, 2023, https://www.chathamhouse.org/about-us/chatham-house-rule.

63. Michael N. Schmitt, ed., *Tallinn Manual 2.0 on the International Law Applicable to Cyber Operations* (Cambridge: Cambridge University Press, 2017), 6.

64. Schmitt, *Tallinn Manual 2.0*, 7.

65. "The Tallinn Manual 2.0 and The Hague Process: From Cyber Warfare to Peacetime Regime," Asser Institute, Center for International and European Law, February 2016, https://www.asser.nl/media/2878/report-on-the-tallinn-manual-20-and-the-hague-process-3-feb-2016.pdf.

66. Schmitt, *Tallinn Manual 2.0*, xxv–xxvii.

67. "Programme of the Netherlands Presidency of the Council of the European Union, 1 January–30 June 2016," Ministry of Foreign Affairs, accessed July 5, 2022, pp. 13–14, http://www.eunec.eu/sites/www.eunec.eu/files/attachment/files/nationaal-programma-engels.pdf.

68. "Non-Paper: Developing a Joint EU Diplomatic Response against Coercive Cyber Operations," 5797/6/16REV6, Netherlands Presidency of the Council of the EU, May 19, 2016, http://statewatch.org/news/2016/jul/eu-council-diplomatic-response-cyber-ops-5797-6-16.pdf.

69. "Draft Council Conclusions on a Framework for a Joint EU Diplomatic Response to Malicious Cyber Activities ('Cyber Diplomacy Toolbox')," 9916/17, Council of the European Union, June 7, 2017, http://data.consilium.europa.eu/doc/document/ST-9916-2017-INIT/en/pdf.

70. Samuel Stolton, "EU Backs Cyber Sanctions Regime, following Dutch and UK Pressure," *Euractive*, May 17, 2019, https://www.euractiv.com/section/cybersecurity/news/eu-backs-cyber-sanctions-regime-following-dutch-and-uk-pressure/.

71. Council of the European Union, "Cyber Attacks: Council Is Now Able to Impose Sanctions," press release, May 17, 2019, https://www.consilium.europa.eu/en/press/press-releases/2019/05/17/cyber-attacks-council-is-now-able-to-impose-sanctions/.

72. "Council Decision Concerning Restrictive Measures against Cyber Attacks Threatening the Union or Its Member States," 7299/19, Council of the European Union, May 14, 2019, http://data.consilium.europa.eu/doc/document/ST-7299-2019-INIT/en/pdf.

73. "Developments in the Field of Information and Telecommunications in the Context of International Security," UN, Office for Disarmament Affairs, accessed July 5, 2022, https://www.un.org/disarmament/ict-security/.

74. "Developments in the Field of Information and Telecommunications in the Context of International Security," UN, Office for Disarmament Affairs.

75. "UN GGE and OEWG," Geneva Internet Platform, Digital Watch Observatory, accessed July 5, 2022, https://dig.watch/processes/un-gge.

76. Broeders, "Aligning the International Protection of 'the Public Core of the Internet,'" 368; interview, employee of the Ministry of Security and Justice of the Netherlands, November 8, 2017.

77. "UN GGE and OEWG," Geneva Internet Platform.

78. "UN GGE and OEWG," Geneva Internet Platform.

79. "UN GGE and OEWG," Geneva Internet Platform.

80. "Open-Ended Working Group," UN, Office for Disarmament Affairs, accessed July 5, 2022, https://www.un.org/disarmament/open-ended-working-group/.

81. Interview with an employee of the GFCE, The Hague, 10th November 2017.

82. Interviews with employees nos. 1 and 2 of the Ministry of Foreign Affairs of the Netherlands, November 8, 2017.

Chapter Five

1. Stephen Krasner, *Sovereignty: Organized Hypocrisy* (Princeton, NJ: Princeton University Press, 1999), 3–4.

2. For more details on the modern trends and developments of state regulations and censorship, see Justin Clark et al., "The Shifting Landscape of Global Internet Censorship," Berkman Klein Center for Internet and Society, Harvard University, June 2017, https://dash.harvard.edu/handle/1/33084425.

3. Sarah K. Harris, "Networked Erasure: Visualizing Information Censorship in Turkey," *Convergence: The International Journal of Research into New Media Technologies* 21, no. 2 (2015): 259.

4. Ronald Deibert et al., *Access Controlled: The Shaping of Power, Rights, and Rule in Cyberspace* (Cambridge, MA: MIT Press, 2010), 342.

5. Doruk Ergun, "National Security vs. Online Rights and Freedoms in Turkey: Moving Beyond the Dichotomy," Center for Economic and Foreign Policy Studies, April 2018, p. 2, https://www.jstor.org/stable/resrep17007.

6. "Freedom on the Net," Freedom House, accessed July 7, 2022, https://freedomhouse.org/report/freedom-net.

7. Sinan Ülgen, ed., "A Primer on Cybersecurity in Turkey and the Case of Nuclear Power," Center for Economic and Foreign Policy Studies, Istanbul, 2015, p. 26, https://www.jstor.org/stable/resrep14043.1.

8. Batu Kinikoglu, "Evaluating the Regulation of Access to Online Content in Turkey in the Context of Freedom of Speech," *Journal of International Commercial Law and Technology* 9, no. 1 (2014): 38.

9. Mehmet Bedii Kaya, "The Law on Regulation of Broadcasts via Internet and Combating Crimes Committed by Means of Such Publications: The Turkish Internet Law (Unofficial Translation)," *İnternet Hukuku*, Mevzuat and İçtihat, v3.0, 2021, arts. 8(3), 8(4), pp. 56–75, https://www.mbkaya.com/hukuk/internetmevzuat.pdf.

10. The TİB was shut down a month after the attempted military coup in mid-2016, on the basis of suspicions and allegations that it was a hub for the coup's instigators. Its powers and responsibilities were transferred to the BTK. Ergun, "National Security vs. Online Rights and Freedoms in Turkey," 14.

11. Ülgen, "A Primer on Cybersecurity in Turkey and the Case of Nuclear Power," 26, 29.

12. Sanja Kelly, Madeline Earp, et al., "Freedom on the Net 2014," Freedom House, 2014, p. 799, https://freedomhouse.org/sites/default/files/2020-02/FOTN_2014_Full_Report_compressedv2.pdf.

13. Kinikoglu, "Evaluating the Regulation of Access," 37.

14. Mustafa Akgül and Melih Kırlıdoğ, "Internet Censorship in Turkey," *Internet Policy Review* 4, no. 2 (June 2015): 3–4.

15. Akgül and Kırlıdoğ, 4.

16. Akgül and Kırlıdoğ, 4.

17. "Binali Yıldırım: Türkiye örnek teşkil edecek," *Sabah*, March 29, 2007, http://arsiv.sabah.com.tr/2007/03/29/gnd87.html; and see "'Temiz İnternet' için Ankara'da buluşalım," *Sabah*, March 29, 2007, http://arsiv.sabah.com.tr/2007/03/29/gun110.html.

18. Akgül and Kırlıdoğ, "Internet Censorship in Turkey," 5.

19. Constitution of the Republic of Turkey, October 18, 1982, https://www.constituteproject.org/constitution/Turkey_2017.pdf?lang=en, art. 41.

20. Constitution of the Republic of Turkey, art. 58.

21. Kaya, "The Law on the Regulation," arts. 2–7, 10.

22. Kaya, art. 8(1).

23. Kaya, art. 8(2).

24. Kaya, art. 8(3).

25. Kaya, art. 8(4).

26. Akgül and Kırlıdoğ, "Internet Censorship in Turkey," 7.

27. Kaya, "The Law on the Regulation," arts. 8(5), 8(10).

28. The exchange rate of the Turkish lira against the euro has fluctuated over time. The conversions within this chapter are approximate and calculated based on "Euro Foreign Exchange Reference Rates," European Central Bank, accessed July 9, 2022, https://www.ecb.europa.eu/stats/policy_and_exchange_rates/euro_reference_exchange_rates/html/eurofxref-graph-try.en.html.

29. Kaya, "The Law on the Regulation," art. 8(11).

30. Yaman Akdeniz, "Report of the OSCE Representative on Freedom of the Media on Turkey and Internet Censorship," Organization for Security and Cooperation in Europe, 2010, p. 18, https://www.osce.org/files/f/documents/a/d/41091.pdf.

31. Kaya, "The Law on the Regulation," arts. 9, 9(1).

32. Akdeniz, "Report of the OSCE," 9.

33. Ergun, "National Security vs. Online Rights and Freedoms in Turkey," 8.

34. Bilge Yesil, Efe Kerem Sozeri, and Emad Khazraee, "Turkey's Internet Policy after the Coup Attempt: The Emergence of a Distributed Network of Online Suppression and Surveillance," Internet Policy Observatory, Annenberg School for Communication, University of Pennsylvania, February 2017, p. 7, https://www.researchgate.net/publication/316015028_Turkey's_Internet_Policy_After_the_Coup_Attempt_The_Emergence_of_a_Distributed_Network_of_Online_Suppression_and_Surveillance.

35. Kaya, "The Law on the Regulation," art. 6/A.

36. Akgül and Kırlıdoğ, "Internet Censorship in Turkey," 11.

37. Kaya, "The Law on the Regulation," art. 9.

38. Kaya, "The Law on the Regulation," art. 9A.

39. Gönenç Gürkaynak, İlay Yılmaz, and Nazlı Pınar Taşkıran, "New Era for Turkish Internet Law: Will Turkey Become Another China or Iran?," *Journal of Business and Economics* 5, no. 11 (November 2014): 1979.

40. Kaya, "The Law on the Regulation," art. 6.

41. Mehmet Bedii Kaya, "The Regulation of Internet Intermediaries under Turkish Law: Is There a Delicate Balance between Rights and Obligations?," *Computer Law and Security Review* 32 (2016): 767.

42. Ergun, "National Security vs. Online Rights and Freedoms in Turkey," 8.

43. Gürkaynak, Yılmaz, and Taşkıran, "New Era for Turkish Internet Law," 1978.

44. Kaya, "The Regulation of Internet Intermediaries under Turkish Law," 766.

45. Gürkaynak, Yılmaz, and Taşkıran, "New Era for Turkish Internet Law," 1978.

46. Uğur Aktekin and Bentley James Yaffe, "Amendments to the Turkish Internet Broadcasts and Publication Law, and the Controversial Application of the New Provisions," *Journal of Internet Law* 18, no. 2 (August 2014): 18.

47. Gürkaynak, Yılmaz, and Taşkıran, "New Era for Turkish Internet Law," 1980; but see also Aktekin and Yaffe, "Amendments to the Turkish Internet Broadcasts and Publication Law," 21.

48. Ergun, "National Security vs. Online Rights and Freedoms in Turkey," 9.

49. Aktekin and Yaffe, "Amendments to the Turkish Internet Broadcasts," 24.

50. Kaya, "The Law on the Regulation," art. 8/A.

51. Kaya, art. 8/A.

52. Nate Schenkkan, Osman Coşkunoğlu, and Aslı Tunç, "The Struggle for Turkey's Internet," Freedom House, 2015, p. 8, https://freedomhouse.org/sites/default/files/2020-02/The_Struggle_for_Turkeys_Internet_Report.pdf.

53. "Milestones," Türk Telekom, accessed July 10, 2022, https://www.turktelekom.com.tr/en/aboutus/pages/milestones.aspx.

54. Schenkkan, Coşkunoğlu, Tunç, "The Struggle for Turkey's Internet," 12.

55. Schenkkan, Coşkunoğlu, Tunç, 5–12.

56. Schenkkan, Coşkunoğlu, Tunç, 12.

57. Sanja Kelly, Mai Truong, et al., "Freedom on the Net 2016," Freedom House, November 2016, p. 833, https://freedomhouse.org/sites/default/files/2020-02/Freedom_on_the_Net_2016_complete_book.pdf.

58. Kelly, Truong, et al., 833.

59. Deibert et al., *Access Controlled*, 353.

60. Deibert et al., 353.

61. Ersu Ablak, "Turkish Telecommunication Infrastructure Reloaded," *Hurriyet Daily News*, July 28, 2016, https://www.hurriyetdailynews.com/opinion/ersu-ablak/turkish-telecommunication-infrastructure-reloaded-102170.

62. Yesil, Sozeri, and Khazraee, "Turkey's Internet Policy after the Coup Attempt," 9.

63. Kaya, "The Regulation of Internet Intermediaries under Turkish Law," 764.

64. Kaya, 765; Yesil, Sozeri, and Khazraee, "Turkey's Internet Policy after the Coup Attempt," 9.

65. Akdeniz, "Report of the OSCE," 11–12.

66. Harris, "Networked Erasure," 257.

67. Engelliweb.com captured by the WayBack Machine, dated May 11, 2014, accessed July 10, 2022, https://web.archive.org/web/20140511111941/http://engelliweb.com:80/istatistikler/.

68. Engelliweb.com captured by the WayBack Machine, dated May 16, 2016, accessed July 10, 2022, https://web.archive.org/web/20160516194730/https://engelliweb.com/istatistikler/.

69. Kelly, Earp, et al., "Freedom on the Net 2014," 800; Akdeniz, "Report of the OSCE," 32.

70. "Removal Requests," Transparency Report, Twitter, accessed July 16, 2022, https://transparency.twitter.com/en/removal-requests.html.

71. Yesil, Sozeri, and Khazraee, "Turkey's Internet Policy after the Coup Attempt," 9.

72. Vijaya Gadde, "Challenging the Access Ban in Turkey," Twitter Blog, March 26, 2014, https://blog.twitter.com/official/en_us/a/2014/challenging-the-access-ban-in-turkey.html.

73. "Twitter Website 'Blocked' in Turkey," *BBC*, March 21, 2014, https://www.bbc.com/news/world-europe-26677134.

74. Internet restrictions such as territorial bans of social networks can be bypassed when using anonymization tools such as the Tor web browser or a virtual private network. Such tools provide users with anonymity and freedom of movement on the internet so that they can, access services and information restricted in their area. Although most internet users do not possess the know-how to use these tools and thus are limited to what is freely accessible online, anonymization tools undermine the government's internet restrictions, making it tricky to exactly measure the efficiency of the restrictions. Nevertheless, certain nondirect indicators, such as the behavior of interested stakeholders, suggest that internet restrictions have a strong impact. One example, mentioned earlier, is the inclination of social networks to comply with a government's demands. Social networks are aware that they might lose followers, and revenue, if they are blocked on a state's territory.

75. Eyüp Can, "Time Ripe for Talking about Presidential Vote, Says Turkish President Gül," *Hürriyet Daily News*, April 3, 2014, https://www.hurriyetdailynews.com/time-ripe-for-talking-about-presidential-vote-says-turkish-president-gul-64477.

76. Akdeniz v. the Presidency of Telecommunication and Communication, Constitutional Court of Turkey, April 2, 2014, https://globalfreedomofexpression.columbia.edu/cases/akdeniz-v-the-presidency-of-telecommunication-and-communication/.

77. Akdeniz v. the Presidency of Telecommunication and Communication; and see "Officials in Turkey 'Lift Twitter Ban,'" *BBC*, April 3, 2014, https://www.bbc.com/news/world-europe-26873603.

78. "Turkey Fines Twitter for Failure to Remove 'Terrorist Propaganda,'" *Hürriyet Daily News*, December 11, 2015, https://www.hurriyetdailynews.com/turkey-fines-twitter-for-failure-to-remove-terrorist-propaganda-official-92387.

79. "Turkey Lifts Two-Year Ban on YouTube," *BBC*, October 30, 2010, https://www.bbc.com/news/technology-11659816.

80. Constitution of the Republic of Turkey, arts. 41, 58; Kinikoglu, "Evaluating the Regulation of Access," 47.

81. Akgül and Kırlıdoğ, "Internet Censorship in Turkey," 10.

82. Kaya, "The Regulation of Internet Intermediaries under Turkish Law," 767.

83. Kinikoglu, "Evaluating the Regulation of Access," 40–41.

84. "New Internet Filtering System Condemned as Backdoor Censorship," Reporters without Borders, December 2, 2011, updated January 20, 2016, https://rsf.org/en/news/new-internet-filtering-system-condemned-backdoor-censorship.

85. Kelly, Earp, et al., "Freedom on the Net 2014," 801.

86. Akgül and Kırlıdoğ, "Internet Censorship in Turkey," 10.

87. For example, the European Court of Human Rights found in December 2012 that Law No. 5651 violated Article 10 of the European Convention on Human Rights, of which Turkey is a signatory. Ahmet Yildirim v. Turkey, European Court of Human Rights, judgment, December 18, 2012, http://hudoc.echr.coe.int/fre?i=001-115705.

88. Among the Venice Commission criticisms was that the two amendments granted the TİB (an administrative body by nature) judicial powers that should have been the sole privilege of judicial bodies. Turkey: Opinion on Law No. 5651 on Regulation of Publications on the Internet and Combating Crimes Committed by Means of Such Publication, Venice Commission, 107th Plenary Session, Venice, June 10–11, 2016, https://www.venice.coe.int/webforms/documents/default.aspx?pdffile=CDL-AD(2016)011-e.

89. Abby Ohlheiser, "How Turkey's Twitter Users Are Working around the Ban," *Atlantic*, March 21, 2014, https://www.theatlantic.com/international/archive/2014/03/how-turkeys-twitter-users-are-working-around-ban/359415/.

90. For more information, see Yesil, Sozeri, and Khazraee, "Turkey's Internet Policy after the Coup Attempt."

Chapter Six

1. Stephen Krasner, *Sovereignty: Organized Hypocrisy* (Princeton, NJ: Princeton University Press, 1999), 4.

2. James Lewis, "Can Telephones Race? 5G and the Evolution of Telecom, Part I," Center for Strategic and International Studies, June 2020, https://www.csis.org/analysis/can-telephones-race-5g-and-evolution-telecom.

3. Cristina Maza, "China Involved in 90 Percent of Espionage and Industrial Secrets Theft, Department of Justice Reveals," *Newsweek*, December 12, 2018, https://www.newsweek.com/china-involved-90-percent-economic-espionage-and-industrial-secrets-theft-1255908.

4. Michael Schuman et al., "Inside the Chinese Company America Can't Trust," *Time*, April 15, 2013, vol. 181, no. 14.

5. Michael R. Pompeo, "The United States Further Restricts Huawei Access to US Technology," press statement, US Department of State, August 17, 2020, https://2017-2021.state.gov/the-united-states-further-restricts-huawei-access-to-u-s-technology/index.html.

6. Theodore H. Moran, "Dealing with Cybersecurity Threats Posed by Globalised IT Suppliers," Policy brief, Peterson Institute for International Economics, May 1, 2013, https://www.piie.com/publications/policy-briefs/dealing-cybersecurity-threats-posed-globalized-information-technology.

7. Kadri Kaska, Henrik Beckvard, and Tomáš Minárik, "Huawei, 5G and China as a Security Threat," NATO CCDCoE, Tallinn, 2019, p. 7, https://ccdcoe.org/library/publications/huawei-5g-and-china-as-a-security-threat/.

8. For more details on why Huawei has been perceived with suspicion by certain other countries, see, for instance, Lucie Kadlecová, "Huawei: A Threat to National Security?," *e-IR*, March 13, 2013, https://www.e-ir.info/2013/03/13/huawei-a-threat-to-national-security/; or Mike Rogers and Dutch Ruppersberger, "Investigative Report on the US National Security Issues Posed by Chinese Telecommunications Companies Huawei and ZTE," US House of Representatives, October 8, 2012, http://intelligence.house.gov/sites/intelligence.house.gov/files/documents/Huawei-ZTE%20Investigative%20Report%20(FINAL).pdf.

9. Murray Scot Tanner, "Beijing's New National Intelligence Law: From Defense to Offense," *Lawfare*, July 20, 2017, https://www.lawfareblog.com/beijings-new-national-intelligence-law-defense-offense; Kaska, Beckvard, and Minárik, "Huawei, 5G and China as a Security Threat," 11.

10. Dustin Volz, "Trump Signs into Law U.S. Government Ban on Kaspersky Lab Software," *Reuters*, December 12, 2017, https://www.reuters.com/article/us-usa-cyber-kaspersky/trump-signs-into-law-u-s-government-ban-on-kaspersky-lab-software-idUSKBN1E62V4.

11. Exec. Order No. 13,636, Improving Critical Infrastructure Cybersecurity, C.F.R. 78, no. 33, February 19, 2013, https://www.govinfo.gov/content/pkg/FR-2013-02-19/pdf/2013-03915.pdf; NIST, Computer Security Resource Center, Glossary, s.v. "critical infrastructure," accessed July 17, 2022, https://csrc.nist.gov/glossary/term/critical_infrastructure.

12. Olav Lysne et al., "Critical Communication Infrastructures and Huawei," July 24, 2019, TPRC47: The 47th Research Conference on Communication, Information and Internet Policy 2019, p. 14, https://papers.ssrn.com/sol3/papers.cfm?abstract_id=3426222.

13. Kaska, Beckvard, and Minárik, "Huawei, 5G and China as a Security Threat," 5.

14. Robert Williams, "Securing 5G Networks," Council on Foreign Relations, July 15, 2019, https://www.cfr.org/report/securing-5g-networks.

15. Kaska, Beckvard, and Minárik, "Huawei, 5G and China as a Security Threat," 20.

16. For more details on the difference between 4G and 5G technologies, see Leigh Hartman, "Get Smarter: Core vs. Edge in 5G Networks," US Embassy and Consulates in the United Kingdom, September 17, 2019, https://uk.usembassy.gov/get-smart-core-vs-edge-in-5g-networks/; for more information on the disappearing distinction between core and edge in 5G technologies, see Cybersecurity and Infrastructure Security Agency, "Edge vs. Core: An Increasingly Less Pronounced Distinction in 5G Networks," 2020, https://www.cisa.gov/sites/default/files/publications/5g_edge-core-computing_508_1.pdf.

17. Keith Krach, "The Free World Must Unite against Huawei," op-ed, *Daily Telegraph* (London), June 25, 2020, https://2017-2021.state.gov/The-free-world-must-unite-against-Huawei/index.html.

18. "National Critical Functions Set," Cybersecurity and Infrastructure Security Agency, accessed July 17, 2022, https://www.cisa.gov/national-critical-functions-set; Williams, "Securing 5G Networks."

19. John T. Watts, "The Battle for 5G Leadership Is Global and the USA Is Behind: The White House's New Strategy Aims to Correct That," Atlantic Council, April 1, 2020, https://www.atlanticcouncil.org/blogs/new-atlanticist/the-battle-for-5g-leadership-is-global-and-the-us-is-behind-the-white-houses-new-strategy-aims-to-correct-that/.

20. "The FCC's 5G FAST Plan," Federal Communications Commission, accessed July 17, 2022, https://www.fcc.gov/5G.

21. National Strategy to Secure 5G of the United States of America, March 2020, preamble, https://trumpwhitehouse.archives.gov/wp-content/uploads/2020/03/National-Strategy-5G-Final.pdf.

22. National Strategy to Secure 5G, 1.

23. National Strategy to Secure 5G.

24. Lysne et al., "Critical Communication Infrastructures and Huawei," 25.

25. Ashlee Vance and Bruce Einhorn, "Would You Buy $1 Billion in China-Made, So-Controversial-IT-Hurts Telecom Equipment from This Guy?," *Bloomberg Businessweek*, September 19–25, 2011, p. 75.

26. Vance and Einhorn, 76–77.

27. Ken Hu, "Huawei Open Letter," February 2011, http://online.wsj.com/public/resources/documents/Huawei20110205.pdf.

28. Mike Rogers and Dutch Ruppersberger, "Investigative Report on the US National Security Issues Posed by Chinese Telecommunications Companies Huawei and ZTE," *Journal of Current Issues in Media and Telecommunications* 4, no. 2 (2012): 59–60.

29. Rogers and Ruppersberger, 69–87.

30. Rogers and Ruppersberger, 60, 69.

31. Rogers and Ruppersberger, 95.

32. Steven Musil, "Sprint, Softbank Vow Not to Use Huawei Gear in Sprint's Network," *CNET*, March 28, 2013, https://www.cnet.com/news/sprint-softbank-vow-not-to-use-huawei-gear-in-sprints-network/.

33. Consolidated and Further Continuing Appropriations Act, Public Law 113-6, March 26, 2013, https://www.congress.gov/113/plaws/publ6/PLAW-113publ6.pdf; Peter Burrows and Bruce Einhorn, "Chinese Spying Crushes Huawei in the US," *Bloomberg Businessweek*, May 6–12, 2013, p. 38.

34. Hamza Shaban, "Pentagon Tells US Military Bases to Stop Selling ZTE, Huawei Phones," *Washington Post*, May 2, 2018.

35. John S. McCain National Defense Authorization Act for Fiscal Year 2019, H.R. 5515, 115th Congress (2017–2018), August 13, 2018, https://www.congress.gov/bill/115th-congress/house-bill/5515/text; Jacob Kastrenakes, "Trump Signs Bill Banning Government Use of Huawei and ZTE Tech," *Verge*, August 13, 2018, https://www.theverge.com/2018/8/13/17686310/huawei-zte-us-government-contractor-ban-trump.

36. Sijia Jiang, "Huawei Challenges U.S. Defense Bill as Sanctions Fight Ramps Up," *Reuters*, May 29, 2019, https://www.reuters.com/article/us-huawei-tech-usa-filing-idUSKCN1SZ08C.

37. Eric Geller, "Trump Signs Order Setting Stage to Ban Huawei from US," *Politico*, May 15, 2019, https://www.politico.com/story/2019/05/15/trump-ban-huawei-us-1042046; Zak Doffman, "Trump Signs Executive Order That Will Lead to US Ban on Huawei," *Forbes*, May 15, 2019, https://www.forbes.com/sites/zakdoffman/2019/05/15/trump-expected-to-sign-executive-order-leading-to-ban-on-huawei-this-week/#56758b3368d9.

38. "Executive Order on Securing the Information and Communications Technology and Services Supply Chain," May 15, 2019, https://trumpwhitehouse.archives.gov/presidential-actions/executive-order-securing-information-communications-technology-services-supply-chain/.

39. Doffman, "Trump Signs Executive Order."

40. "Federal Register: Addition of Entities to the Entity List," Bureau of Industry and Security, US Department of Commerce, accessed July 30, 2022, https://www.federalregister.gov/documents/2019/05/21/2019-10616/addition-of-entities-to-the-entity-list.

41. US Department of Commerce, "Department of Commerce Announces the Addition of Huawei Technologies Co. Ltd. to the Entity List," press release, May 15, 2019, https://2017-2021.commerce.gov/news/press-releases/2019/05/department-commerce-announces-addition-huawei-technologies-co-ltd.html.

42. Adam Satariano, Raymond Zhong, and Daisuke Wakabayashi, "U.S. Tech Suppliers, Including Google, Restrict Dealings with Huawei after Trump Order," *New York Times*, May 20, 2019, https://www.nytimes.com/2019/05/20/technology/google-android-huawei.html.

43. Huawei became the world's number-one phone maker for the first time in its history a year later, overtaking both Samsung and Apple. Although Huawei's overseas exports fell 27 percent in the second quarter of 2020, also due to the US restrictions, the majority of its growth came from mainland China, where it made 70 percent of its sales. Sean Keane, "Huawei Takes Samsung's Crown as World's No. 1 Phone Maker, Analysts Say," *CNET*, July 31, 2020, https://www.cnet.com/news/huawei-takes-samsungs-crown-to-become-worlds-biggest-phone-maker-analysts-say/.

44. Natalie Weinstein, "Google Cuts Off Huawei Phones from Future Android Updates," *CNET*, May 20, 2019, https://www.cnet.com/news/google-reportedly-cuts-off-huawei-phones-from-future-android-updates/.

45. David Shepardson, Karen Freifeld, and Alexandra Alper, "U.S. Moves to Cut Huawei Off from Global Chip Suppliers as China Eyes Retaliation," *Reuters*, May 15, 2020, https://www.reuters.com/article/us-usa-huawei-tech-exclusive/u-s-moves-to-cut-huawei-off-from-global-chip-suppliers-as-china-eyes-retaliation-idUSKBN22R1KC; Ana Swanson, "US Delivers Another Blow to Huawei with New Tech Restrictions," *New York Times*, May 15, 2020, https://www.nytimes.com/2020/05/15/business/economy/commerce-department-huawei.html.

46. Shepardson, Freifeld, and Alper, "U.S. Moves to Cut Huawei Off."

47. Swanson, "U.S. Delivers Another Blow to Huawei."

48. Joe McDonald, "Huawei: Smartphone Chips Running Out under US Sanctions," *AP News*, August 8, 2020, https://apnews.com/270e93e985733a4d086c06a01375ceao.

49. David Shepardson, "U.S. Rural Telecom Networks Need USD 1.8 Billion to Remove Huawei, ZTE Equipment—FCC," *Reuters*, September 15, 2020, https://www.reuters.com/article/us-usa-china-telecom-idUSKBN25V23F?taid=5f52a053b52437000126dd7e&utm_campaign=trueAnthem:+Trending+Content&utm_medium=trueAnthem&utm_source=twitter.

50. Corinne Reichert, "Huawei Gets Another 45-day Reprieve from Commerce Department," *CNET*, February 14, 2020, https://www.cnet.com/news/huawei-gets-another-45-day-reprieve-from-commerce-department/; "Huawei: US Grants More Exemptions to Chinese Phone Ban," *BBC*, November 20, 2019, https://www.bbc.com/news/business-50496639.

51. "Huawei," *BBC*.

52. Reichert, "Huawei Gets Another 45-day Reprieve from Commerce Department."

53. Demetri Sevastopulo, "US Agencies Barred from Buying Huawei Equipment," *Financial Times*, August 7, 2019, https://www.ft.com/content/fc23eebe-b951-11e9-8a88-aa6628ac896c.

54. Federal Communications Commission, "FCC Bars Use of Universal Service Funding for Equipment & Services Posing National Security Risks," press release, November 22, 2019, https://docs.fcc.gov/public/attachments/DOC-360976A1.pdf.

55. Secure and Trusted Communications Networks Act of 2019, H.R. 4998, 116th Congress (2019–2020), December 3, 2020, https://www.congress.gov/bill/116th-congress/house-bill/4998/all-info#.

56. Campbell Kwan, "US Bans Federals Funds from Being Used on Huawei and ZTE Equipment," *ZDNet*, March 16, 2020, https://www.zdnet.com/article/us-bans-federals-funds-from-being-used-on-huawei-and-zte-equipment/.

57. David Shepardson and Karen Freifeld, "Trump Extends U.S. Telecom Supply Chain Order Aimed at Huawei, ZTE," *Reuters*, May 13, 2020, https://www.reuters.com/article/us-usa-trade-china-trump/trump-extends-us-telecom-supply-chain-order-aimed-at-huawei-zte-idUSKBN22P2KG.

58. Tony Capaccio and Jenny Leonard, "Huawei on List of 20 Chinese Companies That Pentagon Says Are Controlled by People's Liberation Army," *Time*, June 25, 2020, https://time.com/5859119/huawei-chinese-military-company-list/.

59. Federal Communications Commission, "FCC Designates Huawei and ZTE as National Security Threats," press release, June 30, 2020, https://www.fcc.gov/document/fcc-designates-huawei-and-zte-national-security-threats.

60. Stephanie Condon, "FCC Officially Designates Huawei, ZTE as National Security Threats," *ZDNet*, June 30, 2020, https://www.zdnet.com/article/fcc-officially-designates-huawei-zte-as-national-security-threats/.

61. Federal Acquisition Regulation: Prohibition on Contracting with Entities Using Certain Telecommunications and Video Surveillance Services or Equipment, Federal Register, July 14, 2020, https://www.federalregister.gov/documents/2020/07/14/2020-15293/federal-acquisition-regulation-prohibition-on-contracting-with-entities-using-certain.

62. Humeyra Pamuk, Alexandra Alper, and Idrees Ali, "Trump Bans U.S. Investments in Companies Linked to Chinese Military," *Reuters*, November 13, 2020, https://www.reuters.com/article/us-usa-china-securities-exclusive-idUSKBN27S2X3.

63. Stu Woo and Kate O'Keeffe, "Washington Asks Allies to Drop Huawei," *Wall Street Journal*, November 23, 2018.

64. "U.S. Will Rethink Cooperation with Allies Who Use Huawei: Official," *Reuters*, April 29, 2019, https://www.reuters.com/article/us-usa-huawei-tech/u-s-will-rethink-cooperation-with-allies-who-use-huawei-official-idUSKCN1S517H.

65. Marco Rubio, "Rubio Joins Cotton, Cruz, Hawley to Introduce Bill Requiring CFIUS to Reexamine U.K. Status after 5G Decision," press release, March 4, 2020, https://www.rubio.senate.gov/public/index.cfm/2020/3/rubio-joins-cotton-cruz-hawley-to-introduce-bill-requiring-cfius-to-reexamine-u-k-status-after-5g-decision.

66. "The Clean Network," US Department of State, accessed July 21, 2023, https://2017-2021.state.gov/the-clean-network/.

67. Michael R. Pompeo, "Announcing the Expansion of the Clean Network to Safeguard America's Assets," press statement, US Department of State, August 5, 2020, https://2017-2021.state.gov/announcing-the-expansion-of-the-clean-network-to-safeguard-americas-assets/index.html.

68. Pompeo, "Announcing the Expansion of the Clean Network."

69. "The Clean Network," US Department of State.

70. CSIS Working Group on Trust and Security in 5G Networks, "Criteria for Security and Trust in Telecommunications Networks and Services," Center

for Strategic and International Studies, May 2020, https://csis-website-prod.s3.amazonaws.com/s3fs-public/publication/200511_Lewis_5G_v3.pdf.

71. "Prague 5G Security Conference 2019," National Cyber and Information Security Agency, accessed July 31, 2022, https://nukib.cz/en/infoservis-en/conferences/prague-5g-security-conference-2019/.

72. Peter Coy, "U.S. Policy on China May Move from 'America First' to America & Co.," *Bloomberg Businessweek*, December 9, 2020, https://www.bloomberg.com/news/articles/2020-12-09/u-s-policy-against-china-america-first-is-becoming-america-and-others?sref=RfJLbe1B.

73. Marguerite Reardon, "Nokia and Ericsson Pitch Themselves as Huawei 5G Alternative," *CNET*, March 4, 2020, https://www.cnet.com/news/nokia-and-ericsson-pitch-themselves-as-huawei-5g-alternative/.

74. Krach, "The Free World Must Unite against Huawei."

75. Sherisse Pham, "Nokia Is Fighting Hard to Steal Huawei's 5G Crown," *CNN*, June 4, 2019, https://edition.cnn.com/2019/06/04/tech/huawei-5g-nokia/index.html.

76. Zak Doffman, "Huawei Confirms $30 Billion Revenue Hit as Smartphone Sales Drop 40–60%," *Forbes*, June 17, 2019, https://www.forbes.com/sites/zakdoffman/2019/06/17/huawei-may-pull-honor-20-and-fears-40-60-drop-in-smartphone-sales-report-claims/?sh=6a2f8e1754d2.

77. Richard Chirgwin, "Huawei: 'Trust Us, We Are Being Transparent,'" *Register*, May 28, 2013, https://www.theregister.co.uk/2013/05/28/huawei_trust_us_we_are_being_transparent/.

Chapter Seven

1. Jan Sedlák, "Ukrajina převezla data v obrněných kufrech a IT funguje i ve válce. Výrazně pomohli také Češi," *Lupa*, December 12, 2022, https://www.lupa.cz/clanky/ukrajina-prevezla-data-v-obrnenych-kufrech-a-it-funguje-i-ve-valce-vyrazne-pomohli-take-cesi/.

2. "The e-Estonia Briefing Centre Is at Your Service," e-Estonia, accessed July 17, 2023, https://e-estonia.com/briefing-centre/about-us/.

3. For example, see "Results of the Accreditation of Stakeholders to the OEWG 2021–2025 Raises Concerns," Geneva Internet Platform, Digital Watch Observatory, July 21, 2022, https://dig.watch/updates/results-of-the-accreditation-of-stakeholders-to-the-oewg-2021-2025-raises-concerns.

4. "The Clean Network," US Department of State, accessed July 21, 2023, https://2017-2021.state.gov/the-clean-network/.

5. World Conference on International Telecommunications, International Telecommunication Union, Dubai, December 2012, https://www.itu.int/en/history/Pages/WorldConferencesInternationalTelecommunications.aspx?conf=4.34.

References

Ablak, Ersu. "Turkish Telecommunication Infrastructure Reloaded." *Hurriyet Daily News*, July 28, 2016. https://www.hurriyetdailynews.com/opinion/ersu-ablak/turkish-telecommunication-infrastructure-reloaded-102170.

Agnew, John. *Globalization and Sovereignty*. Lanham, MD: Rowman & Littlefield, 2009.

Agreement between the Republic of Estonia and the Grand Duchy of Luxembourg on the Hosting of Data and Information Systems. June 20, 2017. https://www.riigiteataja.ee/aktilisa/2280/3201/8002/Lux_Info_Agreement.pdf.

Ahmet Yildirim v. Turkey. European Court of Human Rights. Judgment, December 18, 2012. http://hudoc.echr.coe.int/fre?i=001-115705.

Akdeniz, Yaman. "Report of the OSCE Representative on Freedom of the Media on Turkey and Internet Censorship." Organization for Security and Cooperation in Europe. 2010.

Akdeniz v. the Presidency of Telecommunication and Communication. Constitutional Court of Turkey. April 2, 2014. https://globalfreedomofexpression.columbia.edu/cases/akdeniz-v-the-presidency-of-telecommunication-and-communication/.

Akgül, Mustafa, and Melih Kırlıdoğ. "Internet Censorship in Turkey." *Internet Policy Review* 4, no. 2 (June 2015): 1–21.

Aktekin, Uğur, and Bentley James Yaffe. "Amendments to the Turkish Internet Broadcasts and Publication Law, and the Controversial Application of the New Provisions." *Journal of Internet Law* 18, no. 2 (August 2014): 18–24.

Amsterdam Internet Exchange. "Internet Peering." Accessed January 13, 2020. https://www.ams-ix.net/ams/service/internet-peering.

Arthur, Charles, and agencies. "DigiNotar SSL Certificate Hack Amounts to Cyberwar, Says Expert." *Guardian*, September 5, 2011. https://www.theguardian.com/technology/2011/sep/05/diginotar-certificate-hack-cyberwar.

Asser Institute, Center for International and European Law. "The Tallinn Manual 2.0 and The Hague Process: From Cyber Warfare to Peacetime Regime." February 2016. https://www.asser.nl/media/2878/report-on-the-tallinn-manual-20-and-the-hague-process-3-feb-2016.pdf.

Barlow, John Perry. "A Declaration of the Independence of Cyberspace." Electronic Frontier Foundation, February 8, 1996. https://www.eff.org/cyberspace-independence.

Bartmann, Barry. "Between *De Jure* and *De Facto* Statehood: Revisiting the Status Issues for Taiwan." *Island Studies Journal* 3, no. 1 (2008): 113–128.

BBC. "Huawei: US Grants More Exemptions to Chinese Phone Ban." November 20, 2019. https://www.bbc.com/news/business-50496639.

———. "Officials in Turkey 'Lift Twitter Ban.'" April 3, 2014. https://www.bbc.com/news/world-europe-26873603.

———. "Turkey Lifts Two-Year Ban on YouTube." October 30, 2010. https://www.bbc.com/news/technology-11659816.

———. "Twitter Website 'Blocked' in Turkey." March 21, 2014. https://www.bbc.com/news/world-europe-26677134.

Betz, David, and Tim Stevens. *Cyberspace and the State: Toward a Strategy for Cyber-power.* Abingdon, UK: Routledge, 2011.

Bodin, Jean. *Six Books of the Commonwealth.* Lexington, KY: Seven Treasures, 2009.

Broeders, Dennis. "Aligning the International Protection of 'the Public Core of the Internet' with State Sovereignty and National Security." *Journal of Cyber Policy* 2, no. 3 (2017): 366–376.

———. *The Public Core of the Internet: An International Agenda for Internet Governance.* Amsterdam: Amsterdam University Press, 2015.

Buchanan, Ben. "Cryptography and Sovereignty." *Survival* 58, no. 5 (October–November 2016): 95–122.

Bull, Hedley. *The Anarchical Society.* New York: Palgrave, 1977.

Bureau of Industry and Security, US Department of Commerce. "Federal Register: Addition of Entities to the Entity List." Accessed July 30, 2022. https://www.federalregister.gov/documents/2019/05/21/2019-10616/addition-of-entities-to-the-entity-list.

Burrows, Peter, and Bruce Einhorn. "Chinese Spying Crushes Huawei in the US." *Bloomberg Businessweek*, May 6–12, 2013.

Camilleri, Joseph A., and Jim Falk. *The End of Sovereignty? The Politics of a Shrinking and Fragmenting World*. Hants, UK: Edward Elgar, 1992.

Can, Eyüp. "Time Ripe for Talking about Presidential Vote, Says Turkish President Gül." *Hürriyet Daily News*, April 3, 2014. https://www.hurriyetdailynews.com/time-ripe-for-talking-about-presidential-vote-says-turkish-president-gul-64477.

Capaccio, Tony, and Jenny Leonard. "Huawei on List of 20 Chinese Companies That Pentagon Says Are Controlled by People's Liberation Army." *Time*, June 25, 2020. https://time.com/5859119/huawei-chinese-military-company-list/.

Centrum Wiskunde & Informatica. "CWI History: First European Internet Connection." Accessed June 5, 2022. https://www.cwi.nl/about/history/cwi-achievements-details.

Chatham House. "Chatham House Rule." Accessed September 10, 2023. https://www.chathamhouse.org/about-us/chatham-house-rule.

Chircop, Luke. "Territorial Sovereignty in Cyberspace after 'Tallinn Manual 2.0.'" *Melbourne Journal of International Law* 20, no. 2 (December 2019): 349–377.

Chirgwin, Richard. "Huawei: 'Trust Us, We Are Being Transparent.'" *Register*, May 28, 2013. https://www.theregister.co.uk/2013/05/28/huawei_trust_us_we_are_being_transparent/.

Claessen, Eva. "Reshaping the Internet—the Impact of the Securitisation of Internet Infrastructure on Approaches to Internet Governance: The Case of Russia and the EU." *Journal of Cyber Policy* 5, no. 1 (2020): 140–157.

Clark, Justin, Robert Faris, Ryan Morrison-Westphal, Helmi Noman, Casey Tilton, and Jonathan Zittrain. "The Shifting Landscape of Global Internet Censorship." Berkman Klein Center for Internet and Society, Harvard University. June 2017. https://dash.harvard.edu/handle/1/33084425.

Cohen, Jean L. *Globalization and Sovereignty: Rethinking Legality, Legitimacy and Constitutionalism*. Cambridge: Cambridge University Press, 2012.

Complementary Agreement between the State of the Grand Duchy of Luxembourg and the European Patent Organisation concerning the Inviolability of the Archives of the European Patent Organisation. March 5, 2018. https://treaties.un.org/doc/Publication/UNTS/No%20Volume/55331/Part/I-55331-0800000280518e98.pdf.

Condon, Stephanie. "FCC Officially Designates Huawei, ZTE as National Security Threats." *ZDNet*, June 30, 2020. https://www.zdnet.com/article/fcc-officially-designates-huawei-zte-as-national-security-threats/.

Consolidated and Further Continuing Appropriations Act. Public Law 113-6, March 26, 2013. https://www.congress.gov/113/plaws/publ6/PLAW-113publ6.pdf.

Constitution of the Republic of Turkey. October 18, 1982. https://www.constituteproject.org/constitution/Turkey_2017.pdf?lang=en.

Council of the European Union. "Council Decision Concerning Restrictive Measures against Cyber Attacks Threatening the Union or Its Member States, 7299/19." May 14, 2019. http://data.consilium.europa.eu/doc/document/ST-7299-2019-INIT/en/pdf.

———. "Cyber Attacks: Council Is Now Able to Impose Sanctions." Press release, May 17, 2019. https://www.consilium.europa.eu/en/press/press-releases/2019/05/17/cyber-attacks-council-is-now-able-to-impose-sanctions/.

———. "Draft Council Conclusions on a Framework for a Joint EU Diplomatic Response to Malicious Cyber Activities ('Cyber Diplomacy Toolbox'), 9916/17." June 7, 2017. http://data.consilium.europa.eu/doc/document/ST-9916-2017-INIT/en/pdf.

Coy, Peter. "US Policy on China May Move from 'America First' to America & Co." *Bloomberg Businessweek*, December 9, 2020. https://www.bloomberg.com/news/articles/2020-12-09/u-s-policy-against-china-america-first-is-becoming-america-and-others?sref=RfJLbe1B.

Creemers, Rogier. *China's Approach to Cyber Sovereignty.* Berlin: Konrad Adenauer Stiftung, 2020. https://www.kas.de/documents/252038/7995358/China%E2%80%99s+Approach+to+Cyber+Sovereignty.pdf/2c6916a6-164c-fb0c-4e29-f933f472ac3f?version=1.0&t=1606143361537.

CSIS Working Group on Trust and Security in 5G Networks. "Criteria for Security and Trust in Telecommunications Networks and Services." Center for Strategic and International Studies. May 2020. https://csis-website-prod.s3.amazonaws.com/s3fs-public/publication/200511_Lewis_5G_v3.pdf.

Cybersecurity and Infrastructure Security Agency. "Edge vs. Core: An Increasingly Less Pronounced Distinction in 5G Networks." 2020. https://www.cisa.gov/sites/default/files/publications/5g_edge-core-computing_508_1.pdf.

———. "National Critical Functions Set." Accessed July 17, 2022. https://www.cisa.gov/national-critical-functions-set.

Cybersecurity Week. "Global Forum on Cyber Expertise Stationed in The Hague." April 20, 2015. https://www.cybersecurityweek.nl/2015/pressroom/news/24-global-forum-on-cyber-expertise-stationed-in-the-hague.

Davis, Joshua. "Hackers Take Down the Most Wired Country in Europe." *Wired*, August 21, 2007. https://www.wired.com/2007/08/ff-estonia/.

Declaration of Independence, US Congress, July 4, 1776.

Deibert, Ronald, John Palfrey, Rafal Rohozinski, and Jonathan Zittrain. *Access Controlled: The Shaping of Power, Rights, and Rule in Cyberspace*. Cambridge, MA: MIT Press, 2010.

Deibert, Ronald J., Rafal Rohozinski, and Masashi Crete-Nishihata. "Cyclones in Cyberspace: Information Shaping and Denial in the 2008 Russia-Georgia War." *Security Dialogue* 43, no. 3 (2012): 3–24.

Deloitte Consulting. *Digital Infrastructure in the Netherlands: Driver for the Online Ecosystem*. Netherlands: Deloitte, November 2014.

———. *Dutch Digital Infrastructure 2016: Enabling the Digital Economy and Society*. Netherlands: Deloitte, November 2016.

Demchak, Chris C., and Peter Dombrowski. "Cyber Westphalia: Asserting State Prerogatives in Cyberspace." *Georgetown Journal of International Affairs*, no. 20 (2014): 29–38.

———. "Rise of a Cybered Westphalian Age." *Strategic Studies Quarterly* 5, no. 1 (Spring 2011): 32–61.

Digital Gateway to Europe. "Cloud." Accessed June 4, 2022. http://www.digitalgateway.eu/cloud.html.

———. "Data Centers." Accessed June 4, 2022. http://www.digitalgateway.eu/data-centers.html.

———. "Invest in Holland." Accessed April 27, 2020. http://www.digitalgateway.eu/invest-in-holland.html.

Doffman, Zak. "Huawei Confirms $30 Billion Revenue Hit as Smartphone Sales Drop 40–60%." *Forbes*, June 17, 2019. https://www.forbes.com/sites/zakdoffman/2019/06/17/huawei-may-pull-honor-20-and-fears-40-60-drop-in-smartphone-sales-report-claims/?sh=6a2f8e1754d2.

———. "Trump Signs Executive Order That Will Lead to US Ban on Huawei." *Forbes*, May 15, 2019. https://www.forbes.com/sites/zakdoffman/2019/05/15/trump-expected-to-sign-executive-order-leading-to-ban-on-huawei-this-week/#56758b3368d9.

Dutch Data Center Association. "Collaborations." Accessed April 27, 2020. https://www.dutchdatacenters.nl/en/about-us/collaborations/.

———. "Data Centers: What Is the Economic Impact of Data Centers?" Accessed June 5, 2022. https://www.dutchdatacenters.nl/en/data-centers/what-is-the-economic-impact-of-data-centers/.

———. "Positions: Digital Economy and Gateway." Accessed June 5, 2022. https://www.dutchdatacenters.nl/en/positions/digital-economy-gateway/.

Economist. "A Cyber-Riot." May 10, 2007. https://www.economist.com/europe/2007/05/10/a-cyber-riot.

———. "How Did Estonia Become a Leader in Technology?" July 31, 2013. https://www.economist.com/the-economist-explains/2013/07/30/how-did-estonia-become-a-leader-in-technology?fsrc=scn/fb/te/bl/ed/howdidestoniabecomealeaderintechnology?fsrc=scn/fb/te/bl/ed/howdidestoniabecomealeaderintechnology.

E-Estonia. "The e-Estonia Briefing Centre Is at Your Service." Accessed July 17, 2023. https://e-estonia.com/briefing-centre/about-us/.

———. "E-identity." Accessed November 7, 2019. https://e-estonia.com/solutions/e-identity/id-card.

———. "Estonia to Open the World's First Data Embassy in Luxembourg." June 14, 2017. https://e-estonia.com/estonia-to-open-the-worlds-first-data-embassy-in-luxembourg/.

———. "KSI Blockchain." Accessed May 14, 2022. https://e-estonia.com/solutions/cyber-security/ksi-blockchain/.

———. "KSI Blockchain in Estonia." Accessed May 14, 2022. https://e-estonia.com/wp-content/uploads/2019sept-faq-ksi-blockchain-1-1.pdf.

———. "X-Road." Accessed May 14, 2022. https://e-estonia.com/solutions/interoperability-services/x-road/.

Engelliweb.com captured by the WayBack Machine. Dated May 11, 2014. Accessed July 10, 2022. https://web.archive.org/web/20140511111941/http://engelliweb.com:80/istatistikler/.

———. Dated May 16, 2016. Accessed July 10, 2022. https://web.archive.org/web/20160516194730/https://engelliweb.com/istatistikler/.

Ergun, Doruk. "National Security vs. Online Rights and Freedoms in Turkey: Moving Beyond the Dichotomy." Center for Economics and Foreign Policy Studies. April 2018. https://www.jstor.org/stable/resrep17007.

Estonian Ministry of Economic Affairs and Communications and Microsoft. "Implementation of the Virtual Data Embassy Solution: Summary Report of the Research Project on Public Cloud Usage for Government." 2015.

———. "Transforming Digital Continuity: Enhancing IT Resilience through Cloud Computing." May 2016.

European Central Bank. "Euro Foreign Exchange Reference Rates." Accessed July 9, 2022. https://www.ecb.europa.eu/stats/policy_and_exchange_rates/euro_reference_exchange_rates/html/eurofxref-graph-try.en.html.

European Cybercrime Center. "About." Accessed July 2, 2022. https://www.europol.europa.eu/about-europol/european-cybercrime-centre-ec3.

Executive Order on Securing the Information and Communications Technology and Services Supply Chain. May 15, 2019. https://trumpwhitehouse.archives.gov/presidential-actions/executive-order-securing-information-communications-technology-services-supply-chain/.

Executive Order 13,636. Improving Critical Infrastructure Cybersecurity. C.F.R. 78, no. 33, February 19, 2013. https://www.govinfo.gov/content/pkg/FR-2013-02-19/pdf/2013-03915.pdf.

Fang, Binxing. *Cyberspace Sovereignty: Reflections on Building a Community of Common Future in Cyberspace.* Berlin: Springer, 2018.

Federal Communications Commission. "FCC Bars Use of Universal Service Funding for Equipment & Services Posing National Security Risks." Press release, November 22, 2019. https://docs.fcc.gov/public/attachments/DOC-360976A1.pdf.

———. "FCC Designates Huawei and ZTE as National Security Threats." Press release, June 30, 2020. https://www.fcc.gov/document/fcc-designates-huawei-and-zte-national-security-threats.

———. "The FCC's 5G FAST Plan." Accessed July 17, 2022. https://www.fcc.gov/5G.

Federal Register. Federal Acquisition Regulation: Prohibition on Contracting with Entities Using Certain Telecommunications and Video Surveillance Services or Equipment. July 14, 2020. https://www.federalregister.gov/documents/2020/07/14/2020-15293/federal-acquisition-regulation-prohibition-on-contracting-with-entities-using-certain.

Franzese, Patrick W. "Sovereignty in Cyberspace: Can It Exist?" *Air Force Law Review* 64 (2009): 1–42.

Freedom House. "Freedom on the Net." Accessed July 7, 2022. https://freedomhouse.org/report/freedom-net.

Gadde, Vijaya. "Challenging the Access Ban in Turkey." Twitter Blog. March 26, 2014. https://blog.twitter.com/official/en_us/a/2014/challenging-the-access-ban-in-turkey.html.

GCSC. "About." Accessed July 3, 2022. https://cyberstability.org/about/.

———. "Advancing Cyberstability." Final report. November 2019. https://cyberstability.org/wp-content/uploads/2020/02/GCSC-Advancing-Cyberstability.pdf.

———. "A Call to Action on Advancing Cyber Stability: Global Commission Launches Final Report." Accessed July 3, 2022. https://cyberstability.org/news/a-call-to-action-on-advancing-cyberstability-global-commission-launches-final-report/.

———. "Commissioner." Accessed July 3, 2022. https://cyberstability.org/commissioner/.

———. "Mission Statement." Accessed July 3, 2022. https://cyberstability.org/.

Geller, Eric. "Trump Signs Order Setting Stage to Ban Huawei from US." *Politico*, May 15, 2019. https://www.politico.com/story/2019/05/15/trump-ban-huawei-us-1042046.

Geneva Internet Platform, Digital Watch Observatory. "Results of the Accreditation of Stakeholders to the OEWG 2021–2025 Raises Concerns." July 21, 2022. https://dig.watch/updates/results-of-the-accreditation-of-stakeholders-to-the-oewg-2021-2025-raises-concerns.

———. "UN GGE and OEWG." Accessed July 5, 2022. https://dig.watch/processes/un-gge.

GFCE. "Delhi Communiqué on a GFCE Global Agenda for Cyber Capacity Building." November 24, 2017. https://thegfce.org/wp-content/uploads/2020/04/DelhiCommunique.pdf.

———. "Framework Document GFCE." April 16, 2015. https://thegfce.org/wp-content/uploads/2020/04/framework-document-gfce.pdf.

———. "The Hague Declaration on the GFCE." April 16, 2015. https://thegfce.org/wp-content/uploads/2020/04/the-hague-declaration-on-the-gfce.pdf.

———. "History of the GFCE." Accessed July 3, 2022. https://thegfce.org/about-the-gfce/.

Government of the Grand Duchy of Luxembourg, "E-Embassies in Luxembourg." Luxembourg: Let's Make It Happen. Last updated October 1, 2021. https://luxembourg.public.lu/en/invest/innovation/e-embassies-in-luxembourg.html.

Government of the Netherlands. "'Free, Open and Secure Internet' Focus of Global Conference on CyberSpace 2015 in The Hague." March 27, 2015. https://www.government.nl/latest/news/2015/03/27/free-open-and-secure-internet-focus-of-global-conference-on-cyberspace-2015-in-the-hague.

———. "Koenders Kicks Off Cyber Conference." April 16, 2015. https://www.government.nl/latest/news/2015/04/16/koenders-kicks-off-cyber-conference.

Government of the Netherlands, Ministry of the Interior and Kingdom Relations. "The Constitution of the Kingdom of the Netherlands 2008." Published September 22, 2008. https://www.government.nl/documents/regulations/2012/10/18/the-constitution-of-the-kingdom-of-the-netherlands-2008.

Grande, Edgar, and Louis W. Pauly, eds. *Complex Sovereignty: Reconstituting Political Authority in the Twenty-first Century.* Toronto: University of Toronto Press, 2005.

Gross, Leo. "The Peace of Westphalia." *American Journal of International Law* 42, no. 1 (January 1948): 20–41.

Guardtime. "Keyless Signature Infrastructure." Accessed May 14, 2022. https://m.guardtime.com/files/KSI_data_sheet_201509.pdf.

Gürkaynak, Gönenç, İlay Yılmaz, and Nazlı Pınar Taşkıran. "New Era for Turkish Internet Law: Will Turkey Become Another China or Iran?" *Journal of Business and Economics* 5, no. 11 (November 2014): 1976–1982.

Hague Security Delta. "About HSD." Accessed July 2, 2022. https://securitydelta.nl/about/about-hsd.

———. "Join the Largest Security Cluster in Europe: Factsheet." Accessed July 2, 2022. https://securitydelta.nl/images/HSD_Factsheet_International_DEF.pdf.

Hall, Rodney Bruce, and Thomas J. Biersteker, eds. *The Emergence of Private Authority in Global Governance.* Cambridge: Cambridge University Press, 2002.

Hare, Forrest. "Borders in Cyberspace: Can Sovereignty Adapt to the Challenges of Cybersecurity?" In *The Virtual Battlefield: Perspectives on Cyber Warfare*, edited by Christian Czosseck and Kenneth Geers, 89–106. Amsterdam: IOS Press, 2009.

Harris, Sarah K. "Networked Erasure: Visualizing Information Censorship in Turkey." *Convergence: The International Journal of Research into New Media Technologies* 21, no. 2 (2015): 257–278.

Hartman, Leigh. "Get Smarter: Core vs. Edge in 5G Networks." US Embassy and Consulates in the United Kingdom, September 17, 2019. https://uk.usembassy.gov/get-smart-core-vs-edge-in-5g-networks/.

Heintschel von Heinegg, Wolff. "Legal Implications of Territorial Sovereignty in Cyberspace." In *4th International Conference on Cyber Conflict*, edited by Christian Czosseck, Rain Ottis, and Katharina Ziolkowski, 7–19. Tallinn: NATO CCDCoE, 2012.

Herrera, Geoffrey L. "Cyberspace and Sovereignty: Thoughts on Physical Space and Digital Space." Paper presented at the 1st International CISS/ETH Conference on the Information Revolution and the Changing Face of International Relations and Security, Lucerne, Switzerland, May 2005.

Hobbes, Thomas. *Leviathan*. Oxford: Oxford University Press, 2014.

Hoehne, Markus Virgil. "Somaliland: 30 Years of De Facto Statehood, and No End in Sight." Italian Institute for International Political Studies, May 7, 2021. https://www.ispionline.it/en/publication/somaliland-30-years-de-facto-statehood-and-no-end-sight-30363.

Holsti, K. J. *International Politics: A Framework for Analysis*. Englewood Cliffs, NJ: Prentice Hall, 1988.

Hong, Yu, and Thomas Goodnight. "How to Think about Cyber Sovereignty: The Case of China." *Chinese Journal of Communications* 13, no. 1 (2020): 8–26.

Hu, Ken. "Huawei Open Letter." February 2011. http://online.wsj.com/public/resources/documents/Huawei20110205.pdf.

Hürriyet Daily News. "Turkey Fines Twitter for Failure to Remove 'Terrorist Propaganda.'" December 11, 2015. https://www.hurriyetdailynews.com/turkey-fines-twitter-for-failure-to-remove-terrorist-propaganda-official-92387.

ID, Information System Authority. "Statistics." Accessed November 8, 2019. https://www.id.ee/?lang=en&id=.

Information System Authority, Republic of Estonia. "Data Exchange Layer X-tee." Accessed May 14, 2022. https://www.ria.ee/en/state-information-system/x-tee.html.

International Telecommunication Union. World Conference on International Telecommunications. Dubai, December 2012. https://www.itu.int/en/history/Pages/WorldConferencesInternationalTelecommunications.aspx?conf=4.34.

Invest in Holland. "Europe's Top Location for Data Centers." Accessed January 13, 2020. https://investinholland.com/business-operations/data-centers/.

Jackson, Robert. *Sovereignty: The Evolution of an Idea*. Cambridge, UK: Polity Press, 2007.

Jiang, Sijia. "Huawei Challenges U.S. Defense Bill as Sanctions Fight Ramps Up." *Reuters*, May 29, 2019. https://www.reuters.com/article/us-huawei-tech-usa-filing-idUSKCN1SZ08C.

Johns, Fleur. "Data Territories: Changing Architectures of Association in International Law." *Netherlands Yearbook of International Law*, published July 20, 2016. https://papers.ssrn.com/sol3/papers.cfm?abstract_id=2810897.

John S. McCain National Defense Authorization Act for Fiscal Year 2019. H.R. 5515, 115th Congress (2017–2018), August 13, 2018. https://www.congress.gov/bill/115th-congress/house-bill/5515/text.

Kadlecová, Lucie. "Huawei: A Threat to National Security?" *e-IR*, March 13, 2013. https://www.e-ir.info/2013/03/13/huawei-a-threat-to-national-security/.

Kant, Immanuel. *Toward Perpetual Peace and Other Writings on Politics, Peace, and History*. New Haven, CT: Yale University Press, 2006.

Kaska, Kadri, Henrik Beckvard, and Tomáš Minárik. "Huawei, 5G and China as a Security Threat." NATO CCDCoE, Tallinn, 2019. https://ccdcoe.org/library/publications/huawei-5g-and-china-as-a-security-threat/.

Kastrenakes, Jacob. "Trump Signs Bill Banning Government Use of Huawei and ZTE Tech." *Verge*, August 13, 2018. https://www.theverge.com/2018/8/13/17686310/huawei-zte-us-government-contractor-ban-trump.

Kaya, Mehmet Bedii. "The Law on Regulation of Broadcasts via Internet and Combating Crimes Committed by Means of Such Publications: The Turkish Internet Law (Unofficial Translation)." *İnternet Hukuku*. Mevzuat and İçtihat. v3.0, 2021. https://www.mbkaya.com/hukuk/internetmevzuat.pdf.

———. "The Regulation of Internet Intermediaries under Turkish Law: Is There a Delicate Balance between Rights and Obligations?" *Computer Law and Security Review* 32 (2016): 759–774.

Keane, Sean. "Huawei Takes Samsung's Crown as World's No. 1 Phone Maker, Analysts Say." *CNET*, July 31, 2020. https://www.cnet.com/news/huawei-takes-samsungs-crown-to-become-worlds-biggest-phone-maker-analysts-say/.

Kelly, Sanja, Madeline Earp, Laura Reed, Adrian Shahbaz, and Mai Truong. "Freedom on the Net 2014." Freedom House. 2014. https://freedomhouse.org/sites/default/files/2020-02/FOTN_2014_Full_Report_compressedv2.pdf.

Kelly, Sanja, Mai Truong, Adrian Shahbaz, and Madeline Earp. "Freedom on the Net 2016." Freedom House. November 2016. https://freedomhouse.org/sites/default/files/2020-02/Freedom_on_the_Net_2016_complete_book.pdf.

Kinikoglu, Batu. "Evaluating the Regulation of Access to Online Content in Turkey in the Context of Freedom of Speech." *Journal of International Commercial Law and Technology* 9, no. 1 (2014): 36–55.

Koenders, Bert. "Tallinn Manual 2.0." Speech, The Hague, February 13, 2017.

Kolton, Michael. "Interpreting China's Pursuit of Cyber Sovereignty and Its Views on Cyber Deterrence." *Cyber Defense Review* 2, no. 1 (Winter 2017): 119–154.

Kotka, Taavi, Carlos Ivan Vargas Alvarez del Castillo, and Kaspar Korjus. "Estonian e-Residency: Redefining the Nation-State in the Digital Era." Working Paper Series, No. 3, Cyber Studies Program, University of Oxford, September 2015.

Kotka, Taavi, and Innar Liiv. "Concept of Estonian Government Cloud and Data Embassies." In *Electronic Government and the Information Systems Perspective*, edited by Andrea Kő and Enrico Francesconi, 149–162. Switzerland: Springer, 2015.

Krach, Keith. "The Free World Must Unite against Huawei." Op-ed, *Daily Telegraph*, June 25, 2020. https://2017-2021.state.gov/The-free-world-must-unite-against-Huawei/index.html.

Krasner, Stephen. *Sovereignty: Organized Hypocrisy*. Princeton, NJ: Princeton University Press, 1999.

———. "Think Again: Sovereignty." *Foreign Policy*, November 20, 2009. https://foreignpolicy.com/2009/11/20/think-again-sovereignty/.

Kriener, Florian. "Cyber Space, Sovereignty and the Intricacies of International Law-Making." Völkerrechtsblog, April 16, 2021. https://voelkerrechtsblog.org/cyber-space-sovereignty-and-the-intricacies-of-international-law-making/.

Kwan, Campbell. "US Bans Federals Funds from Being Used on Huawei and ZTE Equipment." *ZDNet*, March 16, 2020. https://www.zdnet.com/article/us-bans-federals-funds-from-being-used-on-huawei-and-zte-equipment/.

Leiter, Andrea. "Cyber Sovereignty: A Snapshot from a Field in Motion." *Harvard International Law Journal Frontiers* 61 (2020). https://journals.law.harvard.edu/ilj/2020/04/cyber-sovereignty-a-snapshot-from-a-field-in-motion/.

Lewis, James. "Can Telephones Race? 5G and the Evolution of Telecom, Part I." Center for Strategic and International Studies. June 2020. https://www.csis.org/analysis/can-telephones-race-5g-and-evolution-telecom.

Liaropoulos, Andrew. "Exercising State Sovereignty in Cyberspace: An International Cyber-Order under Construction?" In *Proceedings of the 8th International Conference on Information Warfare and Security*, edited by Douglas Hart, 136–140. Denver, CO: Regis University, 2013.

Locke, John. *Two Treatises of Government*. New Haven, CT: Yale University Press, 2003.

Lysne, Olav, Ahmed Elmokashfi, Niels Nagelhus Schia, Lars Gjesvik, and Karsten Friis. "Critical Communication Infrastructures and Huawei." July 24, 2019. TPRC47: The 47th Research Conference on Communication, Information and Internet Policy 2019. https://papers.ssrn.com/sol3/papers.cfm?abstract_id=3426222.

Maza, Cristina. "China Involved in 90 Percent of Espionage and Industrial Secrets Theft, Department of Justice Reveals." *Newsweek*, December 12, 2018. https://www.newsweek.com/china-involved-90-percent-economic-espionage-and-industrial-secrets-theft-1255908.

McDonald, Joe. "Huawei: Smartphone Chips Running Out under US Sanctions." *AP News*, August 8, 2020. https://apnews.com/270e93e985733a4d086c06a01375cea0.

McGuiness, Damien. "How a Cyber Attack Transformed Estonia." *BBC*, April 27, 2017. https://www.bbc.com/news/39655415.

Mercier, Jonas, and Jess Bauldry. "2nd Data Embassy for Luxembourg." *Delano*, March 16, 2019. https://delano.lu/d/detail/news/2nd-data-embassy-lux/172985.

Microsoft Corporate Blogs. "Diplomatic Immunity for Data: Estonia Creates a Virtual Embassy." December 14, 2017. https://blogs.microsoft.com/eupolicy/2017/12/14/diplomatic-immunity-data-estonia-creates-virtual-embassy/.

———. "From Submarines to Cyber: Estonia's Innovation Journey." November 29, 2017. https://blogs.microsoft.com/eupolicy/2017/11/29/submarines-cyber-estonias-innovation-journey/.

Ministry of Economic Affairs and Communications. "Digital Agenda 2020 for Estonia." 2014.

Ministry of Foreign Affairs, Netherlands. "International Cyber Strategy: Building Digital Bridges." February 12, 2017. https://www.government.nl/documents/parliamentary-documents/2017/02/12/international-cyber-strategy.

———. "Letter to the Parliament on the International Legal Order in Cyberspace." July 5, 2019. https://www.government.nl/ministries/ministry-of-foreign-affairs/documents/parliamentary-documents/2019/09/26/letter-to-the-parliament-on-the-international-legal-order-in-cyberspace.

———. "Programme of the Netherlands Presidency of the Council of the European Union, 1 January–30 June 2016." Accessed July 5, 2022. http://www.eunec.eu/sites/www.eunec.eu/files/attachment/files/nationaal-programma-engels.pdf.

Ministry of Security and Justice, Netherlands. "National Cybersecurity Strategy 2: From Awareness to Capability." 2013. https://www.enisa.europa.eu/topics/national-cyber-security-strategies/ncss-map/NCSS2Engelseversie.pdf.

Moran, Theodore H. "Dealing with Cybersecurity Threats Posed by Globalised IT Suppliers." Policy brief, Peterson Institute for International Economics, May 1, 2013. https://www.piie.com/publications/policy-briefs/dealing-cybersecurity-threats-posed-globalized-information-technology.

Moynihan, Harriet. "The Application of International Law to Cyberattacks: Sovereignty and Non-intervention." Chatham House, December 2, 2019. https://www.chathamhouse.org/2019/12/application-international-law-state-cyberattacks/2-application-sovereignty-cyberspace.

Musil, Steven. "Sprint, Softbank Vow Not to Use Huawei Gear in Sprint's Network." *CNET*, March 28, 2013. https://www.cnet.com/news/sprint-softbank-vow-not-to-use-huawei-gear-in-sprints-network/.

Nachman, Lev, and Brian Hioe. "No, Taiwan's President Isn't 'Pro-independence.'" *Diplomat*, April 23, 2020. https://thediplomat.com/2020/04/no-taiwans-president-isnt-pro-independence/.

National Cyber and Information Security Agency. "Prague 5G Security Conference 2019." Accessed July 31, 2022. https://nukib.cz/en/infoservis-en/conferences/prague-5g-security-conference-2019/.

National Strategy to Secure 5G of the United States of America. March 2020. https://trumpwhitehouse.archives.gov/wp-content/uploads/2020/03/National-Strategy-5G-Final.pdf.

NATO CCDCoE. "Cyber Law Toolkit: Sovereignty." Last updated May 2, 2023. https://cyberlaw.ccdcoe.org/wiki/Sovereignty.

Netherlands Presidency of the Council of the EU. "Non-Paper: Developing a Joint EU Diplomatic Response against Coercive Cyber Operations," 5797/6/16REV6. May 19, 2016. http://statewatch.org/news/2016/jul/eu-council-diplomatic-response-cyber-ops-5797-6-16.pdf.

Number Resource Organization. "Regional Internet Registries." Accessed July 2, 2022. https://www.nro.net/about/rirs/.

Ohlheiser, Abby. "How Turkey's Twitter Users Are Working around the Ban." *Atlantic*. March 21, 2014. https://www.theatlantic.com/international/archive/2014/03/how-turkeys-twitter-users-are-working-around-ban/359415/.

Osiander, Andreas. "Sovereignty, International Relations, and the Westphalian Myth." *International Organization* 55, no. 2 (2001): 251–287.

Pamuk, Humeyra, Alexandra Alper, and Idrees Ali. "Trump Bans U.S. Investments in Companies Linked to Chinese Military." *Reuters*, November 13, 2020. https://www.reuters.com/article/us-usa-china-securities-exclusive-idUSKBN27S2X3.

Pham, Sherisse. "Nokia Is Fighting Hard to Steal Huawei's 5G Crown." CNN, June 4, 2019. https://edition.cnn.com/2019/06/04/tech/huawei-5g-nokia/index.html.

Philpott, Daniel. *Revolution in Sovereignty: How Ideas Shaped Modern International Relations*. Princeton, NJ: Princeton University Press, 2001.

Pirker, Benedikt. "Territorial Sovereignty and Integrity and the Challenges of Cyberspace." In *Peacetime Regime for State Activities in Cyberspace*, edited by Katharina Ziolkowski, 189–216 Tallinn: NATO CCDCoE, 2013.

Pompeo, Michael R. "Announcing the Expansion of the Clean Network to Safeguard America's Assets." Press statement, US Department of State, August 5, 2020. https://2017-2021.state.gov/announcing-the-expansion-of-the-clean-network-to-safeguard-americas-assets/index.html.

———. "The United States Further Restricts Huawei Access to US Technology." Press statement, US Department of State, August 17, 2020. https://2017-2021.state.gov/the-united-states-further-restricts-huawei-access-to-u-s-technology/index.html.

Reardon, Marguerite. "Nokia and Ericsson Pitch Themselves as Huawei 5G Alternative." *CNET*, March 4, 2020. https://www.cnet.com/news/nokia-and-ericsson-pitch-themselves-as-huawei-5g-alternative/.

Reichert, Corinne. "Huawei Gets Another 45-day Reprieve from Commerce Department." *CNET*, February 14, 2020. https://www.cnet.com/news/huawei-gets-another-45-day-reprieve-from-commerce-department/.

Reporters without Borders. "New Internet Filtering System Condemned as Backdoor Censorship." December 2, 2011, updated January 20, 2016. https://rsf.org/en/news/new-internet-filtering-system-condemned-backdoor-censorship.

Reuters. "U.S. Will Rethink Cooperation with Allies Who Use Huawei." April 29, 2019. https://www.reuters.com/article/us-usa-huawei-tech/u-s-will-rethink-cooperation-with-allies-who-use-huawei-official-idUSKCN1S517H.

Riigikogu Press Service. "The Riigikogu Approved Establishing of Luxembourg Data Embassy." Press release, March 21, 2018. https://www.riigikogu.ee/en/press-releases/plenary-assembly/riigikogu-approved-establishing-luxembourg-data-embassy/.

RIPE NCC. "RIPE Network Coordination Centre." Accessed July 2, 2022. https://www.ripe.net/.

Rogers, Mike, and Dutch Ruppersberger. "Investigative Report on the US National Security Issues Posed by Chinese Telecommunications Companies Huawei and ZTE." US House of Representatives, October 8, 2012. http://intelligence.house.gov/sites/intelligence.house.gov/files/documents/Huawei-ZTE%20Investigative%20Report%20(FINAL).pdf.

———. "Investigative Report on the US National Security Issues Posed by Chinese Telecommunications Companies Huawei and ZTE." *Journal of Current Issues in Media and Telecommunications* 4, no. 2 (2012): 59–100.

Rosecrance, Richard. *The Rise of the Virtual State: Wealth and Power in the Coming Century*. New York: Basic Books, 1999.

Rousseau, Jean-Jacques. *The Social Contract and Discourses*. London: Dant, 1988.

Rubio, Marco. "Rubio Joins Cotton, Cruz, Hawley to Introduce Bill Requiring CFIUS to Reexamine U.K. Status after 5G Decision." Press release, March 4, 2020. https://www.rubio.senate.gov/public/index.cfm/2020/3/rubio-joins-cotton-cruz-hawley-to-introduce-bill-requiring-cfius-to-reexamine-u-k-status-after-5g-decision.

Saalman, Lora, Fei Su, and Larisa Saveleva Dovgal. "Cyber Posture Trends in China, Russia, the United States and the European Union." SIPRI, Stockholm,

December 2022. https://www.sipri.org/publications/2022/other-publications/cyber-posture-trends-china-russia-united-states-and-european-union.

Sabah. "Binali Yıldırım: Türkiye örnek teşkil edecek." March 29, 2007. http://arsiv.sabah.com.tr/2007/03/29/gnd87.html.

———. "'Temiz İnternet' için Ankara'da buluşalım." March 29, 2007. http://arsiv.sabah.com.tr/2007/03/29/gun110.html.

Satariano, Adam, Raymond Zhong, and Daisuke Wakabayashi. "U.S. Tech Suppliers, Including Google, Restrict Dealings with Huawei after Trump Order." *New York Times*, May 20, 2019. https://www.nytimes.com/2019/05/20/technology/google-android-huawei.html.

Schenkkan, Nate, Osman Coşkunoğlu, and Aslı Tunç. "The Struggle for Turkey's Internet." Freedom House. 2015.

Schmitt, Michael N., ed. *Tallinn Manual on the International Law Applicable to Cyber Warfare*. Cambridge: Cambridge University Press, 2013.

———, ed. *Tallinn Manual 2.0 on the International Law Applicable to Cyber Operations*. Cambridge: Cambridge University Press, 2017.

Schuman, Michael, Gu Yongqiang, Massimo Calabresi, Jay Newton-Small, and Krista Mahr. "Inside the Chinese Company America Can't Trust." *Time*, April 15, 2013, vol. 181, no. 14.

Secure and Trusted Communications Networks Act of 2019. H.R. 4998, 116th Congress (2019–2020), December 3, 2020. https://www.congress.gov/bill/116th-congress/house-bill/4998/all-info#.

Sedlák, Jan. "Ukrajina převezla data v obrněných kufrech a IT funguje i ve válce. Výrazně pomohli také Češi." *Lupa*, December 12, 2022. https://www.lupa.cz/clanky/ukrajina-prevezla-data-v-obrnenych-kufrech-a-it-funguje-i-ve-valce-vyrazne-pomohli-take-cesi/.

Sevastopulo, Demetri. "US Agencies Barred from Buying Huawei Equipment." *Financial Times*, August 7, 2019. https://www.ft.com/content/fc23eebe-b951-11e9-8a88-aa6628ac896c.

Shaban, Hamza. "Pentagon Tells US Military Bases to Stop Selling ZTE, Huawei Phones." *Washington Post*, May 2, 2018.

Shepardson, David. "U.S. Rural Telecom Networks Need USD 1.8 Billion to Remove Huawei, ZTE Equipment—FCC." *Reuters*, September 15, 2020. https://www.reuters.com/article/us-usa-china-telecom-idUSKBN25V23F?taid=5f52a053b52437000126dd7e&utm_campaign=trueAnthem:+Trending+Content&utm_medium=trueAnthem&utm_source=twitter.

Shepardson, David, and Karen Freifeld. "Trump Extends U.S. Telecom Supply Chain Order Aimed at Huawei, ZTE." Reuters, May 13, 2020. https://www.reuters.com/article/us-usa-trade-china-trump/trump-extends-us-telecom-supply-chain-order-aimed-at-huawei-zte-idUSKBN22P2KG.

Shepardson, David, Karen Freifeld, and Alexandra Alper. "U.S. Moves to Cut Huawei Off from Global Chip Suppliers as China Eyes Retaliation." *Reuters*, May 15, 2020. https://www.reuters.com/article/us-usa-huawei-tech-exclusive/u-s-moves-to-cut-huawei-off-from-global-chip-suppliers-as-china-eyes-retaliation-idUSKBN22R1KC.

Sierzputowski, Bartołomiej. "The Data Embassy under Public International Law." *International and Comparative Law Quarterly* 68 (January 2019): 225–242.

Soldatov, Andrei, and Irina Borogan. "The New Iron Curtain Part 4: Russia's Sovereign Internet Takes Root." CEPA, April 5, 2022. https://cepa.org/article/the-new-iron-curtain-part-4-russias-sovereign-internet-takes-root/.

Statistics Estonia. "Population." Updated 2021. https://www.stat.ee/en/find-statistics/statistics-theme/population.

Stolton, Samuel. "EU Backs Cyber Sanctions Regime, following Dutch and UK Pressure." *Euractive*, May 17, 2019. https://www.euractiv.com/section/cybersecurity/news/eu-backs-cyber-sanctions-regime-following-dutch-and-uk-pressure/.

Strange, Susan. *The Retreat of the State: The Diffusion of Power in the World Economy.* Cambridge: Cambridge University Press, 1996.

Swanson, Ana. "US Delivers Another Blow to Huawei with New Tech Restrictions." *New York Times*, May 15, 2020. https://www.nytimes.com/2020/05/15/business/economy/commerce-department-huawei.html.

Tanner, Murray Scot. "Beijing's New National Intelligence Law: From Defense to Offense." *Lawfare*, July 20, 2017. https://www.lawfareblog.com/beijings-new-national-intelligence-law-defense-offense.

TeleGeography. "Submarine Cable Map." Accessed June 3, 2022. https://www.submarinecablemap.com/.

Turkey: Opinion on Law No. 5651 on Regulation of Publications on the Internet and Combating Crimes Committed by Means of Such Publication. Venice Commission. 107th Plenary Session, Venice, June 10–11, 2016. https://www.venice.coe.int/webforms/documents/default.aspx?pdffile=CDL-AD(2016)011-e.

Türk Telekom. "Milestones." Accessed July 10, 2022. https://www.turktelekom.com.tr/en/aboutus/pages/milestones.aspx.

Twitter. "Removal Requests." Transparency Report. Accessed July 16, 2022. https://transparency.twitter.com/en/removal-requests.html.

Ülgen, Sinan, ed. "A Primer on Cybersecurity in Turkey and the Case of Nuclear Power." Center for Economics and Foreign Policy Studies, Istanbul. 2015. https://www.jstor.org/stable/resrep14043.1.

UN General Assembly. "Report of the Group of Governmental Experts on Developments in the Field of Information and Telecommunications in the Context of

International Security." A/68/98, June 24, 2013. http://www.un.org/ga/search/view_doc.asp?symbol=A/68/98.
———. "Report of the Group of Governmental Experts on Developments in the Field of Information and Telecommunications in the Context of International Security." A/70/174, July 22, 2015. http://www.un.org/ga/search/view_doc.asp?symbol=A/70/174.
———. "Report of the Group of Governmental Experts on Advancing Responsible State Behavior in Cyberspace in the Context of International Security." A/76/135, July 14, 2021. https://dig.watch/wp-content/uploads/2022/08/UN-GGE-Report-2021.pdf.
UN. "Vienna Convention on Consular Relations." 1963. https://legal.un.org/ilc/texts/instruments/english/conventions/9_2_1963.pdf.
———. "Vienna Convention on Diplomatic Relations." 1961. https://legal.un.org/ilc/texts/instruments/english/conventions/9_1_1961.pdf.
UN, Office for Disarmament Affairs. "Developments in the Field of Information and Telecommunications in the Context of International Security." Accessed July 5, 2022. https://www.un.org/disarmament/ict-security/.
———. "Group of Governmental Experts." Accessed July 5, 2022. https://www.un.org/disarmament/group-of-governmental-experts/.
———. "Official Compendium of Voluntary National Contributions on the Subject of How International Law Applies to the Use of Information and Communications Technologies by States," A/76/136. August 2021. https://front.un-arm.org/wp-content/uploads/2021/08/A-76-136-EN.pdf.
———. "Open-Ended Working Group." Accessed July 5, 2022. https://www.un.org/disarmament/open-ended-working-group/.
Uptime Institute. "Tier Certification Overview." Accessed May 13, 2022. https://uptimeinstitute.com/tier-certification.
US Department of Commerce. "Department of Commerce Announces the Addition of Huawei Technologies Co. Ltd. to the Entity List." Press release, May 15, 2019. https://2017-2021.commerce.gov/news/press-releases/2019/05/department-commerce-announces-addition-huawei-technologies-co-ltd.html.
US Department of State. "The Clean Network." Accessed July 21, 2023. https://2017-2021.state.gov/the-clean-network/.
Vance, Ashlee, and Bruce Einhorn. "Would You Buy $1 Billion in China-Made, So-Controversial-IT-Hurts Telecom Equipment from This Guy?" *Bloomberg Businessweek*, September 19–25, 2011.
van Marissing, Rutger. Panel "International Law and Cyber Operations: Launch of the Tallinn Manual 2.0." Atlantic Council, February 8, 2017. https://www

.atlanticcouncil.org/unused/webcasts/international-law-and-cyber-operations-launch-of-the-tallinn-manual-2-0/.

Vendil Pallin, Carolina, and Mattias Hjelm. "Moscow's Digital Offensive: Building Sovereignty in Cyberspace." Swedish Defense Research Agency, 2021. https://www.foi.se/rapportsammanfattning?reportNo=FOI%20Memo%207521.

Volz, Dustin. "Trump Signs into Law U.S. Government Ban on Kaspersky Lab Software." *Reuters*, December 12, 2017. https://www.reuters.com/article/us-usa-cyber-kaspersky/trump-signs-into-law-u-s-government-ban-on-kaspersky-lab-software-idUSKBN1E62V4.

Walt, Vivienne. "Welcome to Tomorrow Land." *Fortune*, May 1, 2017.

Watts, John T. "The Battle for 5G Leadership Is Global and the USA Is Behind: The White House's New Strategy Aims to Correct That." Atlantic Council, April 1, 2020. https://www.atlanticcouncil.org/blogs/new-atlanticist/the-battle-for-5g-leadership-is-global-and-the-us-is-behind-the-white-houses-new-strategy-aims-to-correct-that/.

Weber, Max. "Politics as a Vocation." In *Max Weber: Essays in Sociology*, edited by Hans Heinrich Gerth and Charles Wright Mills, 77–128. New York: Oxford University Press, 1946.

Weber, Valentin. "The Sinicization of Russia's Cyber Sovereignty Model." Council on Foreign Relations, April 1, 2020. https://www.cfr.org/blog/sinicization-russias-cyber-sovereignty-model.

Weinstein, Natalie. "Google Cuts Off Huawei Phones from Future Android Updates." *CNET*, May 20, 2019. https://www.cnet.com/news/google-reportedly-cuts-off-huawei-phones-from-future-android-updates/.

Williams, Robert. "Securing 5G Networks." Council on Foreign Relations, July 15, 2019. https://www.cfr.org/report/securing-5g-networks.

Woo, Stu, and Kate O'Keeffe. "Washington Asks Allies to Drop Huawei." *Wall Street Journal*, November 23, 2018.

World Government Summit, Organization for Economic Cooperation and Development. "Embracing Innovation in Government: Global Trends 2018." 2018. https://www.oecd.org/innovation/innovative-government/innovation2018.htm.

Wright, Jeremy. "Cyber and International Law in the 21st Century." Speech, May 23, 2018. https://www.gov.uk/government/speeches/cyber-and-international-law-in-the-21st-century.

X-Tee. "Factsheet." Accessed May 14, 2022. https://www.x-tee.ee/factsheets/EE/#eng.

Yesil, Bilge, Efe Kerem Sozeri, and Emad Khazraee. "Turkey's Internet Policy after the Coup Attempt: The Emergence of a Distributed Network of Online Suppression and Surveillance." Internet Policy Observatory, Annenberg School for Communication, University of Pennsylvania. February 2017.

Index

Kolibri 360 GmbH
Ferdinand-Jühlke-Straße 7
99095 Erfurt, Deutschland
produktsicherheit@kolibri360.de